UGC NET Paper I Unlocked

Volume III

Communication and Reading Comprehension

www.nerdschool.online

ANKIT SHARMA

A Complete Guide for UGC NET

TO THE POINT NOTES BASED ON PREVIOUS YEARS QUESTION PAPERS

Foreword

*The **UGC NET Paper I Unlocked: Volume III – Communication and Reading Comprehension** is designed to provide a comprehensive and structured approach to one of the most crucial sections of the UGC NET Paper I syllabus. Communication and Reading Comprehension not only test a candidate's linguistic and analytical abilities but also play a significant role in determining their success in the exam.*

*This book stands apart for its **to-the-point notes**, carefully curated based on the **latest exam trends** and past year question (PYQ) patterns. Every concept is presented concisely, making it easier for aspirants to grasp essential points without unnecessary elaboration. The content is **updated** to align with the most **recent UGC NET exam trends**, ensuring that aspirants stay ahead in their preparation.*

*A key highlight of this book is the inclusion of **detailed explanations for PYQs**. Each answer is supported by a **clear and logical rationale**, helping aspirants understand not just why an answer is correct but also why the other options are incorrect. This **comparative approach** enhances conceptual clarity and eliminates confusion, making the learning process more effective.*

Additionally, this volume features:

✓***Exam-Oriented Summaries*** – *Covering all major topics under Communication and Reading Comprehension, ensuring quick recall.*
✓***Breakdown of Teaching & Communication Theories*** – *With examples to simplify complex concepts.*
✓***Real-Life Applications*** – *Demonstrating how communication theories and comprehension strategies are used in everyday and academic settings.*
✓***Time-Saving Revision Points*** – *Ideal for last-minute preparation.*
✓***Practice Sets and Self-Assessment Questions*** – *To reinforce learning and test progress.*
✓***Error-Analysis Approach*** – *Addressing common mistakes made by aspirants and how to avoid them in the exam.*

[Volume III: Communication and Reading Comprehension]

This book is a ***one-stop solution*** *for candidates who seek* ***structured, precise, and exam-focused*** *preparation material for UGC NET Paper I. Whether you are a first-time aspirant or a repeater aiming for a better score, the strategic layout of this volume will* ***strengthen your conceptual foundation*** *and* ***boost your confidence*** *to excel in the exam.*

I hope this book serves as an effective guide in your journey toward qualifying UGC NET. ***Stay consistent, stay focused, and success will follow!***

Best wishes for your preparation!

Ankit Sharma
Author & Educator

Table of Contents

UNIT IV

COMMUNICATION

- Communication: Meaning, types, and characteristics of communication.
- Effective communication: Verbal and Non-verbal, Inter-Cultural and group communications, Classroom communication.
- Barriers to effective communication.
- Mass-Media and Society.

CHAPTER I

Communication Meaning, Definition, Function, Models and Characteristics

The communication section of the NTA UGC NET Paper 1 syllabus is one of the most exciting topics. There will be four to five questions in the exam from this section. An aspirant can easily score all the marks in this area if he understands communication. The communication section covers all the topics such as the meaning, types, methods, and communication barriers ranging from mass media to stage.

Introduction:

Communication is exchanging ideas and meanings between two or more people. Humans communicate through signs, expressions, utterances, gestures, sounds, and noises. The teaching process should include communication that encourages students to relate what they are learning to their own lives, as these studies will be applied to their everyday lives.

- Communication is inevitable
- Communication is irreversible
- Communication is cultural
- Increase public awareness of educational rights
- Improve the quality of policy preparation
- Improve the educational service delivery
- Primary Orality – No exposure to written language.
- Literacy – Ability to read and write.
- Typography – Printed text's style and design.
- Exclusivity – Not related to oral culture.

Question.

Which of the following are true of communication?

A. Communication is inevitable.
B. Communication is non-social.

C. Communication is irreversible.
D. Communication is cultural.
E. Communication is completely commercial

1. ABC
2. ACD
3. ADE
4. BCE

Explanations
Answer: 2. ACD

A. Communication is inevitable: Communication **cannot be avoided** as humans are constantly sending messages, whether verbal, non-verbal, or through silence.

C. Communication is irreversible: Once a message is communicated, it **cannot be taken back completely**. Even if corrected, the initial message's impact often remains.

D. Communication is cultural: Communication is **shaped by cultural contexts**, with language, symbols

Question

Integrating communication with the educational system will-

A. Increase opportunities for teachers to go abroad
B. Increase public awareness of educational rights
C. Improve the quality of policy preparation
D. Improve the educational service delivery
E. Make teachers have access to better perks.

1. ABC
2. BCD
3. CDE
4. ADE

Explanations
Answer: 2. BCD

Integrating communication with the educational system has the following positive impacts:

B. Increase public awareness of educational rights: Effective communication ensures that **students, parents, and the public are well-informed about their educational rights**, policies, and opportunities.

C. Improve the quality of policy preparation: Clear and transparent communication **helps policymakers gather feedback, share ideas, and create well-informed education policies** that address real needs.

D. Improve the educational service delivery: Good communication **streamlines process, reduces misunderstandings, and enhances collaboration among stakeholders**, leading to better educational services.

Why not the other options?

A. Increase opportunities for teachers to go abroad: This is not a direct result of integrating communication into the educational system.

E. Make teachers have access to better perks: While improved communication may bring better advocacy, it does not directly guarantee better perks for teachers.

Question

Why do we communicate?

A. For social interaction.
B. For happiness's sake.
C. For messages to be understood.
D. For sharing of experience.
E. For protection of traditions.

1. (A), (C), (E) only
2. (B), (C), (D) only
3. (A), (C), (D) only
4. (A), (B), (E) only

Explanations

Answer: 3. (A), (C), (D) only

Communication serves multiple essential purposes, primarily focused on **connection, understanding, and sharing experiences**:

(A) For social interaction: Communication is fundamental for **building relationships, fostering connections, and maintaining social bonds.**

(C) For messages to be understood: The **core goal of communication is clarity and mutual understanding** between sender and receiver.

(D) For sharing of experience: Communication allows individuals to **share stories, knowledge, and life experiences** with others.

Why not the other options?

(B) For happiness's sake: While communication can bring happiness, it is not its primary purpose.

(E) For protection of traditions: Although traditions are passed down through communication, this is a **specific application, not a general reason** for communication.

Meaning of Communication:

In terms of its origin, the word "communication" is "communicare" or "communis", which translates as "to impart", "to share", "to participate", or "to make common." The concept of sharing is inherent in the word "communication." Communicating involves giving, receiving, and sharing information, in other words, speaking, writing, listening or reading. An effective communicator listens carefully, speaks clearly, and respects the opinions of others. Based on the basic concept of communication, it is transmitting and receiving messages from one part (sender) to another (receiver).

- **Network of Inter-relations** – Signs interact to form meaning.
- **Subjectivity of Components** – Interpretation varies by individual.
- **Neutrality of Channel** – Medium does not define meaning.
- **Objectivity of Decoder** – Meaning still shaped by context.
- **Shared Symbolic Environment** – Basis for communication.
- **Sense of Community** – Interaction builds social bonds.
- **Non-participants' Relations** – Symbols extend beyond speakers.

- **Social Interaction** – Builds human relationships.
- **Message Understanding** – Ensures clarity and meaning.
- **Sharing Experiences** – Passed down knowledge and ideas.

Question

Statement I: Communication and socialisation are two non-convergent dimensions of any modern society.
Statement Il: Communication enables the promotion of values that facilitate the process of enculturisation of people in a society.

1. Both Statement I and Statement Il are true
2. Both Statement I and Statement Il are false
3. Statement I is true but Statement Il is false
4. Statement I is false but Statement Il is true

Explanations
Answer: 4. Statement I is false but Statement Il is true

Statement I is false: Communication and socialization are not non-convergent dimensions; rather, they are deeply interconnected. Socialization relies heavily on communication to transmit values, norms, and cultural practices across generations and within social groups.

Statement II is true: Communication plays a **key role in promoting values and norms**, helping individuals internalize cultural practices and facilitating the **enculturation process**, where people learn and adopt their society's culture.

Question

In communication, a text is a product of.

1. Non-responsiveness
2. Military exercises
3. Social interaction
4. Neurological research

Explanations
Answer: 3. Social interaction

A **text** in communication refers to any written, spoken, or visual message created as a result of **social interaction**. It reflects shared meanings, cultural contexts, and intended messages between individuals or groups.

Why not the other options?

- **Non-responsiveness** – No reaction, no meaningful communication.
- **Military exercises** – Drills, not for communication texts.
- **Neurological research** – Studies brain, not communication texts.

Question

Statement I: The words - communication, community and communion are etymologically related.
Statement Il: As human society developed more and more simple systems of communication emerged.

1. Both Statement I and Statement Il are true
2. Both Statement I and Statement Il are false
3. Statement I is true but Statement Il is false
4. Statement I is false but Statement Il is true

Explanations
Answer: 3. Statement I is true but Statement Il is false

Statement I is true: The words **"communication," "community," and "communion"** share a common Latin root, **"communis,"** meaning **"common" or "shared."** This reflects the idea of sharing information, creating connections, and building collective understanding.

Statement II is false: As human society developed, **communication systems became more complex, not simpler.** From basic gestures and oral traditions to written scripts, printing presses, digital media, and advanced virtual communication, communication systems have evolved in sophistication over time.

Question

Statement I: In communication, meaning construction is a process of making choices.

Statement II: Use of language for communication is a restrictive practice in the public domain.

1. Both Statement I and Statement II are true
2. Both Statement I and Statement Il are false
3. Statement l is true but Statement Il is false
4. Statement I is false but Statement Il is true

Explanations
Answer: 3. Statement l is true but Statement Il is false

Statement I is true: In communication, **meaning construction involves making choices** about words, tone, style, and context. Communicators decide how to frame their message to ensure clarity, relevance, and effectiveness based on the audience and situation.

Statement II is false: The **use of language for communication is not inherently restrictive in the public domain**. Public communication often encourages openness, inclusivity, and transparency. Restrictions, when present, are usually context-specific, such as in formal or regulated settings.

Question

Statement I: According to some experts, communication reflects the primary group affiliation of a person.
Statement Il: Communication should be understood within the broad social structure and process.

1. Both Statement I and Statement II are True.
2. Both Statement I and Statement Il are False.
3. Statement I is true but Statement Il is False.
4. Statement I is false but Statement Il is True.

Explanations
Answer: 1. Both Statement I and Statement II are True.

Statement I is true: Communication reflects the primary group affiliation by expressing shared values, norms, and identity linked to an individual's primary social groups, such as family or close friends.

Statement II is true: Communication must be understood within a broad social structure as it involves social dynamics, hierarchies, and processes that shape interaction patterns.

Question

The golden rules that communicators should follow are :

A. They should be aloof
B. They should take sides
C. They must be heard
D. They must be understood
E. They must be appreciated

1. (A), (B), (C) only
2. (B), (C), (D) only
3. (D), (E), (A) only
4. (C), (D), (E) only

Explanations
Answer: 4. (C), (D), (E) only

The **golden rules of communication** emphasize clarity, engagement, and creating a meaningful impact. Effective communicators should ensure:

(C) They must be heard: A communicator's message should **reach the audience clearly and effectively.**

(D) They must be understood: The message must be **interpreted accurately without ambiguity.**

(E) They must be appreciated: The audience should **find value, relevance, and connection in the communication.**

Why not the other options?

(A) They should be aloof: Effective communication requires **engagement and connection, not emotional detachment.**

(B) They should take sides: Communicators should strive for **objectivity and fairness** unless advocating for a specific cause intentionally.

Definition of Communication:

- **Origin** – From Latin *communicare,* meaning "to share."
- **Purpose** – Bridges self-other, private-public divide.
- **Murphy, Hildebrandt & Thomas** – Verbal and non-verbal message exchange.
- **Effectiveness** – Achieves desired receiver response.
- **Keith Davis** – Passing information and understanding.
- **John Adair** – Making contact and being understood.
- **Peter Little** – Transmitting information for understanding.
- **Newman & Summer** – Exchange of ideas and emotions.
- **Louis Allen** – A continuous meaning-making process.
- Communication is a **dynamic exchange of messages.**
- Communication is **social interaction via messages.**
- Communication is **continuously** Evolving
- Language as a tool of communication **provides a grid of reality.**
- Human communication involves **Message Transmission, Reception, Verbal and Non-verbal Messages.**

Question

Communication is continuously-

1. Evolving
2. negative
3. stagnant
4. subliminal

Explanations
Answer: 1. Evolving

Communication is a **dynamic and ever-changing process** that adapts to technological advancements, cultural shifts, and societal changes. It continuously evolves to meet the needs of individuals and groups in different contexts.

Why not the other options?

Negative: Communication is not inherently negative; its impact depends on how it is used.

Stagnant: Communication is never static; it always adapts and grows with time.

Subliminal: Subliminal communication refers to hidden or subconscious messaging, which does not describe the overall nature of communication.

Question

Which of the following are the correct definitions of communication?

A. Process of ideating, searching and telling.
B. Process of sending, receiving, and interpreting the message.
C. Communication is social interaction through messages.
D. Process of thinking, writing, and channelising the messages.

1. AB
2. AC
3. BD
4. BC

Explanations
Answer: 4. BC

Option B: Communication involves the **process of sending, receiving, and interpreting messages**, highlighting the dynamic exchange of information between sender and receiver.

Option C: Communication is indeed **social interaction through messages**, emphasizing its role in building relationships and facilitating interaction in society.

Why not A and D?

Option A: "Ideating, searching, and telling" focuses more on individual thought processes and sharing but misses the two-way interactive aspect of communication.

Option D: "Thinking, writing, and channelizing messages" emphasizes preparation and structuring but does not fully capture the interactive and interpretive nature of communication.

Question

Statement I: Communication can be a path to seek truth.
Statement Il: Communication can also be used to suppress truth.

1. Both Statement I and Statement Il are true
2. Both Statement I and Statement Il are false
3. Statement I is true but Statement II is false
4. Statement I is false but Statement II is true

Explanations
Answer: 1. Both Statement I and Statement Il are true

Statement I is true: Communication can indeed be a **path to seek truth**. Open dialogue, transparent discussions, and the sharing of information allow individuals and societies to uncover facts, clarify misunderstandings, and arrive at informed conclusions.

Statement II is true: Communication can also be **manipulated to suppress the truth**. Misleading information, propaganda, censorship, and deliberate misinformation are ways communication can be used to hide or distort reality.

Question

Language as a tool of communication provides a grid of-

1. Bliss
2. Hidden Secrets
3. Reality
4. Info-paradise

Explanations
Answer: 3. Reality

Language acts as a **tool for constructing, interpreting, and expressing reality**. It helps individuals and societies make sense of the world by framing experiences, sharing knowledge, and establishing common understandings. Through language, abstract and concrete realities are communicated effectively.

Why not the other options?

Bliss: While language can express joy or happiness, it does not inherently create a grid for bliss.

Hidden Secrets: Language may reveal or obscure secrets, but it is primarily a tool for clarity and communication.

Info-paradise: This term is not directly related to the fundamental function of language in shaping reality.

Question

Human communication involves

A. Message Transmission
B. Message reception
C. Verbal and non-verbal messages
D. Power-packed messages only
E. Messages for non-consumption

1. A, B, C Only
2. B, C, D Only
3. B, D, E Only
4. A, C, E Only

Explanations
Answer: 1. A, B, C Only

A. Message Transmission: Communication involves **sending or transmitting messages** from a sender to a receiver using various channels or mediums.

B. Message Reception: Successful communication requires the **receiver to interpret and understand the transmitted message**, completing the communication cycle.

C. Verbal and Non-verbal Messages: Communication is not limited to spoken or written words; it also includes **non-verbal cues such as gestures, facial expressions, posture, and tone of voice.**

Why not the other options?

D. Power-packed messages only: Communication is not restricted to "power-packed" messages; it includes casual, routine, or even simple exchanges.

E. Messages for non-consumption: Communication is meant to **be received, interpreted, and acted upon**, not for "non-consumption."

Question

A competent communicator is

A. Culturally neutral
B. Culturally sensitive
C. Totally ethical
D. Situationally ethical
E. An effective listener

1. A, B and C only
2. B, C and D only
3. B, C and E only
4. A, C and D only

Explanations
Answer: 3. B, C and E only

A **competent communicator** possesses qualities that ensure clarity, cultural awareness, and ethical responsibility in communication. These include:

B. Culturally sensitive: A competent communicator **respects cultural differences, understands diverse perspectives, and adjusts their communication style accordingly.**

C. Totally ethical: Ethical communication involves **honesty, transparency, and integrity** in delivering messages without misleading or harming others.

E. An effective listener: Competent communication requires **active listening to understand others' perspectives, respond appropriately, and avoid misunderstandings.**

Why not the other options?

A. Culturally neutral: No communication is entirely culturally neutral, as communication is inherently influenced by cultural norms and values.

D. Situationally ethical: Ethical communication should not depend solely on the situation but should remain consistent across contexts.

Cultural Aspects of Communication:

Communication between cultures is the practice and study of verbal and nonverbal communication within a community. It is also known as cross-cultural communication or intercultural communication. A culture's philosophy, values, and beliefs are communicated verbally and non-verbally. It is through parenting practices that teach social and communicative behaviours that cultural values are passed from generation to generation.

- **Specific Cultural Context** – Meaning depends on culture.
- **Contrasting Style** – Affects presentation, not meaning.
- **Random Order** – Creates confusion in interpretation.
- **Non-specific Context** – Leads to misinterpretation.
- **Culturally Sensitive** – Respects diverse perspectives.
- **Totally Ethical** – Maintains integrity in speech.
- **Effective Listener** – Understands before responding.

Question

Statement (I): Communication cannot reflect the cultural conduct of people
Statement (II): Communication is a practice integral to formation of social life

1. Both Statement (I) and Statement (II) are correct.
2. Both Statement (I) and Statement (II) are incorrect.
3. Statement (I) is correct but Statement (II) is incorrect
4. Statement (I) is incorrect but Statement (II) is correct

Explanations
Answer: 4. Statement (I) is incorrect but Statement (II) is correct

Statement (I) is incorrect: Communication **does reflect the cultural conduct of people**, as it is deeply influenced by cultural norms, values, and traditions. The way people communicate—language, gestures, tone, and non-verbal cues—often mirrors their cultural background.

Statement (II) is correct: Communication is indeed **integral to the formation of social life**, as it enables interaction, builds relationships, and helps establish societal norms and structures.

Question

From the communication viewpoint which one of the following is a cultural institution?

1. Trade organizations
2. Political parties
3. Military alliances
4. Family

Explanations
Answer: 4. Family

From a **communication viewpoint**, the **family is considered a primary cultural institution** because it is the **first space where individuals learn and practice communication norms, values, and behaviors**. It serves as the foundation for socialization, passing on cultural traditions, language, and communication styles.

Why not the other options?

Trade organizations: These are economic institutions focused on commerce and business, not primarily cultural.

Political parties: While they influence societal norms, they are more aligned with political structures than cultural foundations.

Military alliances: These are strategic and defensive partnerships, not inherently cultural institutions.

Question

Statement I: When messages are delivered by popular sources, they have higher attention and recall of the receivers.
Statement II: A highly credible source may not score much in the areas of expertise, trustworthiness and likability.

1. Both Statement I and Statement Il are true.
2. Both Statement I and Statement Il are false.
3. Statement I is true but Statement Il is false.
4. Statement I is false but Statement Il is true.

Explanations
Answer: 3. Statement I is true but Statement Il is false.

Statement I is true: When messages are **delivered by popular sources (e.g., well-known figures, influencers, or celebrities)**, they tend to **capture higher attention and have better recall** because of the familiarity, relatability, and trust people associate with these sources.

Statement II is false: A **highly credible source inherently scores well in areas of expertise, trustworthiness, and likability.** Credibility is built on these three factors, and a lack of any one of them diminishes overall credibility.

Question

A culture that is not touched by communication of alphabetic writing is known as a culture.

1. Literacy
2. Typography
3. Exclusivity
4. Primary Orality

Explanations
Answer: 4. Primary Orality

A **"Primary Orality"** culture refers to a society that **relies entirely on spoken language for communication and has no exposure to alphabetic writing or written texts.** These cultures pass down knowledge, traditions, and stories orally through speech, chants, and oral narratives rather than written records.

Why not the other options?

Literacy: Refers to the ability to read and write, which does not exist in primary orality cultures.

Typography: Refers to the style, arrangement, and appearance of printed text, irrelevant to oral cultures.

Exclusivity: This term does not directly describe a culture based on oral communication.

Semiotic Aspects of Communication:

A possible definition of communication would be the act of generating meaning among entities or groups by using signs, symbols, and semiotic conventions that both parties mutually understand.

Semiotics

- **Study of Signs** – Examines how signs create meaning.
- **Semiosis** – Any process involving sign interpretation.
- **Sign Interpretation** – Meaning depends on the interpreter.
- **Perception Shaping** – Influences how we see reality.
- **Message Effectiveness** – Ensures signs convey intended meaning.
- **Cultural Impact** – Signs vary across cultures.
- **Linguistic Connection** – Related to language and communication.
- **Visual and Non-Visual** – Includes gestures, symbols, images.
- **Symbolic Communication** – Signs function in multiple contexts.
- **Influences Media** – Used in advertising and storytelling.
- **Inter-subjective Mediation** – Shared meaning through signs.
- **Extra-subjective** – Outside subjective human experience.
- **Non-subjective** – Lacks human perception or emotion.
- **Macro-subjective** – Large-scale subjective interpretations.

Question

Which of the following approaches to the analysis of content is based on the study of signs?

1. Semiotics
2. Ethnography
3. Content Analysis

4. Quantitative Research

Explanations
Answer: 1. Semiotics

Semiotics is the **study of signs, symbols, and their meanings** in communication. It examines how meaning is created and understood through symbols, images, gestures, and language. Semiotics goes beyond the surface content to analyze the deeper cultural and contextual meanings embedded in messages.

Why not the other options?

Ethnography: Focuses on **observing and understanding cultural practices and social interactions** in their natural context.

Content Analysis: Involves a **systematic examination of text or media to identify patterns and themes**, often in a quantitative or qualitative manner.

Quantitative Research: Uses **numerical data and statistical methods** to analyze communication patterns, not signs specifically.

Question

According to the semiotic tradition, communication is ___ mediation of signs.

1. Extra-subjective
2. Non-subjective
3. Inter-subjective
4. Macro-subjective

Explanations
Answer: 3. Inter-subjective

In the **semiotic tradition**, communication is described as **inter-subjective mediation of signs**, meaning it involves a **shared understanding between individuals through the use of signs and symbols**. Inter-subjectivity emphasizes that communication is a **mutual process where meaning is co-created and interpreted by both the sender and receiver** within a shared cultural or social context.

Signs

- **Indicator** – Represents the presence of something.
- **Causal Signs** – Thunder means a storm is coming.
- **Medical Signs** – Symptoms indicate diseases.
- **Gesture-Based** – Many signs are non-verbal.
- **Symbolic Use** – Can function as a communication tool.
- **Enhances Understanding** – Provides additional visual cues.
- **Universal & Contextual** – Some are universal, others contextual.
- **Categories** – Divided into signs and symbols.
- **Preeminent in Communication** – Essential for human interaction.
- **Used Naturally** – Part of everyday life.
- **Internal Relations** – Signs depend on each other.
- **Network of Signs** – Meaning arises through associations.
- **Subjectivity of Components** – Meaning shaped by perceptions.
- **Objectivity of Decoder** – Interpretation still culturally influenced.

Question

Assertion (A): Relationship even among non-participants Communication presupposes a shared, symbolic environment, a social

Reason (R): It leads to social interaction, which in combination with other factors contributes to a sense of community.

Choose the correct option given below :

1. Both (A) and (R) are true but R is the correct explanation of A
2. Both (A) and (R) are true but R is not the correct explanation of A
3. (A) is true but (R) is false
4. (A) is false but (R) is true

Explanations

Answer: 1. Both (A) and (R) are true but R is the correct explanation of A

Assertion (A) is true: Communication relies on a **shared symbolic environment** (e.g., language, gestures, norms) that provides a foundation for mutual understanding, even among those not directly participating in an interaction.

Reason (R) is true: This **shared symbolic environment facilitates social interaction**, and when combined with cultural, emotional, and social factors, it contributes to a **collective sense of community**.

R explains A: The **shared symbolic environment** acts as a bridge that allows communication to transcend direct participation, fostering interaction and strengthening communal bonds.

Question

Statement I: Signs and symbols have internal relations to produce meanings
Statement II: This is possible because of a network of signs through such relations

1. Both Statement I and Statement Il are true
2. Both Statement I and Statement Il are false
3. Statement l is true but Statement Il is false
4. Statement I is false but Statement Il is true

Explanations
Answer: 1. Both Statement I and Statement Il are true

Statement I is true: Signs and symbols do not exist in isolation; they have **internal relationships** with one another, forming patterns and systems that help produce meaning. For example, words in a sentence derive meaning not only from themselves but also from their relationship with other words.

Statement II is true: These relationships are possible because **signs exist within a network or system of interdependent relationships** (as described by Ferdinand de Saussure in semiotics). The meaning of one sign is influenced by its contrast and association with other signs in the system.

Question

Signs are considered as secondary products of:

1. Message
2. Channelisation
3. Semantic accuracy
4. Infotainment

Explanations
Answer: 1. Message

Signs are considered **secondary products of a message** because they **are created or derived during the process of encoding information into a communicable form.** The message serves as the primary element, while signs (e.g., words, symbols, gestures) are used to **represent and transmit the intended meaning.**

Why not the other options?

Channelisation: Refers to the **medium or path through which the message travels,** not the creation of signs.

Semantic accuracy: Deals with the **correct interpretation of meaning,** not the origin of signs.

Infotainment: Refers to **information combined with entertainment,** unrelated to the origin of signs.

The message serves as the core, and signs are the tools through which the message is symbolized and conveyed.

Symbols

- **Representation** – Stands for an idea or concept.
- **Varied Forms** – Can be words, images, sounds.
- **Cultural Connection** – Meanings differ across cultures.
- **Beyond Reality** – Links different experiences.
- **Data Processing** – Essential in communication and computing.
- **Universal Symbols** – Some symbols are globally recognized.
- **Stop Sign Example** – Red octagon means "STOP."
- **Religious & Political Use** – Found in faith and governance.
- **Abstract or Concrete** – Some represent real things, others abstract.
- **Enhances Communication** – Strengthens meaning in messaging.
- **Arbitrary and Conventional Symbols** – Meaning agreed upon culturally.
- **Multiple Symbols for Same Idea** – Different words for same concept.
- **Words as Symbols** – Represent concepts, ideas, or objects.

- **Socio-cultural** – Symbols shaped by culture.
- **Instrumental** – Used for achieving goals.
- **Non-ritualistic** – Lacks cultural significance.
- **Mechanical** – Not interpretive or context-driven.

A communication process can be viewed as the transmission of information governed by three levels of semiotic rules:

1. **Pragmatic**: It concerns the relations between signs/expressions and their users.
2. **Semantic**: It studies relationships between signs and symbols and what they represent.
3. **Syntactic:** It refers to the formal properties of signs and symbols.

Question

Which of the following statements are true in respect of communication?

A. Communicated meanings are always ambiguous.
B. Words are symbols for concepts.
C. Labels may be ambiguous.
D. Symbols are usually understood within a group.
E. Sharing of meaning is not possible in communication.

1. ABC
2. BCD
3. CDE
4. ABE

Explanations
Answer: 2. BCD

B. Words are symbols for concepts: Words function as **symbolic representations of ideas, objects, or concepts**, allowing people to communicate abstract and concrete meanings.

C. Labels may be ambiguous: Labels, whether verbal or symbolic, can sometimes **carry multiple meanings or interpretations**, depending on the context or the audience.

D. Symbols are usually understood within a group: Symbols derive their meaning **from shared understanding within a specific cultural or social group**, enabling common interpretation among its members.

Why not the other options?

A. Communicated meanings are always ambiguous: Meanings can sometimes be ambiguous, but not **always**. Clear communication often reduces ambiguity.

E. Sharing of meaning is not possible in communication: The **core purpose of communication is to share meaning**. While misunderstandings can occur, sharing meaning remains a fundamental goal.

Question

In which of the following categories did Charles Sanders Peirce classify the 'signs'?

A. Object
B. Indices
C. Icons
D. Interpretant
E. Symbols

1. ABC
2. BCE
3. CDE
4. ADE

Explanations
Answer: 2. BCE

- **B (Correct) - Indices**: Signs that have a direct connection to their objects (e.g., smoke for fire).
- **C (Correct) - Icons**: Signs that resemble what they represent (e.g., a picture of a cat represents a real cat).
- **E (Correct) - Symbols**: Signs where meaning is assigned by convention (e.g., words, traffic signals).

A & D (Incorrect): **Object and Interpretant** are parts of Peirce's **semiotic model**, not sign categories.

Question

Statement I: Communication is a social process in which people use symbols to interpret meanings in their own environment
Statement II: People and their interactions are not part of the communication process, because communication cannot be social

1. Both Statement (I) and Statement (Il) are correct.
2. Both Statement (I) and Statement (Il) are incorrect.
3. Statement (I) is correct but Statement (Il) is incorrect
4. Statement (I) is incorrect but Statement (II) is correct

Explanations
Answer: 3. Statement (I) is correct but Statement (Il) is incorrect

Statement (I) is correct: Communication is indeed a **social process** where people use **symbols (words, gestures, images)** to **create, interpret, and share meanings** within their environment. It emphasizes interaction and shared understanding.

Statement (II) is incorrect: Communication is inherently **social**, and people and their **interactions are central to the communication process**.

Question

Symbols provide meaning when used in a

1. Contrasting style
2. Random order
3. Non-specific context
4. Specific cultural context

Explanations
Answer: 4. Specific cultural context

Symbols derive their **meaning within a specific cultural context**, where shared understanding and agreed-upon conventions define their interpretation. Different cultures may assign different meanings to the same symbol, and without cultural context, symbols may lose their intended significance.

Why not the other options?

Contrasting style: Style may enhance presentation, but it does not inherently define symbolic meaning.

Random order: Symbols arranged randomly lack coherence and fail to convey consistent meaning.

Non-specific context: Without a clear context, symbols can be misinterpreted or lose their intended meaning.

Question

The symbolic mode of communication is:

1. Instrumental
2. Non-ritualistic
3. Socio-cultural
4. Mechanical

Explanations
Answer: 3. Socio-cultural

The **symbolic mode of communication** is inherently **socio-cultural** because **symbols derive their meaning from shared cultural norms, values, and social practices.** Communication through symbols—whether language, gestures, or signs—depends on a **common cultural framework** for interpretation and understanding.

Why not the other options?

Instrumental: While communication can serve instrumental purposes, the symbolic mode is not limited to tools or objectives.

Non-ritualistic: Symbolic communication often carries ritualistic significance in cultural and social settings.

Mechanical: Symbolic communication is not mechanical; it is interpretive and context-driven.

Question

Statement I: In communication, codes have never been neutral in their reception.
Statement II: Codes always represent meanings, reflecting partiality.

1. Both Statement I and Statement Il are true
2. Both Statement I and Statement Il are false
3. Statement I is true but Statement Il is false
4. Statement I is false but Statement Il is true

Explanations
Answer: 1. Both Statement I and Statement Il are true

Statement I is true: In communication, **codes (symbols, language, signs)** are **never neutral** because they are interpreted through cultural, social, and personal contexts. The receiver's background, biases, and perceptions always influence how a code is understood.

Statement II is true: Codes inherently carry meaning and reflect partiality, as they are shaped by societal values, cultural norms, and historical contexts. They represent specific perspectives, ideologies, or cultural positions.

Question

Communication stimuli used to convey the message are known as

1. Process
2. Power
3. Channel
4. Codes

Explanations
Answer: 4. Codes

In communication, **codes refer to the stimuli (such as words, gestures, symbols, or images) used to convey a message.** These codes are part of a structured system of signs and symbols shared between the sender and receiver to ensure meaning is effectively communicated.

Why not the other options?

Process: Refers to the overall **sequence of communication events**, not the specific stimuli used to convey meaning.

Power: Refers to the **influence or control dynamics** in communication, not the message carriers.

Channel: Refers to the **medium through which the message travels** (e.g., airwaves, written text, digital platforms), not the symbols themselves.

Question

In verbal communication, words act as:

1. Fillers
2. Decoratives.
3. Symbols
4. Passive barriers

Explanations
Answer: 3. Symbols

In **verbal communication, words act as symbols** because they **represent objects, actions, ideas, or concepts** rather than being directly tied to them. Words are **arbitrary and conventional signs** agreed upon by a community to convey specific meanings, forming the foundation of language and communication.

Why not the other options?

Fillers: Words like *"um," "uh," "well"* serve as fillers in speech but do not represent the symbolic function of language.

Decoratives: Words are not merely decorative; they serve a functional and symbolic purpose.

Passive barriers: Words are not barriers; they are tools for creating and sharing meaning

Question

Statement (I): Communication is a symbolic process and as such depends upon symbols that are both arbitrary and conventional.
Statement (II): Different symbols cannot be selected to represent an object or idea to communicate.

1. Both Statement (I) and Statement (Il) are correct.
2. Both Statement (I) and Statement (Il) are incorrect.
3. Statement (I) is correct but Statement (Il) is incorrect
4. Statement (I) is incorrect but Statement (Il) is correct

Explanations
Answer: 3. Statement (I) is correct but Statement (Il) is incorrect

Statement (I) is correct: Communication is indeed a **symbolic process**, where **symbols (e.g., words, gestures, images)** are used to represent objects, ideas, or feelings. These symbols are often **arbitrary (their meaning isn't inherently tied to what they represent)** and **conventional (agreed upon by a community).**

Statement (II) is incorrect: Different symbols **can be selected to represent the same object or idea** in communication. For example, the word *"water"* in English is symbolized as *"pani"* in Hindi or *"eau"* in French. The choice of symbols varies across languages and cultures.

Question

In the communication process, signs derive meanings through

1. The subjectivity of various components
2. The objectivity of the decoder
3. The network of inter-relations
4. The neutrality of the channel

Explanations
Answer: 3. The network of inter-relations

In the communication process, **signs derive meaning not in isolation but through their relationships with other signs within a system or network.** This principle is central to **semiotic theory**, where the meaning of a sign depends on its **context, contrast, and connection** with other signs in the communication network.

Why not the other options?

The subjectivity of various components: While subjectivity affects interpretation, meaning primarily arises from the **relationships between signs** rather than individual subjective views.

The objectivity of the decoder: Decoding is influenced by context and cultural understanding, not pure objectivity.

The neutrality of the channel: Channels (e.g., text, speech, digital media) are **neutral conduits** and do not actively construct meaning.

Communication Protocol:

The definition of a communication protocol is a set of rules that allow two or more entities of a communication system to exchange information using any variation in a physical quantity. The protocol specifies the rules, syntax, semantics and synchronization of communication, as well as possible error recovery methods. It is possible to implement protocols using either hardware or software.

- **Transmission Control Protocol (TCP)**: It is used for data transmission.
- **User Datagram Protocol (UDP):** It is used by programs to send short datagram messages.
- **Internet Control Message Protocol (ICMP):** It is a message used for diagnostic or error-generating purposes.

The 5 Cs of Communication:

- **Clarity** – The message should be clear and easily understood.
- **Conciseness** – Keep communication brief and to the point.
- **Coherence** – Ensure logical flow and consistency in ideas.
- **Correctness** – Use accurate language, facts, and grammar.

- **Courtesy** – Be respectful and considerate in tone and delivery.

Question

Arrange the sequence the 5 Cs (Elements) of communication-

A. Compassionate
B. Curious
C. Compelling
D. Concise
E. Clear

1. A, B,C,D, E
2. B, A, C, D, E
3. E, D, C, B, A
4. D, E, C, A, B

Explanations
Answer: 3. E, D, C, B, A

The **5 Cs of communication** are often arranged in the following order to ensure clarity and effectiveness:

1. **Clear**
2. **Concise**
3. **Compelling**
4. **Curious**
5. **Compassionate**

This sequence ensures that the message is first clear and brief, followed by engagement, curiosity, and emotional connection.

Question

Sequential accounts, told from a particular viewpoint are called:

1. Situational actions
2. Social themes
3. Narratives
4. Dignified discourse

Explanations
Answer: 3. Narratives

A **narrative** refers to a **sequential account of events or experiences told from a particular viewpoint**. It involves a clear structure with a beginning, middle, and end, often providing context, perspective, and meaning to the events described.

Why not the other options?

Situational actions: These refer to specific behaviors in response to particular situations, not structured storytelling.

Social themes: These are overarching ideas or topics in society, not sequential accounts.

Dignified discourse: This refers to respectful and formal communication, not necessarily sequential storytelling.

Question

Many modern scholars consider the following as positive aspects of communication. Which of them are true?

A. Communication helps create knowledge
B. It defines the human goals
C. It supports efforts to change social norms
D. It makes simple tasks complex
E. It promotes propaganda techniques all the time

1. ABC
2. BCD
3. DE
4. ACE

Explanations
Answer: 1. ABC

Modern scholars view communication as a **powerful tool for societal and personal development** through the following aspects:

A. Communication helps create knowledge: It facilitates the **exchange of ideas, sharing of information, and building collective understanding**, contributing to knowledge creation.

B. It defines human goals: Communication allows individuals and groups to **express aspirations, set objectives, and align efforts** toward shared goals.

C. It supports efforts to change social norms: Communication plays a key role in **raising awareness, challenging stereotypes, and promoting social change** through dialogue and campaigns.

Why not the other options?

D. It makes simple tasks complex: Effective communication simplifies tasks rather than complicating them.

E. It promotes propaganda techniques all the time: While communication can be used for propaganda, it is not inherently tied to it or used exclusively for that purpose.

Roles and Forms of Communication

Communication Roles

- **Disruptive Role** – Blocks effective communication flow.
- **Promotive Role** – Encourages constructive group discussions.
- **Counteractive Role** – Fixes communication breakdowns.
- **Devotional Role** – Reinforces commitment to values.

Question

When communication helps a group to achieve its goals, it is known as

1. Disruptive role
2. Promotive role
3. Counteractive role
4. Devotional role

Explanations

Answer: 2. Promotive role

When communication **facilitates coordination, clarity, and understanding within a group to achieve its goals**, it serves a **promotive role**. This type of communication focuses on encouraging productive discussions, resolving conflicts, and aligning group members toward shared objectives.

Forms of Communication

- **Personal Address** – Direct communication between individuals.
- **Social Drama** – Conflict-driven public interactions.
- **Narratives** – Storytelling to convey ideas.
- **Silence** – Expresses meaning without words.

Question

List - I (Communication form)	List - II (Description)
A. Personal address	I. Sequential accounts told and retold from a particular viewpoint
B. Social drama	II. Subject to a community's rules for appropriate conduct
C. Narratives	Ill. Points to self and others in interaction
D. Silence	IV. Invokes local socio-cultural rules for behavior

Choose the correct answer from the options given below:

1. A-,I B-III, C-IV, D-II
2. A-II, B-I, C-III, D-IV
3. A-III, B-IV, C-I, D-II
4. A-IV, B-I, C-II, D-III

Explanations

Answer: 3. A-III, B-IV, C-I, D-II

A. Personal address → III. Points to self and others in interaction

Personal address refers to the use of names, titles, or pronouns to **identify and address individuals in conversation**, establishing relationships and context.

B. Social drama → IV. Invokes local socio-cultural rules for behavior

Social drama refers to **performative actions that follow cultural or social norms**, often reflecting societal values or addressing conflicts.

C. Narratives → I. Sequential accounts told and retold from a particular viewpoint
Narratives are **structured stories or accounts that present events sequentially** from a specific perspective.

D. Silence → II. Subject to a community's rules for appropriate conduct
Silence in communication carries **cultural and contextual meanings**, often shaped by societal norms about when and how silence is appropriate.

Discipline of Communication Process

- **Anthropology → Culture** – Studies symbols and traditions.
- **Sociology → Society** – Analyzes social structures.
- **Psychology → Motivation** – Examines internal drive and influence.
- **Management → System** – Organizes communication processes.

Question

Match the column:

LIST 1: Discipline	LIST 2: Focus of Communication Process
A. Anthropology	I. motivation
B. Sociology	II. system
C. Psychology	III. culture
D. Management	IV. society

1. A-II B-III C-IV D-I
2. A-III B-IV C-I D-II
3. A-I B-II C-III D-IV
4. A-IV B-I C-II D-III

Explanations
Answer: 2. A-III B-IV C-I D-II

A. Anthropology → III. Culture: Anthropology studies **human societies, their cultures, and development over time**, focusing on how culture shapes communication practices and behaviors.

B. Sociology → IV. Society: Sociology examines **how individuals interact within societies and how social structures influence communication patterns.**

C. Psychology → I. Motivation: Psychology focuses on **individual behavior, thoughts, emotions, and motivations,** which play a crucial role in how and why people communicate.

D. Management → II. System: Management views communication as a **structured system for coordination, control, and achieving organizational goals.**

Language as a Communication Tool

- **Expressing Emotions** – Words convey feelings effectively.
- **Manipulating Perceptions** – Shapes opinions and beliefs.
- **Influencing Relationships** – Builds or damages connections.
- **Gaining Sympathy** – Elicits emotional support.
- **Avoiding Confrontation** – Reduces conflict in discussions.
- **Consoling Friends** – Provides comfort through words.
- **Embarrassing Adversaries** – Uses language to demean.

Question

Statement I: Communicative language is used by people to get sympathy, ignore fellow travelers, placate or embarrass enemies, and comfort friends.
Statement II: As a tool of communication, language suffers from emotional loadings, polar words and fictitious concepts.

1. Both Statement I and Statement II are true
2. Both Statement I and Statement II are false
3. Statement I is true but Statement II is false
4. Statement I is false but Statement II is true

Explanations
Answer: 1. Both Statement I and Statement II are true

Statement I is true: Language is not just a tool for sharing information but also a **means to express emotions, manipulate perceptions, and influence**

relationships. People use language to **gain sympathy, avoid confrontation, console friends, or even embarrass adversaries.**

Statement II is true: Language, as a tool of communication, is often **laden with emotional weight, polarized terms (e.g., good vs. evil, right vs. wrong), and abstract or fictitious concepts** that may not have a clear reference in reality. These aspects can sometimes distort communication or influence interpretations.

Language and Communication Distortions

- **Emotional Weight** – Words carry deep feelings.
- **Polarized Terms** – Oppositional language influences thought.
- **Abstract Concepts** – Meaning varies by interpretation.
- **Fictitious Constructs** – Imaginary ideas shape reality.
- **Distorted Communication** – Bias affects message clarity.
- **Influenced Interpretations** – Context alters message meaning.

Question

Statement I: Language and other symbolic means of communication are surely social products.
Statement II: Communication media always provide the feel-good-factor to their users

1. Both Statement I and Statement Il are true
2. Both Statement I and Statement Il are false
3. Statement I is true but Statement Il is false
4. Statement I is false but Statement ll is true

Explanations
Answer: 3. Statement I is true but Statement Il is false

Statement I is true: Language and other symbolic means of communication (e.g., gestures, signs, and symbols) are inherently **social products**. They evolve through collective societal interactions, cultural norms, and shared experiences over time.

Statement II is false: Communication media do not **always provide a feel-good factor**. While they can entertain, inform, and uplift, they can also spread misinformation, provoke anxiety, or amplify negative emotions, depending on the content and usage.

Question

Communicative power is meaningful only in the network of-

1. Social relations
2. Ethical resistance
3. Restrictive freedom
4. Political one upmanship

Explanations
Answer: 1. Social relations

Communicative power derives its **meaning and effectiveness from social relations**, as communication is fundamentally about **building connections, sharing meanings, and influencing behaviors within a social context**. Social structures, norms, and relationships shape how messages are interpreted and acted upon.

Why not the other options?

Ethical resistance: While ethics play a role in communication, they don't form the primary framework for communicative power.

Restrictive freedom: Communication thrives in an open exchange, not under restrictive conditions.

Political one-upmanship: While political tactics use communication, they represent a subset and not the core foundation of communicative power.

Models of Communication:

Communication models are conceptual representations of the human communication process. A major model for communication was developed in 1948 by Claude Shannon and published by Bell Laboratories with an introduction by Warren Weaver. Also worth mentioning is Lasswell's communication model, which Harold Lasswell developed in 1948. Communication can be described along a few major dimensions: message

/content (what information is communicated), origin/source/sender /encoder (who sent it), signal/format (how it was transmitted), channel (how it was received), destination/sink/receiver /decoder (to whom).

Linear Model of Communication:

- **Basic Concept**: The linear model of communication is a one-way process where a sender transmits a message to a receiver through a communication channel. It involves five basic elements: sender, message, encoding, medium, and receiver.
- **Characteristics**:
    - **One-way flow**: The message flows in a straight line from sender to receiver.
    - **Simple**: It doesn't account for feedback or any kind of interaction during the process.
    - **Noise**: External factors (like physical noise or technical issues) can interfere with the message.
- **Example**: A television broadcast, where information flows from the TV station (sender) to the audience (receiver) without direct feedback.

Question

What are the advantages of linear communication?

A. It is best suited for persuasion
B. It quickens the process of feedback
C. It facilitates a two-way exchange of information
D. It is extensively used in international propaganda
E. It provides demarcated results

1. (A), (B) and (C) only
2. (B), (C) and (D) only
3. (C), (D) and (E) only
4. (A), (D) and (E) only

Explanations
Answer: 4. (A), (D) and (E) only

A. Best for persuasion: Focuses on influencing the receiver.

D. Used in propaganda: Effective for controlled one-way messaging.

E. Clear results: Provides measurable outcomes.

Feedback and two-way exchange are absent in linear communication.

Question

Which of the following are the key features of linear model of communication?

A. One-way communication
B. Manipulated feedback
C. Absence of noise
D. Used for mass communication
E. Sender-centric communication

1. A, B and C only
2. B, C and D only
3. D, C and E only
4. A, D and E only

Explanations
Answer: 4. A, D and E only

The **linear model of communication** is characterized by its **one-way, sender-focused nature**, often used in mass communication.

A. One-way communication: Information flows **in a single direction** from sender to receiver.

D. Used for mass communication: Effective for **broadcast media, speeches, and public announcements.**

E. Sender-centric communication: The **sender controls the message**, with little to no emphasis on receiver feedback.

Why not the other options?

B. Manipulated feedback: Feedback is **not part of the linear model.**

C. Absence of noise: Noise is always present in **any communication process**, even in linear models.

Question

Match column:

A. Encoding	I. Many meanings
B. Decoding	II. A linguistics system
C. Polysemy	III. Process of creating a message according to a particular code
D. Langue	IV. Process of using a code to decipher a message

1. A-I B-III C-III D-IV
2. A-II B-III C-IV D-I
3. A-III B-IV C-I D-II
4. A-IV B- I C-II D-III

Explanations

Answer: 3. A-III B-IV C-I D-II

Question

A university teacher makes a very effective expository presentation in his/her class without caring for its effect on the students. This is an example of a/an :

1. Linear Communication Model
2. Interactive Communication Model
3. Transactional Communication Model
4. Authoritarian Communication Model

Explanations
Answer: 1. Linear Communication Model

In the **Linear Communication Model**, communication flows **one-way** from the **sender (teacher)** to the **receiver (students)** without expecting or prioritizing **feedback**.

One-Way Process: The teacher delivers the presentation without actively engaging with the students' responses.

No Feedback Loop: There's no mechanism to ensure students understood the message or to allow interaction.

Sender-Centric: The focus is entirely on the **teacher delivering the message.**

Why not the other options?

Interactive Communication Model: Includes **feedback and interaction**, which is absent here.

Transactional Communication Model: Focuses on **simultaneous feedback and role exchange** between sender and receiver.

Authoritarian Communication Model: This is not a recognized communication model but more about **power dynamics** in communication.

Question

The sequence of elements in linear model of communication is

A. Message
B. Decoder
C. Encoder
D. Medium
E. Noise

1. ACBED
2. BDCAE
3. CADEB
4. DECAB

Explanations
Answer: 3. CADEB

C. Encoder: The **sender encodes the message** into a form suitable for transmission.
A. Message: The **encoded information** is structured as a message.
D. Medium: The message is **transmitted through a chosen medium or channel** (e.g., speech, writing).

E. Noise: External or internal interference might distort the message during transmission.
B. Decoder: The **receiver decodes the message** to understand its meaning.

Interactive Model of Communication:

- **Basic Concept**: The interactive model improves on the linear model by introducing feedback, making communication a two-way process. Both the sender and receiver act as communicators, allowing for interaction.
- **Characteristics**:
    - **Two-way communication**: Both parties (sender and receiver) share messages, and feedback is returned.
    - **Encoding and decoding**: The sender encodes the message, and the receiver decodes it, then may respond with feedback.
    - **Context**: This model incorporates the context in which the communication takes place (environment, culture, etc.).
    - **Noise**: It also accounts for noise (disturbances) affecting both the message and feedback.
- **Example**: A video call where both people communicate and respond to each other.

Transaction Model of Communication:

- **Basic Concept**: The transactional model views communication as a dynamic and continuous process where both participants are simultaneously senders and receivers of messages. It emphasizes the simultaneous exchange of messages.
- **Characteristics**:
    - **Simultaneous roles**: Both parties send and receive messages at the same time.
    - **No clear distinction between sender and receiver**: The roles of sender and receiver are interdependent and fluid.
    - **Continuous process**: Communication occurs in a continuous, ongoing process, where feedback and interaction are part of the message flow.
    - **Noise**: It considers both physical and psychological noise that can affect communication.

- **Context**: This model recognizes the importance of context (personal, cultural, etc.) in communication.

➢ **Example**: A face-to-face conversation where both individuals are talking and listening at the same time.

Question

The important features of the transactional model of communication are-

A. Feedback is repetitive.
B. It is mostly used for inter-personal communication.
C. The senders and the receivers of messages can inter-change their roles.
D. Feedback is simultaneous.
E. The heavy dose of noise provides a message.

1. ABC
2. BCD
3. CDE
4. ADE

Explanations
Answer: 2. BCD

The **transactional model of communication** emphasizes the **simultaneous exchange of messages and feedback**, making it highly dynamic and suitable for **interpersonal communication**.

Key Features:

B. It is mostly used for interpersonal communication: The model focuses on **real-time, two-way communication** between individuals.

C. The senders and the receivers of messages can interchange their roles: Communication roles **constantly switch between sender and receiver.**

D. Feedback is simultaneous: Feedback occurs **instantly and continuously**, making communication interactive and dynamic.

Why not the other options?

A. Feedback is repetitive: Feedback in the transactional model is **simultaneous, not repetitive.**

E. The heavy dose of noise provides a message: Noise **interferes with communication; it doesn't provide a message.**

Question

Which of the following are determinants in transactional communication?

A. Social context
B. Cultural context
C. Relational context
D. Legal context
E. Delayed context

1. 1. A, B and C only
2. 2. B, C and D only
3. 3. C, D and E only
4. 4. A, B and E only

Explanations
Answer: 1. 1. A, B and C only

In the **transactional model of communication**, communication is seen as a **dynamic, simultaneous process** influenced by multiple **contexts** that shape meaning.

A. Social context: Refers to the **social environment, norms, and expectations** that influence communication.

B. Cultural context: Includes **shared beliefs, traditions, and values** that guide how messages are interpreted.

C. Relational context: Focuses on the **relationship between the sender and receiver** (e.g., friends, colleagues, or strangers).

Why not the other options?

D. Legal context: While important in formal settings, it's not a key determinant in the **transactional communication model.**

E. Delayed context: Communication in this model focuses on **immediate, real-time interaction.**

Question

In communication process, when the sender and the receiver interchange their roles in respect of sending and receiving the message, it is called

1. Universal model
2. Transactional model
3. Singular-flow model
4. Pluralistic model B

Explanations
Answer: 2. Transactional model

In the **transactional model of communication**, the **sender and receiver interchange their roles** simultaneously, with both actively **sending and receiving messages in real-time.**

Dynamic Process: Communication happens **continuously and simultaneously.**

Role Reversal: The **sender becomes the receiver and vice versa** throughout the conversation.

Feedback Loop: Immediate feedback is **integrated into the process.**

Why not the other options?

Universal model: Not a recognized communication model.

Singular-flow model: Refers to **one-way communication**, not role interchange.

Pluralistic model: More related to **diverse perspectives,** not interactive role switching.

Question

A teacher decides to form six groups of students and assigns a sub-theme to each group for discussion and reporting. Which kind of communication model will best describe his/her strategy in this regard?

1. Linear model
2. Horizontal model
3. Interactional model
4. Transactional model

Explanations

Answer: 4. Transactional model

The **Transactional Model of Communication** best fits this scenario because:

Simultaneous Exchange: Communication happens **simultaneously** as students discuss, share ideas, and provide feedback within their groups.

Role Interchangeability: Students act as both **senders and receivers** during discussions.

Interactive Feedback: Continuous feedback loops are present as group members exchange thoughts and refine their understanding.

Dynamic Process: Communication adapts to the **group dynamics and ongoing discussion.**

Why not the other options?

Linear model: One-way communication; **no feedback or interaction** is emphasized.

Horizontal model: Refers to communication **between peers at the same level**, but doesn't fully capture group interaction.

Interactional model: Includes feedback but lacks the **simultaneous exchange of messages** seen in the transactional model.

I. Aristotle Model of Communication:

- Aristotle's Model is mainly focused on speaker and speech.
- It can be broadly divided into five primary elements: **Speaker, Speech, Occasion, Audience and Effect**.
- For instance, a politician **(speaker)** gives a grand message **(speech)** to get votes at the time of an election **(occasion)** from the civilians **(audience)**. The civilians only vote if they are influenced by what the politician says in his speech, so the content must be awe-inspiring and influential **(effect)**.

Question

Match the column:

A. Aristotle	I. SMCR- sender, message, channel, receiver-model
B. Shannon and Weaver	II. circular communication
C. Wilbur Schramm	III. Speaker- centered communication
D. David Berlo	IV. Top-down, linear communication

1. A-I B-II C-III D-IV
2. A-II B-III C-IV D-I
3. A-III B-IV C-II D-I
4. A-IV B-I C-III D-II

Explanations
Answer: 3. A-III B-IV C-II D-I

A. Aristotle → III. Speaker-centered communication: Aristotle's model emphasizes the **speaker as the central figure**, focusing on **persuasion and audience influence.**

B. Shannon and Weaver → IV. Top-down, linear communication: Their model is **linear**, focusing on the **one-way transmission of messages** from sender to receiver, with noise as an interference.

C. Wilbur Schramm → II. Circular communication: Schramm introduced the **circular model**, highlighting **feedback and interaction** in the communication process.
D. David Berlo → I. SMCR model:

Berlo developed the **SMCR (Sender, Message, Channel, Receiver) model**, emphasizing the **key elements of communication.**

II. Shannon and Weaver Linear Model of Communication:

- Shannon and Weaver first introduced the linear communication model in 1949.
- In this model, **the message travels one direction from the sender to the receiver**.
- In other words, the communication process ends once the sender sends the message to the receiver.
- Shannon and Weaver were American engineers who worked for Bell Telephone Labs.
- Their work aimed to ensure that telephone cables and radio waves operated as efficiently as possible.
- Shannon-Weaver developed a mathematical theory of communication that expanded upon the Shannon–Weaver model.
- It is widely accepted that the Shannon-Weaver model, developed in 1949, is the mother of all models.
- There were four primary components to the initial model:
    i. Sender,
    ii. Message,
    iii. Channel,
    iv. Receiver.

Their conceptualization of communication was based on **the following steps**:

1. **Sender**: The formation of communicative motivation or reason.
2. **Message**: The composition of the message (a further internal or technical explanation of what the message is intended to express).
3. **Encoding:** The process of encoding a message (for instance, digital data, written text, speech, pictures, gestures, and so on).
4. **Channel:** The method of transmitting encoded messages as a sequence of signals over a particular channel or medium.
5. **Noise**: External factors such as natural forces and human activity (intentional and accidental) affect the quality of signals propagating from the sender to the receiver.
6. **Reception:** The act of receiving signals and assembling the encoded message from the sequence of signals received.
7. **Decode**: The process of decoding the reassembled encoded message.

8. **Interpretation:** Interpretation and making sense of the presumed original message.

Question

The Shannon and Weaver model of communication has which of the following characteristics?

A. It is linear.
B. It focusses on transmission of information
C. It is concerned with reproduction of messages from one point to another.
D. It offers a meta model of communication
E. The feedback component is circular.

1. A,B and C only
2. B,C and D only
3. C,D and E only
4. A,D and E only

Explanations
Answer: 1. A,B and C only

The **Shannon and Weaver model of communication** is a **linear model** developed to explain **how information is transmitted from a sender to a receiver** using a channel and addressing potential noise.

Characteristics:

A. It is linear: The model follows a **straightforward, one-way process** from sender to receiver.

B. It focuses on the transmission of information: The primary emphasis is on **how information flows** and the potential disruptions (noise) during transmission.

C. It is concerned with the reproduction of messages from one point to another: The model explains **how a message is encoded, transmitted, and decoded** accurately from the sender to the receiver.

Why not the other options?

D. It offers a meta model of communication: The model is **not meta**; it primarily addresses **technical aspects of communication.**

E. The feedback component is circular: Shannon and Weaver's model does not include feedback, making it strictly **linear.**

III. Lasswell's Model of Communication:

- Harold Lasswell is an eminent Yale University professor.
- According to Lasswell, communication has three functions.
    i. The surveillance of the environment,
    ii. The correlation of components of society,
    iii. The cultural transmission between generations.
- In contrast to Shannon-Weaver's communication model, Lasswell's model provides a different perspective on communication.
- Using his model below, he describes an act of communication by answering specific questions. Each stage of communication has the potential to alter an individual's response:
    - Who -> Says what -> In which Channel? -> To Whom -> With what kind of effect
- Example: Who – TEPC Operator What – Radioactive material flowing into the sea Channel – BBC News (Television news medium) Whom – Public Effect – giving warning to the people of japan from the radiation

IV: Berlo's Sender-Message-Channel-Receiver (SMCR) Model of Communication:

David Berlo, a professor at Michigan State University, expanded Shannon and Weaver's 1949 linear communication model. In 1960, Berlo developed the sender-message-channel-receiver (SMCR) communication model.

1. **Source/Sender:** A source, whether represented by a person or by a body such as the United Nations, produces a message based on its communication skills, attitude, knowledge, social system, and culture.
2. **Message:** The message is developed, elements in a set of symbols, and the sender step begins. Messages are what are being transferred in the model. The message consists of many aspects that contribute to

its completion and understanding: the code, the content, and the treatment.

3. **Channel:** The encoding process involves the motor skills of speaking, writing, touching, etc. The message is transmitted through the channel. The channel carries messages through the use of five sensory factors, namely: hearing, sight, touch, taste, and smell.
4. **Receiver:** Following the channel step, the receiver step is carried out. **In the decoding process, sensory skills are utilized through hearing, seeing, feeling, etc.** The communication process concludes at the destination, which is the part that interprets the message by using its communication skills, attitude, knowledge, and social system. Several factors influence the receiver's interpretation of a message, such as communication skills, attitude, knowledge, social design and cultural aspects.

V. Schramm Model of Communication:

- According to Wilbur Schramm (1954), examining a message's impact on its target is also important.
- Communicating between parties involves sharing knowledge and experiences, giving advice and commands, and asking questions.
- There may be many forms of communication in which these acts may be performed.
- The form of communication depends on the abilities of the group.
- Communication content and form work together to create messages sent towards a particular destination.
- The target may be oneself, another person or being, or another entity.
- There are three levels of semiotic rules that govern communication:
    - i. **Syntactic:** It is concerned with the relations between signs.
    - ii. **Pragmatic:** It is concerned with the relations between signs and their users.
    - iii. **Semantic:** It is concerned with the relations between signs and their referents.

Question

Statement I: Wilbur Schramm's model of communication had interpreters acting as both encoders and decoders.
Statement II: Wilbur Schramm was one of the first scholars to consider communication as an interactive process.

1. Both Statement I and Statement I are true
2. Both Statement I and Statement II are false
3. Statement I is true but Statement Il is false
4. Statement I is false but Statement Il is true

Explanations

Answer: 1. Both Statement I and Statement I are true

Statement I: Wilbur Schramm's **model of communication introduced the concept of interpreters** who act as both **encoders and decoders**, emphasizing that **communication is a two-way process.**

Statement II: Schramm was **one of the first scholars to highlight communication as an interactive process**, moving beyond linear models like Shannon and Weaver. He recognized the **importance of feedback** in ensuring effective communication.

Question

Which are the main components of a language?

A. Phonetics
B. Syntactic
C. Discourse
D. Semantics
E. Pragmatics

1. ABCD
2. BCDE
3. ABDE
4. CE

Explanations

Answer: 3. ABDE

- **A (Correct) - Phonetics**: Study of speech sounds and pronunciation.
- **B (Correct) - Syntactic**: Rules governing sentence structure.
- **D (Correct) - Semantics**: Meaning and interpretation of words.

- **E (Correct) - Pragmatics**: Contextual use of language in communication.

C (Incorrect) - Discourse: Refers to language use beyond sentences, not a core linguistic component.

VI. Interaction Model of Communication:

According to the communication interaction model, communication involves sending and receiving messages and receiving feedback within a physical and psychological context in which participants alternate roles as sender and receiver.

Question

The key features of the interaction model of communication are:

A. It is a two-way process.
B. The physical context of communication is unimportant.
C. The psychological context of communication is always taken into account.
D. Feedback is not a response to the message received.
E. It is less message-focussed.

1. A, B and C only
2. B, C and D only
3. A, C and E only
4. C, D and E only

Explanations
Answer: 3. A, C and E only

The **interaction model of communication** emphasizes **two-way communication** with a focus on **context and feedback**.

A. It is a two-way process: Both the **sender and receiver actively participate**, exchanging roles during feedback.

C. The psychological context of communication is always taken into account: Emotional states, attitudes, and perceptions **affect communication effectiveness.**

E. It is less message-focused: The model **considers interaction and feedback equally important** alongside the message.

Why not the other options?

B. The physical context of communication is unimportant: Physical context **remains relevant** in interaction models.

D. Feedback is not a response to the message received: Feedback **is always a response** to the message in interaction models

VII. Barnlund's Transactional Model of Communication:

- Barnlund (1970) proposed a transactional communication model in light of these weaknesses.
- The basic premise of the transactional communication model is that individuals are simultaneously engaging in sending and receiving messages.
- According to Barnlund's Transactional Model of Communication, messages are reciprocal.
- Consequently, both communicators (sender and receiver) are responsible for the impact and effectiveness of the communication.
- Meaning is not simply sent from one person to another and then returned. The message must have a shared purpose.
- Barnlund's model illustrates communication as a complex, multi-layered process where the feedback from the sender becomes the message for the receiver.
- Dance's helical model is another example, which suggests communication is continuous, dynamic, evolutionary, and non-linear.
- A sender and a receiver can be linked reciprocally in a slightly more complex manner.
- The second approach to communication is known as the constitutive or constructionist approach.
- How a message is communicated determines how the receiver will interpret it.
- Communication is considered a conduit, a passage through which information is conveyed from one person to another, and the information is deemed separate from the communication itself.

- The model has multiple layers and is a feedback system. Both parties provide constant feedback. Barnlund's model comprises public, private, and behavioural cues.
    i. **Public Cues:** They are those in the environment or can be man-made.
    ii. **Private Cues:** It includes senses and can be verbal or non-verbal,
    iii. **Behavioural Cue:** It is concerned with behaviour and can be verbal and non-verbal.

VIII. Helical Model of Communication:

- Frank Dance proposed the Helical Model of communication **in 1967** to shed more light on the communication process.
- Dance thought of a communication process similar to the helix.
- The name helical comes from "Helix, " which refers to an object with a three-dimensional shape, such as a wire wound uniformly around a cylinder or cone.
- A child starts communicating from the very moment he enters this world. A nurse rubs a baby's back to make the child cry when he is born. If the child doesn't cry, it indicates a stillborn child.

IX. The Constructionist Model of Communication:

- The Constructionist View can also define how you say something and determines the message.
- According to the Constructionist View, "truth" and "ideas" emerge from the social process of communication.
- Robert T. Craig believed that the Constructionist View, or the constitutive view, is "...an ongoing process that symbolically forms and re-forms our personal identities." (Craig, 125).
- The Constructionist View sees communication as, "...in human life, the information does not behave as simply as bits in an electronic stream. In human life, information flow is far more like an electric current running from one landmine to another" (Lanham, 7).
- Constructionist views of communication are more realistic because they involve human interaction and the free exchange of ideas.

X. Transmission Communication Model:

- The Transmission Model, on the other hand, views communication as a robotic and computerized process.
- In the Transmission Model, communication is viewed as the process of transmitting and receiving messages and perfection.
- The transmission model describes communication as a one-way, linear process in which a sender encodes a message and transmits it through a channel to a receiver.
- Environmental or semantic noise may disrupt the transmission of the message.

Characteristics of Communication:

Exchange of Ideas: Communication cannot be considered without the exchange of ideas. To complete the communication process, there must be an exchange of thoughts, orders, feelings, etc., among two or more persons.

Continuous Process: Communication is a continuous process, as in business, where the manager continuously assigns tasks to his subordinates and monitors their progress.

Two Process: Communication requires a minimum of two persons because an individual cannot exchange ideas with himself alone. A listener is necessary to receive one's ideas. In communication, at least two people must be involved in the exchange of information- the sender and the receiver.

Anticipatory Excitement: Anticipation is a feeling of excitement about something pleasant or exciting that you know will happen. Anticipatory communication is the process of identifying areas of interest an individual or group will be interested in discussing and preparing responses based upon those expected interests.

Communication is an art and science: The art and science of effective communication go hand in hand. The process of telling stories involves both the expression of sentiment and the creation of new ideas, but it also involves a systematic and rigorous evaluation of those ideas. Led Zeppelin even composed a song called "Communication Breakdown." Communication requires creativity.

Complex Process: There is no denying that communication is a complex discipline as it involves the study of how a sender encodes information to be transmitted, how a receiver decodes received data, and barriers to communication which are the influences in the environment that affect the whole process of how information is communicated.

Dynamic Process: Communication is a dynamic process. There is much more to it than what we say. It is common for people to use the words communication, language, and speech interchangeably, but these terms are not synonymous. The word speech refers to the words or sounds produced by the mouth. The language combines grammar, meaning, and the ability to use words. Language refers to both verbal and non-verbal communication. Language and speech are both components of communication, but communication is much more than that. Sharing thoughts and experiences in a meaningful way while taking in, processing, and responding to the person you are conversing with makes a conversation meaningful.

Cooperative Process: Communication through exchanging ideas and information helps bring unity of action in pursuing a common purpose. It facilitates coordination between individuals and binds them together.

Direct and Indirect: It is not necessary to communicate that the receiver and giver of information should be face-to-face. Communication can be both direct and indirect. Direct communication occurs through face-to-face interaction, while indirect communication occurs through other means.

Formal and Informal: Formal communication is also known as official communication, and informal communication is known as grapevine communication. Examples of formal communication are business letters, reports, orders, etc., while informal communication is face-to-face communication, telephonic conversations, etc.

Horizontal and Vertical Process: Horizontal communication is established with people on the same hierarchical level within the company (or project). Vertical communication is established with people who belong to a different hierarchical group.

Universal Process: The act of communication is a fundamental, universal process that connects senders and receivers of messages across space and time. Communication relates to many kinds of senders and receivers, including ones that are not human and even ones that are not alive.

Mutual Understanding: Mutual understanding implies that the receiver should receive the information in the same spirit it is being given. Understanding the information in the communication process is more important than carrying it out.

Questions

Question

Without whom the communication process cannot be completed?

1. Receiver
2. Media
3. Writer
4. Expert

Explanations
Answer: 1. Receiver

The **communication process** cannot be completed **without a receiver** because:

Essential Role: The receiver is the **intended target of the message**, and their understanding or interpretation completes the communication cycle.

Message Interpretation: Communication is only effective when the **receiver decodes and understands the message** sent by the sender.

Feedback Loop: The receiver's **response or feedback** ensures that the sender knows whether the message was understood correctly.

Core Component: In any communication model (e.g., Shannon-Weaver model), the **receiver is a fundamental element.**

Why not the other options?

Media: It acts as a **channel** for communication but is not the endpoint of the communication process.

Writer: A writer is essentially a **sender**, not the one completing the communication.

Expert: An expert may or may not be part of the communication process.

Question

Arrange the following four stages of communication in a proper sequence:

A. Transmission
B. Encoding
C. Sender
D. Feedback

1. C, B, A, D
2. B, A, C, D
3. D, C, B, A
4. A, B, C, D

Explanations
Answer: 1. C, B, A, D

C. Sender: The communication process begins with the **sender**, who has an idea, message, or information to communicate.

B. Encoding: The sender **encodes the message** using symbols, words, or gestures to convey the intended meaning.

A. Transmission: The **encoded message is transmitted** through a medium or communication channel (e.g., speech, email, phone).

D. Feedback: After receiving the message, the **receiver decodes it and provides feedback**, completing the communication loop.

Question

The context in which communication takes place is termed as -

1. Historical background
2. Objectification
3. Environment
4. Media sphere

Explanations
Answer: 3. Environment

The **context or setting in which communication takes place** is referred to as the **environment**. It encompasses all the **external and internal factors** that influence how messages are **sent, received, and interpreted** during communication.

Physical Setting: Includes the **location, space, lighting, and noise levels** where communication happens.

Psychological Factors: Emotional states, moods, and attitudes of participants.

Social and Cultural Context: Social norms, cultural expectations, and relationships between participants.

Technological Context: Tools and channels (e.g., online platforms, emails) used for communication.

Question

Basic factors of listening are:

A. Self interest
B. Speaker
C. Facts
D. Style of speaking
E. Atmosphere

1. ABD
2. ACE
3. BCE
4. BDE

Explanations
Answer: 1. ABD

Effective **listening** depends on several key factors that influence how well a listener understands and processes a message. The **basic factors of listening** are:

A. Self-interest:

- A listener's **motivation and personal interest** in the topic greatly influence their attention and engagement.
- Example: A student pays more attention to a topic they find personally relevant.

B. Speaker:

- The **speaker's clarity, credibility, and speaking style** affect how well their message is received.
- Example: A confident and articulate speaker can hold the audience's attention better.

D. Style of speaking:

- The **tone, pitch, pace, and delivery style** of the speaker influence how effectively the listener engages with the content.
- Example: A monotonous delivery may cause the listener to lose focus.

Question

What do people basically want to extract from the communicated message?

1. Compulsions
2. Meaning
3. Synergy
4. Behavioural pattern

Explanations
Answer: 1. Meaning

At the core of every communication process, **people seek to extract meaning from the communicated message.** Communication is not just about transmitting words or signals; it's about ensuring that the **receiver understands the intended message** and derives **relevant meaning** from it.

Why Meaning?

Purpose of Communication: The primary goal is to **convey a clear idea, information, or emotion** that the receiver can understand.

Interpretation: Effective communication depends on how **accurately the receiver decodes the message** and derives meaning.

Clarity: The sender's role is to **encode the message clearly** to reduce ambiguity.

Why not the other options?

Compulsions: Communication is not about **forcing or compelling someone** but about conveying meaning.

Synergy: Refers to **collaboration or combined effort**, not the core purpose of extracting meaning from a message.

Behavioral pattern: Refers to **observable actions or habits**, not the fundamental outcome of communication.

Question

Match the column:

A. Physical situation	I. participants
B. Persons involved in interaction	II. key
C. Manner of communication enacted	III. instrumentality
D. Channels of communication	IV. scene or setting

1. A-I B-II C-III D-IV
2. A-II B-III C-IV D-I
3. A-III B-IV C-I D-II
4. A-IV B-I C-II D-III

Explanations
Answer: 4. A-IV B-I C-II D-III

Each element in communication corresponds to a specific aspect of the communication process, forming a coherent structure:

A. Physical situation → IV. Scene or setting:

- The **physical situation** refers to the **environment or location** where communication takes place, including **lighting, noise levels, and spatial arrangement.**
- Example: A classroom, conference room, or outdoor setting.

B. Persons involved in interaction → I. Participants:

- The **people participating in the communication process** are referred to as **participants (sender and receiver).**
- Example: A teacher and students in a lecture.

C. Manner of communication enacted → II. Key:

- The **manner or tone of communication** reflects the **mood, style, or attitude** in which the message is conveyed.
- Example: Formal, casual, sarcastic, or serious tone.

D. Channels of communication → III. Instrumentality:

- The **channels or tools used to deliver messages** represent the **instrumentality** of communication.
- Example: Spoken words, written text, video calls, or emails.

Question

The general context of communication is known as communication -

1. situation
2. position
3. praxis
4. convention

Explanations

Answer: 1. Situation

The **general context of communication** is referred to as the **communication situation** because it encompasses the **environment, setting, and conditions** in which communication occurs. It includes **who is communicating, where, when, and under what circumstances.**

Why Situation?

Contextual Relevance: The **situation sets the stage for communication**, determining how messages are framed and interpreted.

Elements Included: The **participants, physical setting, social environment, and objectives** all contribute to the communication situation.

Examples: A classroom discussion, a boardroom meeting, or a casual chat at a cafe all represent distinct **communication situations.**

Why not the other options?

Position: Refers to **a specific role or stance**, not the broader context of communication.

Praxis: Refers to **practical application or practice**, not the situational context of communication.

Convention: Refers to **established norms, rules, or traditions** in communication, not the immediate context.

Question

Three major actions in the process of Communication are:

A. Receiving
B. Sending
C. Reviewing
D. Interpreting
E. Analysing

1. CDE
2. ACD

3. ABD
4. ADE

Explanations
Answer: 3. ABD

The **three major actions in communication** are:

A. Receiving: Actively perceiving or listening to the message.

B. Sending: Conveying the message to the intended audience.

D. Interpreting: Decoding and understanding the received message.

Why not C (Reviewing) and E (Analysing)?

C. Reviewing: This is more about **evaluating** rather than an essential action in the communication process.

E. Analysing: This involves **reflecting on the content** after communication, not part of the core cycle.

Question

Arrange the following in correct sequence in the process of Communication

A. Transmitter
B. Destination
C. Channel
D. Receiver
E. Information Source

1. AECDB
2. EACDB
3. EADBC
4. ACEDB

Explanations
Answer: 2. EACDB

- **E (Information Source)** – The origin of the message.
- **A (Transmitter)** – Encodes and sends the message.
- **C (Channel)** – The medium through which the message travels.
- **D (Receiver)** – Decodes the message.
- **B (Destination)** – The final recipient of the message.

Question

Who sends what to whom in a communication process?

(A) Channel sends the message to sender.
(B) Sender sends messages to receiver.
(C) Sender sends the feedback receiver.
(D) Receiver sends messages to sender.

1. (A) Only
2. (B) Only
3. (A) and (D) Only
4. (B) and (C) Only

Explanations
Answer: 2. (B) Only

In the **communication process:**

B. Sender sends messages to receiver: The **sender initiates the communication** by encoding and transmitting a message to the **receiver** through a chosen channel.

Why not the other options?

A. Channel sends the message to sender: The **channel carries the message**, but it doesn't initiate communication.

C. Sender sends the feedback to receiver: Feedback comes from the receiver, not the sender.

D. Receiver sends messages to sender: This happens during **feedback**, not the initial communication process.

Question

Which of the following physical environmental factors affect the communicators' behaviour during interaction?

A. Smiling face
B. Melodious voice
C. Temperature
D. Lighting conditions
E. Loud noise

1. (A), (B) and (C) only.
2. (B), (C) and (D) only.
3. (C), (D) and (E) only.
4. (A), (B) and (E) only.

Explanations
Answer: 3. (C), (D) and (E) only.

Physical environmental factors are **external conditions** that influence communication behavior:

C. Temperature: Extreme heat or cold can cause **discomfort and distraction** during communication.

D. Lighting conditions: Poor or harsh lighting can **affect visibility and focus.**

E. Loud noise: Excessive noise can **distort messages and reduce concentration.**

Why not the other options?

A. Smiling face: This is a **non-verbal cue**, not a physical environmental factor.

B. Melodious voice: This refers to **vocal tone**, not an external physical factor.

Question

Which of the following contextual factors determine meaning in communication behaviour ?

A. Physical location
B. Participants
C. Preceding events
D. Nonfunctional goals
E. Absence of audience

1. ABC
2. BCD
3. CDE
4. ADE

Explanations
Answer: 1. ABC

Contextual factors play a crucial role in determining **meaning in communication behavior**:

A. Physical location: The **setting or place** (e.g., classroom, office, or outdoor) affects how messages are interpreted.

B. Participants: The **people involved** (sender and receiver) and their relationship influence meaning.

C. Preceding events: Events that occurred **before the communication** shape perceptions and context.

Why not the other options?

D. Nonfunctional goals: These are **irrelevant objectives** and do not determine meaning in communication.

E. Absence of audience: Communication typically requires an **audience for meaningful interaction.**

Question

Feedback is immediate in________Communication.

1. Print
2. Broadcast
3. Top-down
4. Face-to-face

Explanations
Answer: 4. Face-to-face

In **face-to-face communication**, feedback is **immediate** because:

Real-time Interaction: The sender and receiver are **physically or virtually present** at the same time.

Non-verbal Cues: Immediate feedback is given through **gestures, facial expressions, and tone of voice.**

Instant Clarification: Misunderstandings can be **addressed on the spot.**

Why not the other options?

Print: Feedback is **delayed** since readers cannot respond immediately.

Broadcast: Communication is typically **one-way**, with no direct feedback.

Top-down: Feedback might occur, but it is often **hierarchical and not instant.**

Question

Statement I: The physical context of communication must be tangible.
Statement II: The temporal context of the message deals with the sequence of events.

1. Both Statement I and Statement II are true.
2. Both Statement I and Statement II are false,
3. Statement I is true but Statement II is false
4. Statement I is false but Statement II is true

Explanations
Answer: 1. Both Statement I and Statement II are true.

Statement I: The physical context of communication must be tangible.

The **physical context** refers to the **tangible, observable environment** where communication occurs, such as a classroom, office, or park.

Statement II: The temporal context of the message deals with the sequence of events.

The **temporal context** refers to the **time-related sequence of events** surrounding communication, including **past experiences, timing, and order of events.**

Why are both true?

Physical context deals with **real, observable factors.**

Temporal context deals with **timing and sequence**, impacting how messages are understood

Question

In communication, channel richness is highest in the case of-

1. Television
2. Newspapers
3. Face-to-face conversation
4. Formal reports

Explanations
Answer: 3. Face-to-face conversation

Channel richness refers to the **capacity of a communication channel to convey information effectively, including verbal and non-verbal cues.**

Face-to-face conversation has the **highest channel richness** because:

It includes **verbal and non-verbal cues** (tone, facial expressions, gestures).

Provides **immediate feedback** for clarification.

Allows for **emotional expression and personal connection.**

Why not the other options?

Television: One-way communication with **limited feedback and interaction.**

Newspapers: Static and **lack immediate interaction.**

Formal reports: Written documents with **no immediate feedback** or non-verbal cues.

Question

In communication, the test of parsimony will have the element of-

1. Logical simplicity
2. Complex validity
3. Susceptible generalisability
4. Abstraction

Explanations
Answer: 1. Logical simplicity

In communication, the **test of parsimony** refers to the principle of **choosing the simplest explanation or model that effectively explains a phenomenon.**

Logical simplicity: Parsimony emphasizes **clarity, precision, and avoiding unnecessary complexity** in communication theories or explanations.

Efficiency: It focuses on **using the fewest assumptions** while maintaining accuracy.

Question

Match the list:

List I (Communication context)	List II (Related factor)

A. Physical	(I) Group norms
B. Cultural	(II) Sequential positioning
C. Social and Psychological	(III) Tangible environment
D. Temporal	(IV) Value system

1. A-II B-III C-IV D-I
2. A-III B-IV C-I D-II
3. A-IV B-I C-II D-III
4. A-I B-II C-III D-IV

Explanations
Answer: 2. A-III B-IV C-I D-II

A. Physical → III. Tangible environment:

Refers to the **physical setting** where communication occurs, including **lighting, space, noise, and location.**

B. Cultural → IV. Value system:

Cultural context relates to the **beliefs, traditions, and value systems** that shape communication norms.

C. Social and Psychological → I. Group norms:

The **social and psychological context** involves **group dynamics, relationships, and emotional states** affecting communication.

D. Temporal → II. Sequential positioning:

The **temporal context** deals with the **timing and sequence of communication events**, influencing meaning and interpretation.

Question

In communication. meanings refer to a person's-

1. Notions about the world
2. Internal responses to a message
3. Subsuming messages for suppression
4. External responses only

Explanations

Answer: 2. Internal responses to a message

In communication, **meanings are formed based on how an individual internally processes and interprets a message.**

Internal responses: Meanings are shaped by **thoughts, emotions, perceptions, and personal experiences** triggered by the message.

Subjective Nature: Different individuals may derive **different meanings** from the same message due to their **internal contexts.**

Why not the other options?

Notions about the world: These are **pre-existing beliefs**, not the active response to a message.

Subsuming messages for suppression: Refers to **hiding or disregarding messages**, not deriving meaning.

External responses only: External responses show **visible reactions**, but meaning is first created internally.

Question

Identify the correct sequence of information processing in communication

A. Input
B. Output
C. Data entry
D. Processing
E. Storage

Choose the correct answer from the options given below :

1. ABEDC
2. BDEAC
3. CADEB
4. ACDEB

Explanations
Answer: 4. ACDEB

The **correct sequence of information processing in communication** follows a **logical flow** from data entry to output:

A. Data entry: Information is **entered or captured** into the system or communication process.

C. Input: The **entered data becomes input** for processing.

D. Processing: The input data is **analysed, interpreted, or transformed** into meaningful information.

E. Storage: Processed information is **stored for future retrieval** or reference.

B. Output: The final **information is delivered or presented** to the receiver.

Question

Match the column:

List I (Elements of Human Communication)	**List II (Representational Description)**
A. People	(I) Semanticism
B. Ideas	(Il) Lead to modification of Physical environment
C. Noise	(III) Information processors
D. Language	(IV) Expression of creativity

1. A-II B-III C-IV D-I
2. A-I B-II C-IV D-III
3. A-IV B-I C-III D-II
4. A-III B-IV C-II D-I

Explanations
Answer: 4. A-III B-IV C-II D-I

Each **element of human communication** corresponds to a specific representational description:

A. People → III. Information processors:

People act as **information processors**, encoding, decoding, and interpreting messages in communication.

B. Ideas → IV. Expression of creativity:

Ideas represent the **creative and innovative aspects** of human thought expressed through communication.

C. Noise → II. Lead to modification of physical environment:

Noise, whether **physical or psychological**, can **disturb communication and alter the environment** to address or reduce interference.

D. Language → I. Semanticism:

Language is a **semantic tool** used to convey meaning through **symbols, words, and gestures.**

Question

Match the column:

A. phatic	I. decoder becomes encoder
B. feedback	II. communication about communication
C. meta message	III. between equals
D. lateral communication	IV. To greet

1. A-I B-II C-IV D-III
2. A-II B-III C-IV D-I
3. A-III B-IV C-I D-II
4. A-IV B-I C-II D-III

Explanations
Answer: 4. A-IV B-I C-II D-III

A. Phatic → IV. To greet:

Phatic communication is used for **social pleasantries or greetings**, such as "Hello" or "How are you?"

It focuses on **maintaining social relationships** rather than sharing content.

B. Feedback → I. Decoder becomes encoder:

Feedback occurs when the **receiver (decoder) responds back to the sender (becoming an encoder)** to complete the communication loop.

C. Meta message → II. Communication about communication:

A **meta message** refers to **messages about communication itself,** such as tone, body language, or indirect implications.

D. Lateral communication → III. Between equals:

Lateral communication happens **between peers or individuals at the same level** within an organization or structure.

Question

In describing elements of communication, a person or an event which provides verbal or non-verbal cues to which someone can respond is known as

1. Message
2. Source
3. Channel
4. Communication context

Explanations
Answer: 2. Source

In communication, the **source** refers to the **person or event** that initiates the communication process by **providing verbal or non-verbal cues** to which someone can respond.

The **source encodes the message** and selects the appropriate **channel** for delivery.

It can be **a person, event, or medium** generating the communication.

Why not the other options?

Message: Refers to **the content or information** being communicated, not the initiator.

Channel: The **medium or pathway** through which the message travels.

Communication context: Refers to the **setting or environment** where communication occurs.

Question

A student greets his teacher with 'Good Morning'. Here the channel of communication is:

1. The effect
2. The source
3. The speech
4. The intent

Explanations
Answer: 3. The speech

In communication, the **channel** refers to the **medium through which the message travels from the sender to the receiver.**

In this example, the **student's speech ("Good Morning") serves as the channel** through which the message is conveyed.

Speech uses **spoken words and vocal tones** to deliver the message to the teacher.

Why not the other options?

The effect: Refers to the **impact or result of communication,** not the channel.

The source: Refers to the **sender of the message** (the student).

The intent: Refers to the **purpose or reason** behind the communication (greeting the teacher).

Question

In a classroom, transforming verbal and non-verbal signs back into messages is known as

1. Feedback
2. Encoding
3. Decoding
4. Reverse communication

Explanations
Answer: 3. Decoding

In communication, **decoding** refers to the **process of interpreting or translating verbal and non-verbal signs back into meaningful messages** by the receiver.

In a **classroom setting**, students **decode the teacher's verbal words and non-verbal cues** (gestures, tone, facial expressions) to understand the message.

Why not the other options?

Feedback: Refers to the **receiver's response** to the message, not interpreting it.

Encoding: Refers to the **sender creating and delivering the message.**

Reverse communication: Not a standard term in communication theory.

Question

The sequence of the stages of communication process is:

(A) Level of acceptance
(B) Transmission of cognitive data
(C) Message reception
(D) Understanding
(E) Reaction

1. (A), (B), (C), (D), (E)

2. (B), (C), (D), (E), (A)
3. (C), (E), (D), (A), (B)
4. (B), (C), (D), (A), (E)

Explanations
Answer: 4. (B), (C), (D), (A), (E)

(B) Transmission of cognitive data: The **sender transmits information or data** to the receiver through a chosen channel.
(C) Message reception: The **receiver receives the transmitted message** through hearing, seeing, or other sensory means.
(D) Understanding: The receiver **decodes the message** to derive meaning from the transmitted data.
(A) Level of acceptance: The receiver **accepts or rejects the message** based on understanding and relevance.
(E) Reaction: The receiver **responds to the message**, completing the communication loop through feedback.

Question

According to the behavioural model, the communication approach is considered as:

1. Contrived
2. Natural
3. Reward-punishment based
4. Innate

Explanations
Answer: 3. Reward-punishment based

In the **behavioral model of communication**, the focus is on **observable behavior and responses** rather than internal thought processes. Communication is seen as a **stimulus-response activity**, where behavior is shaped by **rewards and punishments.**

Reward: Positive reinforcement encourages **desired communication behavior**.

Punishment: Negative consequences discourage **undesirable communication behavior**.

Conditioning: The model often draws from **behavioral psychology principles** (e.g., Skinner's Operant Conditioning).

Why not the other options?

Contrived: Behavioral communication isn't artificial; it focuses on **observable outcomes.**

Natural: The approach is **learned and conditioned**, not inherently natural.

Innate: Communication in this model is viewed as **acquired through experience, not as an inborn trait.**

CHAPTER II

Types of Communication

Types of Communication

I. Verbal Communication and Non-Verbal Communication:

Verbal Communication

- **Uses Spoken and Written Words** – Expresses thoughts clearly.
- **Relies on Language and Vocabulary** – Meaning depends on words.
- **Direct Form of Communication** – Clear message delivery.
- **Includes Conversations, Speeches, and Texts** – Various formats.
- **Essential for Formal Communication** – Used in business and academics.

Nonverbal Communication

- **Uses Gestures and Body Language** – Expresses emotions visually.
- **Relies on Facial Expressions** – Shows hidden feelings.
- **Can Include Silence or Eye Contact** – Conveys unspoken messages.
- **Supports or Contradicts Verbal Messages** – Enhances meaning.
- **Essential in Cross-Cultural Communication** – Varies by culture.

Question

Non-verbal communication is mostly-

A. Descriptive
B. Aggressive
C. Involuntary
D. Contextual
E. Symbolic

1. ABC
2. BCD
3. ADE
4. CDE

Explanations
Answer: 4. CDE

Non-verbal communication is primarily characterized by the following traits:

C. Involuntary: Many non-verbal cues, such as **facial expressions, body posture, or micro-expressions**, happen **unconsciously** and are difficult to control.

D. Contextual: Non-verbal communication **depends heavily on context**, including cultural, social, and situational factors, to be correctly interpreted.

E. Symbolic: Non-verbal cues often **function as symbols**, conveying meaning through gestures, eye contact, body language, and other non-verbal signs.

Why not the other options?

A. Descriptive: Non-verbal cues might describe feelings or intentions but are not inherently descriptive.

B. Aggressive: Non-verbal communication is not necessarily aggressive; it can also be calm, neutral, or friendly.

Question

Under which type of communication 'House Journals' fall?

1. Oral Communication
2. Intercultural Communication
3. Written Communication
4. Group Communication

Explanations
Answer: 3. Written Communication

Question

Statement I: Non-verbal signals are used to emphasize and support verbal communication.
Statement II: Non-verbal signals are not a substitute for verbal communication.

1. Both Statement I and Statement II are true
2. Both Statement I and Statement II are false
3. Statement I is true but Statement II is false
4. Statement I is false but Statement II is true

Explanations
Answer: 3. Statement I is true but Statement II is false

Statement I is true: Non-verbal signals (e.g., gestures, facial expressions, tone of voice) **often emphasize and support verbal communication.** They can add clarity, highlight key points, and reinforce the emotional tone of a spoken message. For example, nodding while saying "Yes" reinforces agreement.

Statement II is false: Non-verbal signals **can indeed serve as a substitute for verbal communication.** For example:

- A thumbs-up gesture can replace the spoken word "okay."
- A glare can communicate disapproval without speaking.

Question

Assertion A: Smiles and laughter should be avoided when messages are serious.
Reason R: Non-verbal cues are always contextual like verbal communication

1. Both A and R are true and R is the correct explanation of A
2. Both A and R are true but R is NOT the correct explanation of A
3. A is true but R is false
4. A is false but R is true

Explanations
Answer: 1. Both A and R are true and R is the correct explanation of A

Assertion (A) is true: In serious or formal communication settings, **smiles and laughter can undermine the gravity of the message** and cause misunderstandings. Maintaining appropriate non-verbal cues ensures the message aligns with the intended tone.

Reason (R) is true: Non-verbal cues are highly contextual, just like verbal communication. Their meaning depends on **cultural norms, situational context, and the relationship between the sender and receiver.** For example, a smile might indicate friendliness in one situation but seem inappropriate in another, such as during a serious announcement.

R explains A: The **contextual nature of non-verbal communication explains why certain cues, like smiles or laughter, may not be appropriate in serious situations.**

Question

Statement I: People use non-verbal cues more than verbal cues.
Statement II: Non-verbal cues have better believability than spoken words.

1. Both Statement I and Statement II are true
2. Both Statement I and Statement II are false
3. Statement I is true but Statement II is false
4. Statement I is false but Statement II is true

Explanations
Answer: 1. Both Statement I and Statement II are true

Statement I is true: Research suggests that **a significant portion of communication is non-verbal** (e.g., body language, facial expressions, gestures, and tone of voice). People often rely more on these non-verbal cues, especially in emotionally charged situations, as they convey meaning beyond words.

Statement II is true: Non-verbal cues are generally perceived as more believable than verbal messages because they are harder to fake or control consciously. For example, a person's facial expressions or body posture often reveal their true feelings, even if their words say otherwise.

Question

Thums up is a kind of communication

1. Verbal
2. Non-Verbal
3. Transpersonal
4. Intrapersonal

Explanations
Answer: 2. Non-Verbal

Question

Match the column:

A. Verbal communication	I. use of spoken or written words
B. Non-verbal communication	II. facial expression and body language
C. Encoding	III. converting thoughts into message
D. Decoding	IV. interpreting the message

1. A-II B-I C-III D-IV
2. A-I B-II C-IV D-III
3. A-I B-II C-III D-IV
4. A-II B-I C-IV D-III

Explanations
Answer: 3. A-I B-II C-III D-IV

A. Verbal communication → I: Uses **spoken or written words** for communication.
B. Non-verbal communication → II: Includes **facial expressions and body language**.
C. Encoding → III: The process of **converting thoughts into a message**.
D. Decoding → IV: The process of **interpreting the received message**.

II. Intrapersonal Communication:

- **Communication Within Oneself** – Engages in self-talk.
- **Uses Unspoken Words Internally** – Inner speech process.
- **Forms an Internal Monologue** – Continuous thought stream.
- **Shapes Self-Identity & Emotions** – Influences self-perception.

- **Affects Planning & Problem-Solving** – Enhances critical thinking.

Question

Match the column:

A. One-to-one	I. Network (translational)
B. One-to-many	II. Intra-personal
C. Man-to-many	III. Inter-personal
D. One-to-none	IV. Mass communication especially print

1. A-I B-II C-III D-IV
2. A-II B-III C-IV D-I
3. A-III B-IV C-I D-II
4. A-IV B-I C-II D-III

Explanations
Answer: 3. A-III B-IV C-I D-II

A. One-to-one → III. Inter-personal: One-to-one communication refers to **interpersonal communication**, where two individuals exchange messages directly, such as in a conversation, interview, or counselling session.

B. One-to-many → IV. Mass communication (especially print): One-to-many communication happens in **mass communication**, where one source (e.g., an author, public speaker, or broadcaster) communicates with a **large audience**, often through mass media channels like newspapers or television.

C. Many-to-many → I. Network (translational): Many-to-many communication occurs in **networks**, where multiple individuals or groups interact in a **collaborative and interconnected system** (e.g., social media platforms, group discussions).

D. One-to-none → II. Intra-personal: One-to-none communication is essentially **intra-personal communication**, where an individual communicates with themselves, often through **self-talk, reflection, or inner dialogue.**

Question

Which of the following is a stage of intrapersonal communication?

1. Phatic stage
2. Intimate stage
3. Personal stage
4. Transcendental communication

Explanations
Answer: 4. Transcendental communication

Transcendental communication is considered a **stage of intrapersonal communication** where an individual engages in **deep self-reflection, inner dialogue, or a connection with a higher state of consciousness or purpose.**

It goes **beyond everyday self-talk** and involves a **deeper, more abstract level of communication** within oneself. Often associated with **spiritual experiences, meditation, or profound self-awareness.** Involves **examining personal beliefs, values, and existence** on a deeper level.

Why not the other options?

Phatic stage: Refers to **social communication focused on small talk or establishing connections**, not intrapersonal communication.

Intimate stage: Related to **deep emotional connections in interpersonal relationships**, not inner communication.

Personal stage: Refers to **self-disclosure in interpersonal communication**, not self-reflective dialogue.

Question

The paradoxical relationship between body and mind in a communication environment results in

1. Mindfulness
2. Self-importance
3. Obedience
4. Humour

Explanations
Answer: 4. Humour

The **paradoxical relationship between body and mind in a communication environment** often leads to **humor** because it arises from the **unexpected alignment or misalignment between verbal and non-verbal cues** or between what is said and how it is expressed.

For example, when someone's **body language contradicts their spoken words** (e.g., saying they are fine while visibly showing stress), it can create an unintentional humorous effect.

Humor also emerges from the **playful or exaggerated interaction of mental intent and physical expression**, often breaking tension and building rapport.

Why not the other options?

Mindfulness: Refers to **awareness and focus**, not directly tied to the body-mind paradox.

Self-importance: Relates to an **exaggerated sense of one's value**, not humor.

Obedience: Refers to **compliance with authority or instructions**, unrelated to the paradoxical body-mind dynamic.

III. Interpersonal Communication:

- It is an **exchange of information** between two or more people.
- There are at least **six categories of inquiry** in interpersonal communication research:
    i. How do humans adapt their verbal and nonverbal communication during face-to-face communication?
    ii. How messages are produced.
    iii. How uncertainty influences behaviour and information-management strategies.
    iv. Deceptive communication
    v. Relational dialectics.
    vi. Social interactions are mediated by technology.

- Interpersonal communication process principles:
- **Communication is transactional:** Transactional communication implies that the sender and the receiver are jointly responsible for its effect and effectiveness.
- **Direct face-to-face**: A key feature of interpersonal communication.
- **Between two persons**: Defines interpersonal communication.
- **Communication can be intentional and unintentional.**
- **Communication Is Irreversible:** A person can wish he hadn't said something and apologize for something he said and later regret it, but he is aware that he can't take it back.
- The three stages of **Interpersonal Communication** are:
    - **The Phatic Stage**: Initial small talk to establish connection.
    - **The Personal Stage**: Exchange of personal information and deeper interaction.
    - **The Intimate Stage**: Deep trust and emotional bonding in communication.
- **Communication Is Unrepeatable:** A communication act can never be replicated. Therefore, it is unrepeatable. We may be in a different mood at the time, our audience may be diverse, or our relationship may be different at the time. In short, you don't get a second chance to make a first impression.
- **Examples:** Active listening, Teamwork, Responsibility, Leadership, Motivation, Flexibility, and Patience.

Question

What are the three stages of Interpersonal Communication?

A. The Phatic Stage
B. The Plato Stage
C. The Personal Stage
D. The proxemics Stage
E. The Intimate Stage

1. ABC
2. ACE
3. CDE
4. BCD

Explanations

Answer: 2. ACE

The three stages of **Interpersonal Communication** are:

- **A (Correct) - The Phatic Stage**: Initial small talk to establish connection.
- **C (Correct) - The Personal Stage**: Exchange of personal information and deeper interaction.
- **E (Correct) - The Intimate Stage**: Deep trust and emotional bonding in communication.

B & D (Incorrect): **Plato Stage and Proxemics Stage** are not part of interpersonal communication stages.

Question

Interpersonal communication.

A. Direct face to face
B. With group of people
C. With large number of anonymous persons
D. Between two persons
E. Within ourselves or self-communication

1. (A) and (D) only
2. (A) and (B) only
3. (C) and (A) only
4. (D) and (E) only

Explanations
Answer: 1. (A) and (D) only

Interpersonal communication occurs **directly between two individuals**, involving **face-to-face interaction** and **mutual exchange of messages**.

- **A (Correct) - Direct face-to-face**: A key feature of interpersonal communication.
- **D (Correct) - Between two persons**: Defines interpersonal communication.
- **B (Incorrect) - With a group**: Falls under **group communication**.
- **C (Incorrect) - With anonymous persons**: Part of **mass communication**.

- **E (Incorrect) - Self-communication**: Considered **intrapersonal communication**.

Question

Statement (I): The disadvantage of inter-personal communication is the availability of immediate feedback.
Statement (II): The greatest advantage of mass communication is its delayed feedback

1. Both Statement I and Statement Il are true
2. Both Statement I and Statement Il are false
3. Statement I is true but Statement Il is false
4. Statement I is false but Statement Il is true

Explanations
Answer: 2. Both Statement I and Statement Il are false

Statement I is false: Immediate feedback is **not a disadvantage** in **interpersonal communication**; it is one of its **greatest strengths**. Real-time responses allow for **clarification, adjustment, and better understanding** between participants, making the communication more effective.

Statement II is false: Delayed feedback is not considered an advantage in **mass communication**. In fact, it is seen as a **limitation** because it reduces the ability to **adjust or respond to audience reactions in real-time.**

Question

Homogeneity of opinion among groups of people is mostly caused by

1. Mass communication
2. Intra-personal communication
3. Inter-personal communication
4. Abstraction in communication

Explanations
Answer: 3. Inter-personal communication

Homogeneity of opinion refers to the **alignment of thoughts, beliefs, or perspectives within a group.** This is primarily achieved through **inter-**

personal communication, where individuals directly **exchange ideas, share perspectives, and influence each other's opinions** in a close or familiar setting.

Why Inter-personal Communication?

Inter-personal communication involves **dialogue, discussion, and persuasion**, allowing individuals to align their viewpoints.

It fosters **trust and emotional connections**, making people more open to adopting shared opinions.

Group discussions, debates, and one-on-one conversations often create **consensus and shared understanding** among members.

Why not the other options?

Mass communication: Targets **large, diverse audiences**, which may result in varied interpretations, not homogeneity.

Intra-personal communication: Happens **within an individual's mind** and doesn't involve group influence.

Abstraction in communication: Refers to **vague or generalized communication**, which often creates ambiguity, not uniformity.

Question

The communication between two persons through letters is an instance of:

1. Intrapersonal verbal communication
2. Intrapersonal nonverbal communication
3. Interpersonal verbal communication
4. Interpersonal nonverbal communication

Explanations

Answer: 3. Interpersonal verbal communication

Communication through letters involves **written language**, which is a form of **verbal communication**, even though it is not spoken. It also happens between **two individuals**, making it **interpersonal communication**.

Why is it Interpersonal Verbal Communication?

Interpersonal: Communication occurs **between two people** (the sender and receiver of the letters).

Verbal: Written language is considered **verbal communication** because it uses words, grammar, and structure to convey meaning.

Question

Write the following types of communication in proper sequence:

A. Group
B. Public
C. Mass communication
D. Intrapersonal
E. Interpersonal

1. DEABC
2. EDCBA
3. ABCED
4. BACDE

Explanations
Answer: 1. DEABC

The **proper sequence of communication types** follows the progression from **individual communication to broader audience communication**, arranged by complexity and audience size:

D. Intrapersonal Communication: Communication **within oneself** (e.g., self-reflection, internal dialogue).

E. Interpersonal Communication: One-on-one communication between two people (e.g., a conversation with a friend).

A. Group Communication: Communication within a **small group of people** (e.g., team discussions, study groups).

B. Public Communication: One person communicates with a **large audience directly** (e.g., a public speech).

C. Mass Communication: Communication through **mass media to a very large audience** (e.g., TV broadcasts, online content).

Question

Which of the following are social emotions displayed during inter-personal communication?

A. Embarrassment
B. Guilt
C. Shame
D. Pride
E. Jealousy

1. ABC
2. ACD
3. BCD
4. ABCDE

Explanations
Answer: 4. ABCDE

Social emotions are emotions that arise from an individual's interactions with others and are influenced by **social norms, relationships, and expectations.** These emotions play a significant role in **interpersonal communication** as they affect how messages are sent, received, and interpreted.

The following are **examples of social emotions:**

A. Embarrassment: A reaction to **social awkwardness or perceived social mistake.**

B. Guilt: Feeling responsible for **causing harm or breaking social rules.**

C. Shame: A sense of **humiliation or distress** due to failing to meet social or personal standards.

D. Pride: A positive emotion arising from **achievements or being recognized by others.**

E. Jealousy: A feeling of **insecurity or resentment** over perceived rivalry or lack of attention.

Question

Which of the following are the two basic psychological functions of intra-personal communication?

A. Internalisation of culturally organised ways of thinking
B. Promotion of leader centric speech
C. Regulation of one's own mental activity
D. Orientation towards enhancing social disorders

1. AB
2. AC
3. BC
4. CD

Explanations
Answer: 2. AC

Intrapersonal communication refers to the **internal dialogue and self-reflection** within an individual. It serves two primary **psychological functions**:

A. Internalization of culturally organized ways of thinking: Intrapersonal communication helps individuals **adopt and internalize cultural norms, values, and organized patterns of thinking.** This internal dialogue shapes perceptions, behavior, and decision-making.

C. Regulation of one's own mental activity: Intrapersonal communication plays a key role in **self-regulation, emotional control, and managing thoughts and actions effectively.** It helps individuals plan, evaluate, and monitor their own behavior and reactions.

Why not the other options?

B. Promotion of leader-centric speech: This is not related to internal communication but rather to interpersonal or public communication.

D. Orientation towards enhancing social disorders: Intrapersonal communication **does not promote social disorders** but instead contributes to mental and emotional balance.

Question

Sharing of meaning between two positions of thought within-person is called

1. Selfish communication
2. Intra-personal communication
3. Inter-personal communication
4. Spiritual communication

Explanations
Answer: 2. Intra-personal communication

Intra-personal communication refers to the **internal dialogue or conversation that occurs within an individual's mind.** It involves **sharing meaning between two positions of thought**—for example, weighing pros and cons, reflecting on a decision, or questioning one's actions.

- It helps in **self-awareness, self-regulation, and problem-solving.**
- It often manifests as **inner speech, reflection, or self-questioning.**

Example:

When someone thinks, *"Should I take this opportunity, or should I wait for a better one?"* they are engaging in **intra-personal communication.**

Why not the other options?

Selfish communication: This term is not recognized in communication theory.

Inter-personal communication: Refers to **communication between two or more people**, not within oneself.

Spiritual communication: Refers to **communication based on spiritual or transcendental experiences,** not internal dialogue.

Question

In intra-personal communication, the medium that carries the messages is

1. The personal ego
2. The central nervous system
3. The physical surrounding
4. The symbol system

Explanations
Answer: 2. The central nervous system

In **intra-personal communication**, the **central nervous system (CNS)** acts as the **medium that carries messages** within an individual's mind. It processes thoughts, emotions, and self-talk through **neuronal activity, brain functions, and internal signals.**

The **brain processes information**, interprets meanings, and regulates internal dialogue.

Neural pathways enable **the transmission of thoughts, memories, and emotions**, forming the foundation of intra-personal communication.

Why not the other options?

The personal ego: Refers to **self-identity or self-perception**, not a medium for message transmission.

The physical surrounding: Refers to **external environmental factors**, unrelated to internal message transmission.

The symbol system: Refers to **language, signs, or representations** used in communication, but it does not act as a biological medium for intra-personal messages.

Question

Match the column:

A. intra-personal	I. between persons
B. inter-personal	II. within a small organisation
C. group	III. Large number of unknown audience
D. mass	IV. within oneself

1. A-I B-II C-III D-IV
2. A-II B-III C-IV D-I
3. A-III B-IV C-I D-II
4. A-IV B-I C-II D-III

Explanations
Answer: 4. A-IV B-I C-II D-III

A. Intra-personal → IV. Within oneself: Intra-personal communication refers to **self-talk, reflection, or internal dialogue** that happens within an individual.

B. Inter-personal → I. Between persons: Inter-personal communication takes place **between two or more individuals**, often in face-to-face conversations, phone calls, or video calls.

C. Group → II. Within a small organization: Group communication occurs within **small groups or teams**, such as in meetings, classroom discussions, or project collaborations.

D. Mass → III. Large number of unknown audience: Mass communication is directed toward a **large, often anonymous audience** through mediums like television, radio, or social media.

IV. Formal Communication:

- **Follows Organizational Rules & Policies** – Structured communication.
- **Governed by Chain of Command** – Hierarchical flow.
- **Ensures Information Flow in Organizations** – Controlled messaging.

- **Regulated by Conventional Rules** – Standardized processes.
- **Includes Vertical & Horizontal Communication** – Flows per hierarchy.
- These are the following **types of formal communication** which are given below:

Horizontal or Lateral:

- Horizontal or lateral communication is established between individuals or departments at the same hierarchical level.
- The role of this type is to facilitate the coordination of activities aimed at common objectives.
- Information that flows laterally or from left to right and vice versa follows a horizontal path.
- **Example:** Think about brainstorming sessions, department-wide meetings and group discussions with your coworkers.

Vertical Communication:

Vertical communication is a business communication strategy in which information, tasks, and requests move **upward and downward** between senior management and lower-level employees.

Downward Communication:

- Flows from a higher to a lower level is a downward communication.
- Occurs between superiors and subordinates in a chain of command.
- The managers use this communication flow to transmit work-related information to the employees at lower levels.
- The managers use downward communication for the following purposes:
    - Providing feedback on employees' performance.
    - Giving job instructions.
    - **Clarifies Employee Roles & Responsibilities** – Defines job expectations.
    - **Explains Job Interconnection** – Shows teamwork importance.
    - Providing employees with information about the organization's mission and vision.
    - Highlighting the areas of attention.

Upward Communication.

- **Flows from Subordinates to Superiors** – Bottom-to-top structure.
- **Provides Feedback on Organization's Functioning** – Helps improvements.
- **Allows Employees to Express Concerns** – Shares workplace issues.
- **Encourages Idea Sharing & Participation** – Enhances decision-making.
- **Strengthens Employer-Employee Relationship** – Improves communication trust.

Diagonal Communication:

- **Combines Vertical and Horizontal Communication** – Cross-hierarchy exchange.
- **Direct Dialogue Across Different Levels** – Bypasses formal structure.
- **Used When Other Channels Are Ineffective** – Ensures efficiency.
- **Facilitates Interdepartmental Collaboration** – Enhances teamwork.
- **Example: Developer & Marketing Manager Interaction** – Cross-functional communication.

Question

In the line organisation, the best suited communication (flow) is

1. Horizontal
2. Upward
3. Downward
4. Gestural

Explanations
Answer: 3. Downward

In a **line organization**, communication follows a **hierarchical structure**, where **instructions, decisions, and policies flow from higher to lower levels** in a **downward** direction. This ensures **clear authority and responsibility**.

Question

The communication among persons working at different levels who have no direct reporting relationship is called:

1. Intrapersonal communication
2. Upward communication
3. Horizontal communication
4. Diagonal communication

Explanations

Answer: 4. Diagonal communication

Diagonal communication refers to the **flow of information between individuals or departments who are at different levels in the organizational hierarchy and do not have a direct reporting relationship.**

It cuts across traditional **vertical (upward and downward) and horizontal communication lines** in an organization.

It often happens to **improve efficiency, share expertise, or resolve issues quickly** without going through hierarchical structures.

Example:

A **marketing executive communicating directly with a finance analyst** without involving their respective managers.

Why not the other options?

Intrapersonal communication: Refers to **communication within oneself**, not between individuals in an organization.

Upward communication: Refers to **information flowing from subordinates to superiors** in a hierarchy.

Horizontal communication: Happens **between individuals or departments at the same hierarchical level.**

Question

The advantages of diagonal communication are:

A. Resistance,
B. Side-tracking
C. Anomie
D. Morale boosting
E. Co-ordination

1. A, B and C only
2. B, C and D only
3. C, D and E only
4. B, D and E only

Explanations
Answer: 4. B, D and E only

Diagonal communication occurs across different levels and departments without adhering strictly to the traditional chain of command. It offers several advantages:

(B) Side-tracking: Diagonal communication **can bypass unnecessary hierarchical steps**, speeding up decision-making and problem-solving.

(D) Morale boosting: It **encourages collaboration and direct interaction**, making employees feel more involved and valued.

(E) Coordination: Diagonal communication improves **coordination between different levels and departments**, enhancing teamwork and organizational efficiency.

Why not the other options?

(A) Resistance: Resistance is usually a **disadvantage** in communication, not an advantage.

(C) Anomie: Anomie refers to a **sense of normlessness or disconnection**, which is not an advantage of diagonal communication.

Question

The communication between two or more persons who are subordinates working under the same person is an example of :

1. Lateral communication
2. Upward communication
3. Diagonal communication
4. Downward communication

Explanations
Answer: 1. Lateral communication

Lateral communication, also known as **horizontal communication**, refers to the **exchange of information between individuals or departments at the same hierarchical level within an organization.**

In this case, **subordinates working under the same superior** communicate directly with each other to **coordinate tasks, share information, or solve problems** without involving their manager.

It helps **promote teamwork, reduce misunderstandings, and improve efficiency** among team members.

Example:

Two project team members discussing task progress or coordinating deadlines under the supervision of the same project manager.

Why not the other options?

Upward communication: Refers to information **flowing from subordinates to superiors.**

Diagonal communication: Involves communication **across different hierarchical levels and departments** without direct reporting relationships.

Downward communication: Refers to information **flowing from superiors to subordinates.**

Question

Match the column:

A. Vertical	I. Feedback oriented
B. Horizontal	II. Inter-personal
C. Circular	III. Top-down
D. Transactional	IV. Rumour-oriented

1. A-I B-II C-III D-IV
2. A-II B-III C-IV D-I
3. A-Ill B-IV C-I D-II
4. A-IV B-I C-II D-III

Explanations
Answer: 3. A-Ill B-IV C-I D-II

A. Vertical → III. Top-down: Vertical communication refers to the **flow of information in a hierarchical structure**, either **top-down (from superiors to subordinates)** or **bottom-up (from subordinates to superiors).**

B. Horizontal → IV. Rumor-oriented: Horizontal communication occurs **among peers or employees at the same level** and can sometimes be **informal, leading to the spread of rumors** due to casual conversations and a lack of official channels.

C. Circular → I. Feedback-oriented: Circular communication is **cyclical** and emphasizes **continuous feedback and clarification** to ensure effective understanding and message delivery.

D. Transactional → II. Inter-personal: Transactional communication occurs in **inter-personal contexts**, involving **mutual exchange, real-time feedback, and shared understanding.**

Question

When there is an animated discussion between a teacher and his or her students in the classroom. it can be classified as :

1. Horizontal communication
2. Mechanical communication

3. Linear communication
4. Categorical communication

Explanations
Answer: 1. Horizontal communication

In a **classroom setting**, when there is **animated discussion and active interaction between a teacher and students**, it often resembles **horizontal communication** because:

Both the teacher and students are **engaged in an exchange of ideas on an equal platform** during discussions.

Horizontal communication focuses on **collaboration, sharing perspectives, and mutual understanding** rather than a one-way flow of information.

The flow of communication becomes **less hierarchical and more interactive**, resembling peer-level interaction even though the teacher holds authority.

Question

Match the column:

List I (Features)	List II (Communication Types)
A. A company boss telephones his/her secretary for some help from outside	I. marketing communication
B. A company issues a circular of guidelines for its employees	II. horizontal communication
C. Employees discuss certain issues among themselves	III. veritcal communication
D. A company sends a formal letter to its retailers and wholesalers	IV. informal communication

1. A-IV B-III C-II D-I
2. A-I B-II C-III D- IV
3. A-II B-III C-IV D-I
4. A-III B-IV C-I D-II

Explanations
Answer: 1. A-IV B-III C-II D-I

A. A company boss telephones his/her secretary for some help from outside → IV. Informal communication: A casual phone call, even in a professional context, often falls under **informal communication** as it bypasses formal procedures.

B. A company issues a circular of guidelines for its employees → III. Vertical communication: A circular from management to employees represents **downward vertical communication**, where information flows from higher levels to lower levels in the hierarchy.

C. Employees discuss certain issues among themselves → II. Horizontal communication: When employees at the **same hierarchical level** interact and discuss work-related topics, it is classified as **horizontal communication.**

D. A company sends a formal letter to its retailers and wholesalers → I. Marketing communication: A formal letter aimed at **retailers and wholesalers** serves as **marketing communication**, focused on promoting or managing business relationships

V. Informal Communication:

- **Casual Information Sharing** – No formal structure.
- **Occurs in Social Groups** – Includes friends and colleagues.
- **Happens in Everyday Situations** – Common daily interactions.
- **Examples: Small Talk & Emails** – Includes casual messages.
- **Gestures Also Convey Messages** – Nonverbal communication.
- **Workplace Informal Communication = Grapevine** – Spreads news quickly.
- **Lacks Official Approval** – Unregulated and spontaneous.

Grapevine:

- **Exists as an Informal Information Network** – Unofficial communication.
- **Spreads Through Casual Conversations** – Workplace social interactions.
- **Information Travels Quickly & Widely** – Rapid dissemination.
- **May Include Rumors & Misinformation** – Facts get distorted.

- **Not Part of Formal Hierarchy** – Unstructured flow.
- **Occurs Outside Official Channels** – Based on relationships.
- **Influences Workplace Culture & Morale** – Affects employee perceptions.
- Keith Davis found **four primary informal communication networks**:

Single Strand Network

- **Information Passes Linearly** – One person to another.
- **Serialized Transmission** – Follows a step-by-step process.
- **Slow and Distorted Over Time** – Message may change.

Gossip Chain

- **One Person Spreads Information** – Multiple people receive it.
- **Informal & Unverified Information** – Lacks factual confirmation.
- **Common in Workplace Conversations** – Spreads quickly.

Probability Chain

- **Message Spread Randomly** – No fixed pattern.
- **Each Person Selects Others** – Unstructured communication.
- **Example: Internet Spam** – Mass, uncontrolled dissemination.

Cluster Chain

- **Message Passed to Selected Individuals** – More organized flow.
- **Each Person Shares with a Group** – Expands systematically.
- **Used in Workplace Networks** – Efficient for quick updates

Question

Which of the following are the advantages of grapevine communication?

A. A Smooth float of adverse comments
B. Knowing the morale in the organisation
C. Spead of propagandist views
D. To know the important issues faced by the employees
E. Assessment of employee anxiety

1. A, B and C only
2. B, C, and D only
3. D, C, and E only
4. B, D, and E only

Explanations

Answer: 4. B, D, and E only

Grapevine communication refers to **informal and unofficial channels of communication** within an organization, often spreading through casual conversations, rumors, or word-of-mouth. While it can sometimes lead to misinformation, it also has distinct advantages:

(B) Knowing the morale in the organization: Grapevine communication **reveals the general mood, satisfaction, or dissatisfaction** of employees, offering insight into workplace morale.

(D) To know the important issues faced by the employees: It can **highlight underlying problems or concerns** that may not surface in formal communication channels.

(E) Assessment of employee anxieties: Informal conversations often **reflect employee fears, uncertainties, or anxieties,** helping management address these concerns proactively.

Why not the other options?

(A) Smooth float of adverse comments: Negative or adverse comments spreading informally can harm the organization's atmosphere rather than be an advantage.

(C) Spread of propagandist views: Propaganda or misinformation is generally seen as a **disadvantage of grapevine communication.**

Question

What is Grapevine communication?

1. Corporate Communication
2. Agri based Communication

3. Formal Communication
4. Informal Communication

Explanations

Answer: 4. Informal Communication

Grapevine communication refers to the **informal flow of information** within an organization, often through **rumors, gossip, or casual conversations**. It is **unstructured, spontaneous, and not officially controlled** by management.

Question

The grapevine communication is often driven by

1. External professional agencies
2. Competing organisations
3. Top management of an organisation
4. Social networks of employees

Explanations

Answer: 4. Social networks of employees

Grapevine communication thrives within the **informal social networks of employees** in an organization. It arises from **casual interactions, friendships, and trust built among colleagues**, rather than official communication channels.

Employees naturally form **informal groups or networks** where they share information, opinions, rumors, or concerns, leading to the spread of grapevine communication.

These networks are **unstructured, spontaneous, and often rapid**, making grapevine a powerful medium for sharing information—both accurate and inaccurate.

Why not the other options?

External professional agencies: They are not part of internal organizational grapevine networks.

Competing organizations: External competitors do not drive internal grapevine communication.

Top management of an organization: While management may sometimes use informal channels, grapevine communication **originates organically from employees.**

VI. Direct Communication:

- **Conveys Clear Messages & Instructions** – Avoids confusion.
- **Expresses Thoughts Without Ambiguity** – Ensures clarity.
- **Clarifies Authority in Workplaces** – Defines leadership roles.
- **Reduces Misunderstandings** – Prevents communication errors.
- **Builds Trust in Relationships** – Strengthens connections.
- **Prioritizes Clarity Over Comfort** – Ensures honesty.
- **May Seem Rude or Argumentative** – Can appear harsh.
- **Encourages Brutal Honesty** – Direct, no sugarcoating.
- **Active Listening is Essential** – Shows engagement.
- **Requires Effective Feedback** – Improves communication.
- **Enhances Workplace Efficiency** – Streamlines processes.
- **Examples:**
    - Honestly, telling another person, you appreciate their work ethic.
    - Telling your boss that you are sick and can't make it to work.

VII. Indirect Communication:

- **Uses Facial Expressions & Gestures** – Nonverbal cues matter.
- **Relies on Tone Instead of Words** – Meaning is implied.
- **Intentions Are Not Explicitly Stated** – Message is indirect.
- **Expectations Are Hinted, Not Expressed** – Requires interpretation.
- **Can Lead to Miscommunication** – Lacks direct clarity.
- **Increases Tension in Conversations** – Causes uncertainty.
- **Common Among Hesitant Individuals** – Fear of speaking directly.
- **Avoids Confrontation in Discussions** – Prefers subtlety.
- **Used by Socially Anxious People** – Reduces personal stress.
- **Can Be Ineffective in Workplaces** – Needs clarity.
- **Requires Awareness to Understand Meaning** – Demands attentiveness.

- Indirect communication allows you to say "No" non-offensive, especially when working with cultures that communicate indirectly, such as **India, China, Japan, Asia, and many countries in the Middle East**.

VIII. Continuous Communication:

- **Keeps Communication Flowing Constantly** – Ensures ongoing exchange.
- **Enhances Motivation & Collaboration** – Strengthens partnerships.
- **Develops Common Vocabulary & Goals** – Improves coordination.
- **Maintains Direct Contact Between Parties** – Ensures clarity.
- **Functions Like a Flowing River** – Never stops.
- **Allows Simultaneous Responses to Information** – Quick adaptability.
- **Enables Rapid Feedback & Insights** – Supports decision-making.
- **Example:** Face-to-face interaction, chat sessions and so on.

IX. Non-continuous Communication:

- The sender and receiver are not in direct touch.
- It can have a greater reach.
- **Example:** Reading a book, listening to the radio, and watching TV.

X. Intra group Communication:

- Intra-group communication means communication **within a group**.
- It usually happens in **small groups**.
- **Occurs Between Social Groups** – Facilitates interaction.
- **Includes Organizations, Families, or Classes**.
- **Can Foster Dialogue or Rivalry** – Strengthens or divides groups.
- **Example**: Intergroup communication scholars argue that much of our communication is intergroup where groups include age, ethnicity, sexual orientation, or political party.

XI: Intergroup Communication:

- **Involves Communication Between Groups** – Connects multiple groups.

- ➢ **Example: Classroom Group Discussions** – Encourages collaboration.
- ➢ **Guided by Intergroup Communication Theory** – Focuses on social identity.
- ➢ **Social Memberships Influence Interaction** – Shapes communication.
- ➢ **Can Strengthen or Divide Groups** – Affects relationships.

Question

Match the column:

A. Formal communication	I. Religious discourses
B. Informal communication	II. Questioning oneself after doing a mistake
C. Group communication	III. taking part in meeting
D. Intra-personal communication	IV. Conservation in canteen

1. A-I, B-II, C-III, D-IV
2. A-II, B-III, C-I, D-IV
3. A-III, B-IV, C-I, D-II
4. A-IV, B-I, C-II, D-II

Explanations

Answer: 3. A-III, B-IV, C-I, D-II

A. Formal communication → III. Taking part in a meeting: Formal communication happens in **structured, official settings**, like meetings, where information follows a defined protocol.

B. Informal communication → IV. Conversation in canteen: Informal communication occurs in **casual or unofficial settings,** like a friendly conversation in a canteen.

C. Group communication → I. Religious discourses: Group communication involves **one person addressing a group or interaction within a group**, such as religious sermons or group discussions.

D. Intrapersonal communication → II. Questioning oneself after doing a mistake: Intrapersonal communication happens **within an individual's mind**, such as reflecting or questioning oneself.

Question

Match the column:

A. Interviews	(I) Group Communication
B. Newspaper	(II) Intrapersonal Communication
C. Classroom	(III) Interpersonal Communication
D. Meditation	(IV) Mass Communication

1. A-I, B-III, C-II, D-IV
2. A-II, B-IV, C-III, D-I
3. A-IV, B-I, C-II, D-III
4. A-Ill, B-IV, C-I, D-II

Explanations
Answer: 4. A-Ill, B-IV, C-I, D-II

A. Interviews → III. Interpersonal Communication: An interview involves **one-on-one interaction between two or more individuals**, making it a clear example of **interpersonal communication**.

B. Newspaper → IV. Mass Communication: Newspapers serve as a platform for **mass communication**, delivering information to a **large, widespread audience.**

C. Classroom → I. Group Communication: Classroom communication involves a teacher interacting with a **group of students**, making it **group communication**.

D. Meditation → II. Intrapersonal Communication: Meditation is an **internal process of self-reflection and communication with oneself**, fitting the definition of **intrapersonal communication**.

XII. Synchronous Communication:

- **Happens in Real-Time** – Instant interaction occurs.
- **Requires Immediate Response** – No delays in replies.
- **Involves Two or More Participants** – Interactive exchange.
- **Examples: Calls, Video Meetings, Chats** – Live communication.
- **Differs from Asynchronous Communication** – No time gap.

- **Ensures Quick Decision-Making** – Speeds up processes.
- **Examples:** Video conferencing, instant messaging, and telephone conversations.

XIII. Asynchronous Communication:

- **No Immediate Response Required** – Happens with delay.
- **Occurs Out of Sync** – Not in real-time.
- **Transmits Data Intermittently** – Irregular flow.
- **Lacks Continuous Interaction** – No instant feedback.
- **Example: Emails & Recorded Messages** – Used in delayed communication.
- **Example**: An email to a colleague would be classed as asynchronous communication. Messages via any instant messaging app (e.g. WhatsApp messenger

Question

Match the column:

A. synchronous media	I. application of muti-media
B. asynchronous media	Il. interactive multi-media
C. rich media	III. e-mail
D. hyper media	IV. telephone

1. A-I B-II C-III D-IV
2. A-IV B-III C-II D-I
3. A-Il B-IV C-I D-III
4. A-III B-I C-IV D-II

Explanations
Answer: 2. A-IV B-III C-II D-I

A. Synchronous media → IV. Telephone: Synchronous media requires **real-time interaction**, and the telephone is a prime example of such communication.

B. Asynchronous media → III. E-mail: Asynchronous media does not require real-time interaction, like **email**, where participants can respond at their convenience.

C. Rich media → II. Interactive multi-media: Rich media refers to **interactive multi-media** that includes dynamic elements like video, animations, and sound.

D. Hypermedia → I. Application of multi-media: Hyper media involves **multi-media applications** that integrate text, audio, and visuals, often used in educational or web-based environments.

Question

Which of the following are examples of Asynchronous communication?

A. Blog
B. Podcast
C. Electronic Mail
D. Discussion Forum
E. Phone calls

1. BE
2. CDE
3. ACD
4. ABCD

Explanations
Answer: 4. ABCD

Asynchronous communication refers to communication that **does not happen in real-time**. Participants can **send, receive, and respond to messages at their convenience**, without requiring simultaneous interaction.

Examples of Asynchronous Communication:

A. Blog: Readers can access and respond to blog posts **at any time** after publication.

B. Podcast: Podcasts are **pre-recorded audio content** that listeners can access at their convenience.

C. Electronic Mail (Email): Emails allow individuals to **send messages without requiring an immediate response.**

D. Discussion Forum: Participants can **post messages, ask questions, or provide answers** without everyone being present simultaneously.

Why not Phone Calls (E)?

Phone Calls: These are an example of **synchronous communication** because they require **both participants to be present simultaneously** for interaction.

Question

Which of the following tools are used by learners and teachers for Asynchronous Interaction?

A. Web conferencing
B. E-mail
C. Wikis and collaborative documents
D. Discussion Boards
E. Live Streaming.

1. B, C and D only
2. C, D and only
3. A, C, D and E only
4. A and B only

Explanations
Answer: 1. B, C and D only

Asynchronous interaction refers to communication or collaboration that does not require participants to be online or available simultaneously. It allows learners and teachers to **engage, share resources, and collaborate at their convenience.**

Tools for Asynchronous Interaction:

B. E-mail: Emails allow teachers and learners to **exchange messages, share resources, and provide feedback** without being online simultaneously.

C. Wikis and collaborative documents: Tools like **Google Docs or collaborative platforms** enable multiple users to **edit, comment, and share resources asynchronously.**

D. Discussion Boards: Platforms like **Moodle or online forums** allow participants to **post questions, comments, and responses at different times.**

Why not the other options?

A. Web conferencing: This is a **synchronous tool**, requiring participants to be present online in real-time.

E. Live streaming: This also happens **in real-time**, making it synchronous communication.

Question

An example of asynchronous media is -

1. The television
2. The radio
3. The cinema
4. The newspaper

Explanations
Answer: 4. The newspaper

Asynchronous media refers to communication or content delivery that **does not require the sender and receiver to be engaged simultaneously.** The **newspaper** is an example of asynchronous media because:

Time Independence: Readers can access and read the newspaper **at their convenience**, long after it has been printed and distributed.

No Real-Time Interaction: There is **no immediate feedback loop** between the content creator (journalist) and the reader.

Static Content: Once printed, the information remains **unchanged** until the next edition.

Why not the other options?

Television: Often used for **live broadcasts**, making it synchronous communication.

Radio: Live radio broadcasts rely on **real-time interaction** with listeners.

Cinema: Movies are scheduled, and audiences **experience them simultaneously**, aligning more with synchronous media.

Question

Which of the following systems use synchronous communication?

A. Skype video call
B. Facebook Chat
C. Email
D. Messaging on Snap chat
E. Telephone call

1. ABE
2. ABDE
3. ACDE
4. BC

Explanations
Answer: 2. ABDE

Synchronous communication occurs in **real-time**, where participants are actively engaged simultaneously, allowing for immediate feedback and interaction.

Systems that use synchronous communication:

A. Skype video call: A **real-time audio and video interaction** tool, enabling live conversation.

B. Facebook Chat: Real-time messaging platform where participants **respond instantly** through text or video chat.

D. Messaging on Snapchat: Snapchat's messaging feature supports **instant messaging and video chats**, happening in real-time when both users are online.

E. Telephone call: Telephone communication happens **live and in real-time**, enabling instant feedback and conversation.

Why not C. Email?

Email is an **asynchronous communication tool**, where messages are sent and received **at different times**, without requiring both parties to be online simultaneously.

Question

What are the benefits of asynchronous mode of online learning-

A. Self-pacing
B. Immediate Feedback
C. Self-engagement
D. Flexibility
E. Presence of Teacher and student at the same time

1. (A), and (D) only
2. (B) and (D) only
3. (A), (C), and (D) only
4. (A), (C), and (E) only

Explanations
Answer: 3. (A), (C), and (D) only

Asynchronous online learning allows students to access learning materials, complete tasks, and engage with course content **at their own convenience** without requiring real-time interaction with instructors or peers.

Benefits of Asynchronous Learning:

(A) Self-pacing: Learners can **progress through course materials at their own speed**, revisiting content as needed.

(C) Self-engagement: Students are **responsible for managing their learning schedule**, fostering independent study habits.

(D) Flexibility: Learners can **access course content anytime, anywhere**, accommodating diverse schedules and time zones.

Why not the other options?

(B) Immediate Feedback: Asynchronous learning does not provide **instant feedback**, as interactions happen with delays.

(E) Presence of Teacher and Student at the Same Time: This is characteristic of **synchronous learning**, not asynchronous.

Question

In terms of communication, most online platforms of teaching and learning are:

1. Synchronous
2. Asynchronous
3. One-to-none
4. Tied to specific timeframe

Explanations
Answer: 2. Asynchronous

Most **online teaching and learning platforms** operate in an **asynchronous mode**, allowing learners and instructors to **access, share, and respond to content at different times** without the need for real-time interaction.

Flexibility: Students can **access lectures, assignments, and resources at their convenience.**

Self-Paced Learning: Learners can **progress through the material at their own speed.**

No Time Zone Constraints: Participants from different geographical locations can **engage without scheduling conflicts.**

Resource Availability: Recorded lectures, documents, and resources remain **available for repeated access.**

Question

Which of the following statements are true in the context of Web Conferencing?

A. It uses the Internet to permit conferencing to take place.
B. Multiple computers are used with this system, all connected over the Internet.
C. Delegates cannot leave the conference once they join.
D. It is carried out in real-time.

1. AB
2. ABC
3. CD
4. ABD

Explanations
Answer: 4. ABD

Web conferencing refers to **virtual meetings or conferences conducted over the Internet** using tools like Zoom, Google Meet, or Microsoft Teams. The following statements are true:

A. It uses the Internet to permit conferencing to take place: Web conferencing **relies on the Internet** as its primary platform to enable real-time virtual communication.

B. Multiple computers are used with this system, all connected over the Internet: Web conferencing involves **multiple devices (computers, tablets, smartphones)** connected via the Internet, allowing participants from different locations to join.

D. It is carried out in real-time: Web conferencing is typically **synchronous (real-time)** communication, enabling live interaction, discussion, and collaboration.

Question

In which mode of leaning, leaners participate in active discussion and get immediate feedback from the teachers?

1. Synchronous mode of learning
2. Asynchronous mode of learning
3. Spatial mode of learning
4. Relativist mode of learning

Explanations

Answer: 1. Synchronous mode of learning

In the **synchronous mode of learning**, learners and teachers interact **in real-time**, enabling **immediate feedback, active discussions, and direct clarification of doubts.** This mode mirrors the traditional classroom environment but takes place in an **online or virtual setting** using platforms like **Zoom, Google Meet, or Microsoft Teams**.

Immediate Feedback: Teachers can provide **instant responses** to students' queries.

Real-time Interaction: Learners can **actively participate in live discussions.**

Dynamic Environment: Encourages **collaborative activities, group discussions, and brainstorming sessions.**

Instant Clarification: Any doubts or misunderstandings can be addressed **on the spot.**

Question

Chatting on WhatsApp is an example of

1. Synchronous communication
2. Asynchronous communication
3. Non-verbal communication
4. Friendly communication

Explanations
Answer: 1. Synchronous communication

Chatting on WhatsApp is an example of **synchronous communication** because it allows for **real-time interaction between participants.** Both sender and receiver can **exchange messages instantly, respond immediately, and have ongoing conversations without significant delays.**

Real-time Interaction: Messages are sent and received **almost instantaneously.**

Instant Feedback: Participants can respond **immediately**, mimicking face-to-face conversations.

Dynamic Exchange: Conversations flow naturally, with a **back-and-forth interaction.**

Question

Asynchronous communication takes place through which of the following technologies?

A. Teleconferencing
B. Virtual classroom
C. Video chat
D. Blogs
E. Discussion boards
F. Vlog

1. ABC
2. BCD
3. DEF
4. CDE

Explanations
Answer: 3. DEF

Asynchronous communication happens when **participants do not need to be present simultaneously** for communication to occur. It allows users to **engage with content, respond, and interact at their convenience.**

D. Blogs: Blogs allow content creators to **publish written posts or articles**, and readers can **comment or respond later** without real-time interaction.

E. Discussion boards: These platforms enable participants to **post messages, ask questions, and respond asynchronously**, fostering ongoing discussions over time.

F. Vlogs: Video blogs are **pre-recorded video content** that viewers can watch and respond to **at their convenience**, often through comments.

Question

Synchronous communication takes place through which of the following technologies?

A. Video chat
B. Virtual classrooms
C. Audio conferencing
D. Wikis
E. Electronic mail

1. ABC
2. BCD
3. CDE
4. ADE

Explanations
Answer: 1. ABC

Synchronous communication occurs in **real-time**, where participants are **actively engaged simultaneously**, enabling immediate interaction, feedback, and collaboration.

A. Video chat: Platforms like **Zoom, Google Meet, and Microsoft Teams** enable **live video communication** between participants.

B. Virtual classrooms: Online platforms such as **Google Classroom or Blackboard** allow **teachers and students to interact in real-time.**

C. Audio conferencing: Tools like **teleconferencing or voice calls** facilitate **real-time audio discussions** among participants.

Question

Which of the following communication technologies employ only asynchronous communication?

a. Video conferencing
b. Email
c. Forums
d. Instant messaging

1. ac
2. bd
3. bc
4. ad

Explanations
Answer: 3. bc

Asynchronous communication refers to communication that does not require participants to be online or available simultaneously. Responses can be delayed, and interaction happens at each participant's convenience.

B. Email: Emails allow users to send and receive messages at different times, making them a classic example of asynchronous communication.

C. Forums: Discussion forums enable users to post questions, share opinions, and respond later without requiring all participants to be online simultaneously.

Question

Instructions which encourage live participation and interaction through online classes are called

1. Synchronous instructions

2. Asynchronous instructions
3. Traditional instructions
4. Theoretical instructions

Explanations
Answer: 1. Synchronous instructions

Synchronous instructions refer to **live, real-time teaching and learning sessions** conducted through online platforms where students and teachers interact simultaneously.

Live Participation: Students and teachers are **present online at the same time** for real-time interaction.

Instant Feedback: Teachers can **immediately respond to questions, clarify doubts, and provide feedback.**

Engagement: Activities like **live discussions, Q&A sessions, and collaborative exercises** encourage participation.

Platforms Used: Tools like **Zoom, Google Meet, and Microsoft Teams** facilitate synchronous instructions.

XIV. Classroom Communication

- Verbal Communication Uses Speech & Language – Facilitates learning.
- Nonverbal Communication Includes Gestures & Expressions – Supports teaching.
- Written Communication Uses Text & Symbols – Enhances clarity.
- Teachers Address Individuals or Entire Class – Ensures engagement.
- Communication Makes Learning More Accessible – Improves understanding.
- Expands Opportunities for Knowledge – Encourages deeper learning.
- Strengthens Student-Teacher Relationships – Builds trust.

XV. Public Communication:

- **Reaches Multiple People Simultaneously** – Delivered in identical form.

- **Includes Broadcasts, Newspapers, and Advertisements** – Covers mass media.
- **Uses Various Communication Channels** – TV, radio, and digital platforms.
- **Essential for Public Speaking** – Involves structured messaging.
- **Requires Understanding of Different Speech Types** – Enhances effectiveness.
  - Speaking to Inform.
  - Speaking to Persuade.
  - Speaking to Actuate.
  - Speaking to Entertain.
- **Example**: Advertisements, magazine articles, website information, presentations, website matters, conference attendance, membership in organizations, town hall meetings, newsletter distribution, activity updates, and other publications are included, as well as the approval of related proposals, contracts, and contract amendments.

Question

Announcement of arrival and departure of trains at railway stations is:

1. Spatial communication
2. Organisational communication
3. Public communication
4. Sectional communication

Explanations

Answer: 3. Public communication

The **announcement of train arrivals and departures at railway stations** is an example of **public communication** because:

Target Audience: The information is addressed to a **large, general audience** present at the station.

Purpose: The goal is to **inform and guide the public** about train schedules.

Medium: It typically uses **public address systems (loudspeakers)** to reach everyone in the area.

One-Way Communication: The announcement is **primarily one-way**, with minimal or no immediate feedback from the audience.

Why not the other options?

Spatial communication: Refers to the **use of space and physical distance** to convey meaning, not announcements.

Organizational communication: Involves **internal communication within an organization**, not broadcasting to the public.

Sectional communication: Refers to communication within **specific sections or departments**, not public-facing announcements.

XVI. Political Communication:

- **Spreads Information Influencing Politics & Citizens** – Shapes opinions.
- **Uses Mass Media & Interpersonal Channels** – Disseminates messages.
- **Connects Politics & Citizens Through Interaction** – Builds engagement.
- **Persuasion Uses Pathos, Ethos, & Logos** – Influences decisions.
- **Strategic Communication Serves Organizational Goals** – Fulfills missions.
- **Campaigns Gain Public Support for Leaders** – Strengthens influence.
- **Social Media Transforms Political Campaigning** – Expands reach.
- **Digital-Native Voters Prefer Online Engagement** – Modernizes politics.
- **Political Messages Spread Through Multiple Channels** – Includes media.
- **Print, Broadcast, & Digital Platforms Used** – Ensures visibility.

XVII. Intercultural Communication: (Discussed in Depth Later)

- **Interaction Between Different Cultures** – Cross-cultural exchange.
- **Involves Symbolic & Interpretive Process** – Meaning varies.

- **Transactional & Contextual Communication** – Influenced by culture.
- **Cultural Awareness is Essential** – Avoids misunderstandings.
- **Different Cultures Have Unique Norms** – Varies by region.

XVIII. Organizational communication:

- Manages Information Flow Within Organizations
- Sustains Organizations Through Continuous Communication.
- Involves Internal & External Stakeholders.
- Can Be Formal or Informal
- Supports Shared Organizational Objectives.
- There are four categories of organizational culture:
    - i. Formal and informal communication.
    - ii. Directional communication.
    - iii. Internal and external communication.
    - iv. Oral and written communication.

Question

One of the major barriers in organisational communication is-

1. Semantic distortion
2. Effective downward communication
3. Immediate feedback
4. Flexible human environment

Explanations
Answer: 1. Semantic distortion

Semantic distortion occurs when **misinterpretation of words, jargon, or symbols** creates confusion in communication. This is a **major barrier in organizational communication**, leading to misunderstandings and inefficiencies.

Question

Organisational communication is ____in nature.

1. Obtrusive
2. Contradictory

3. Non-behavioural
4. Applied

Explanations
Answer: 4. Applied

Organizational communication is considered **applied in nature** because it involves **practical implementation of communication principles, theories, and strategies** to achieve specific organizational goals. It focuses on **effective message flow, collaboration, conflict resolution, and team management** within an organizational structure.

Why not the other options?

Obtrusive: Suggests something **intrusive or forceful,** which does not describe the nature of organizational communication.

Contradictory: Effective communication within organizations aims to **reduce contradictions and confusion,** not promote them.

Non-behavioral: Organizational communication is inherently **behavioral** as it involves human interaction, attitudes, and relationships.

Question

Match the column:

A. Dyadic communication	I. messages flow through a network of inter-dependent relationships
B. Public communication	II. uses a medium to reach a large anonymous audience
C. Organisational communication	III. provides equal opportunity to communicate
D. Mass communication	IV. occurs within a formal and structured setting

1. A-II B-III C-IV D-I
2. A-III B-IV C-I D-II
3. A-IV B-I C-II D-III
4. A-I B-II C-III D-IV

Explanations
Answer: 2. A-III B-IV C-I D-II

A. Dyadic communication → III. Provides equal opportunity to communicate: Dyadic communication refers to **two-person communication** (e.g., a conversation or interview) where **both participants have an equal chance to share thoughts.**

B. Public communication → IV. Occurs within a formal and structured setting: Public communication happens in **formal, organized settings** where one person addresses an audience, such as in a **public speech, lecture, or presentation.**
C. Organizational communication → I. Messages flow through a network of inter-dependent relationships: Organizational communication involves **information flow within formal structures and networks** of an organization, often interconnecting various departments or levels.

D. Mass communication → II. Uses a medium to reach a large anonymous audience: Mass communication relies on **mass media (e.g., television, radio, social media)** to reach a **large, often anonymous audience.**

XIX. Family Communication:

Communication skills influence relationships in families, children, friends, and work. According to the Family Communication Patterns Theory, there are different types of family communication patterns:

1. **Conversation:** Families can have open discussions and freely discuss any topic.
2. **Conformity:** Families with individuals (a parent usually) who have the authority to make final decisions.
3. **Pluralistic:** Families engage in open discussions in which every family member has an equal opportunity to share their opinions when deciding on a unit.
4. **Consensual:** With conversation and conformity, family members can openly communicate their thoughts and feelings and value conformity within the family unit. The parents or caregivers usually make the final decision.

5. **Laissez-Fair:** Families are emotionally detached from each other without conversation or conformity. Children are typically free to make their own choices without interest from parents/caregivers.
6. **Protective:** Without conversation but with conformity, parents or caregivers expect their children to obey the rules and do not usually trust their children to make their own decisions.

XX. Metacognition Communication

- **Metacognition communication** involves thinking about thinking.
- **Enhances** self-awareness in learning and communication.
- **Encourages** reflection on one's communication process.
- **Helps** in monitoring and adjusting speech patterns.
- **Develops** better problem-solving and reasoning skills.
- **Involves** evaluating how messages are perceived.
- **Supports** active listening and critical thinking.
- **Improves** clarity and effectiveness in discussions.
- **Strengthens** self-regulation in social interactions.
- **Affects** decision-making and message interpretation.

Question

Which of the following are true in the case of metacommunication?

A. It is intentional
B. It is not always intentional
C. It often takes place spontaneously.
D. It can modify itself.
E. It decontextualized itself

1. (A), (B) and (C) only
2. (B), (C) and (D) only
3. (C), (D) and (E) only
4. (A), (D) and (E) only

Explanations
Answer: 2. (B), (C) and (D) only

Metacommunication refers to **communication about communication** — it includes messages that **convey meaning beyond the literal content of the words spoken.** It can occur both verbally and non-verbally.

(B) It is not always intentional: Metacommunication **can happen unconsciously** through tone, facial expressions, or gestures.

(C) It often takes place spontaneously: Many metacommunicative cues are **unplanned and occur naturally** in interaction.

(D) It can modify itself: Metacommunication can **adjust, clarify, or contradict the primary message,** influencing its interpretation.

Why not the other options?

(A) It is intentional: While metacommunication can sometimes be intentional, it is **not always deliberate.**

(E) It decontextualized itself: This is incorrect. Metacommunication is **highly context-dependent** and relies on the interaction's social and emotional setting.

Question

Communication about communication is called -

1. Communication narrative
2. Communication narrative
3. Metacognition
4. Metacommunication

Explanations
Answer: 4. Metacommunication

Metacommunication refers to **"communication about communication."** It involves **conveying messages about how to interpret other messages,** often through **tone of voice, body language, facial expressions, or explicit statements about communication itself.**

For example:

Saying, *"Don't take this the wrong way, but..."* is metacommunication because it **guides how the following message should be interpreted.**

A sarcastic tone while saying "Great job!" changes the meaning of the words and serves as metacommunication.

Why not the other options?

Communication narrative: This refers to **telling stories or structuring communication in a narrative format**, not about communication itself.

Metacognition: Refers to **thinking about one's own thinking processes,** not about communication.

Question

Among the following skills, which are considered as soft skills?

A. Decision making
B. Marketing
C. Communication
D. Conflict resolution
E. Leadership

1. B & E only
2. A, C & E only
3. A, C, D & E only
4. B & D only

Explanations
Answer: 3. A, C, D & E only

Soft skills refer to **personal attributes, communication abilities, and emotional intelligence** that enable individuals to interact effectively and harmoniously with others. The following are considered soft skills:

A. Decision making: The ability to **make informed and effective choices** in different situations.

C. Communication: Essential for **expressing ideas clearly and understanding others.**

D. Conflict resolution: Involves **managing and resolving disputes** effectively.

E. Leadership: The ability to **guide, motivate, and inspire others** toward shared goals.

Why not the other option (B - Marketing)?

Marketing is typically considered a **hard skill**, as it involves technical knowledge, strategies, and tools specific to the field.

Question

Skills to face job interviews and getting employed are part of:

1. Livilhood skill
2. Life skill
3. Soft skill
4. Learning skill

Explanations

Answer: 3. Soft skill

Skills to face job interviews and getting employed **are part of Soft skill**

Question

Negative communicators usually express

A. Verbal softness
B. Optimism
C. Pessimism
D. Resentment
E. Distrust

1. A, B, C only
2. B, C, D only
3. C, D, E only
4. A, B, E only

Explanations
Answer: 3. C, D, E only

Negative communicators often exhibit behaviors and attitudes that reflect a **lack of confidence, hostility, or distrust** in communication. The following traits are common in negative communicators:

C. Pessimism: They tend to have a **negative outlook** and focus on problems rather than solutions.

D. Resentment: Negative communicators often express **bitterness or anger** through their words or tone.

E. Distrust: They frequently **doubt others' intentions** and may resist collaboration or open dialogue.

Why not the other options?

A. Verbal softness: This suggests politeness or gentle communication, which is not characteristic of negative communicators.

B. Optimism: Optimism is a positive trait, opposite to the nature of negative communication.

XXI. Mass Communication: (Discussed in Depth Later)

- Imparts Information to Large Audiences – Reaches many people.
- Influences Behavior, Attitudes & Opinions – Shapes perceptions.
- Uses Various Media Platforms – TV, radio, internet.
- Includes Print & Digital Formats – Newspapers, books, films.
- Affects Public Emotion & Awareness – Impacts society.

Question

Match the column:

A. Addressing the nation over national TV network	I. horizontal communication
B. Conducting a workshop for a select number of teachers	II. intra-personal communication

C. Internal conversation with fellow workers	III. mass communication
D. Recollection of past events	IV. group communication

1. A-I B-II C-III D-IV
2. A-II B-III C-IV D-I
3. A-III B-IV C-I D-II
4. A-IV B-I C-II D-III

Explanations
Answer: 3. A-III B-IV C-I D-II

A. Addressing the nation over a national TV network → III. Mass communication: Speaking to a **large, anonymous audience** via a national TV network is an example of **mass communication**, where the message is broadcasted to a vast audience.

B. Conducting a workshop for a select number of teachers → IV. Group communication: A workshop involves **direct interaction within a small group**, where participants engage in discussions, activities, and learning, fitting the definition of **group communication**.

C. Internal conversation with fellow workers → I. Horizontal communication: Conversations among colleagues or fellow workers at the **same hierarchical level** represent **horizontal communication**, aimed at coordination and collaboration.

D. Recollection of past events → II. Intra-personal communication: Reflecting on past events happens **internally within one's mind**, which is characteristic of **intra-personal communication**.

Question

The communication which happens outside the realm of interpersonal communication is called:

1. Interpersonal communication
2. Intrapersonal communication
3. Mass communication
4. Upward communication

Explanations
Answer: 3. Mass communication

Mass communication refers to the exchange of information with a large audience, typically through mass media channels like television, radio, newspapers, or the internet. It occurs outside the realm of interpersonal communication, which focuses on one-on-one or small group interactions.

Why Mass Communication?

Audience: Targets a **large, diverse audience**, not just individuals.

Medium: Often mediated through **radio, TV, newspapers, or digital platforms.**

Feedback: Feedback is often **delayed or indirect**, unlike immediate feedback in interpersonal communication.

Question

Match the column:

A. network communication	I. formal and planned
B. mass communication	II. creates identity and unique dynamics
C. public communication	III. inter-dependent relations
D. small group communication	IV. anonymous audience

1. A-II B-III C-IV D-I
2. A-III B-IV C-I D-II
3. A-IV B-I C-II D-III
4. A-I B-II C-III D-IV

Explanations
Answer: 2. A-III B-IV C-I D-II

A. Network Communication → III. Inter-dependent relations: Network communication refers to **interconnected communication channels where individuals or groups depend on each other** for information flow, collaboration, and coordination.

B. Mass Communication → IV. Anonymous audience: Mass communication targets a **large, anonymous audience** through media channels like television, newspapers, and the internet.

C. Public Communication → I. Formal and planned: Public communication, such as a speech or presentation, is **formal, structured, and planned** to address a larger audience in a direct manner.

D. Small Group Communication → II. Creates identity and unique dynamics: In small group communication, members **develop shared identities, norms, and dynamics** to achieve collective goals and maintain group cohesion.

Question

Match the column:

List I: Types of communication	List II: Function served
A. Mass communication	(I) Corridor discussion
B. Intrapersonal communication	(II) Classroom Teaching
C. Group communication	(III) For communicates with oneself
D. Interpersonal communication	(IV) For mechanical message transmission

1. (A)-(IV), (B)-(III), (C)-(II), (D)-(I)
2. (A)-(I), (B)-(II), (C)-(III), (D)-(IV)
3. (A)-(II), (B)-(III), (C)-(IV), (D)-(I)
4. (A)-(III), (B)-(II), (C)-(I), (D)-(IV)

Explanations
Answer: 1. (A)-(IV), (B)-(III), (C)-(II), (D)-(I)

A. Mass communication → (IV) For mechanical message transmission: Mass communication relies on **mechanical or technological channels** (e.g., television, radio, internet) to deliver messages to **large, anonymous audiences.**

B. Intrapersonal communication → (III) For communicates with oneself: Intrapersonal communication involves **self-talk, reflection, and internal dialogue**, serving the purpose of **introspection and self-regulation.**

C. Group communication → (II) Classroom teaching: Group communication takes place in **small to medium-sized groups**, like classroom teaching, where **a teacher interacts with multiple students.**

D. Interpersonal communication → (I) Corridor discussion: Interpersonal communication happens **one-on-one or in informal small conversations,** such as casual chats in a corridor.

Question

Statement I: The art of Mass Communication is much simpler than of face to face communication or any type of communication
Statement II: Each of us uses 35 (Sight, Sound and Smell and 2T (Touch and Taste) when we communicate with others.

1. Both Statement I and Statement Il are correct
2. Both Statement I and Statement Il are incorrect
3. Statement I is correct but Statement Il is incorrect
4. Statement I is incorrect but Statement Il is correct

Explanations
Answer: 4. Statement I is incorrect but Statement Il is correct

Statement I is incorrect: Mass communication is far more complex than face-to-face or interpersonal communication. It involves **reaching large, diverse audiences across different geographic and cultural boundaries.** Additionally, mass communication often requires **advanced technologies, strategic planning, and careful message crafting** to be effective.

Statement II is correct: Human communication relies on the **five senses—sight, sound, smell, touch, and taste** (referred to as **3S and 2T**). Each sense contributes to how we **perceive, interpret, and respond to messages** during communication. For example:

- **Sight:** Observing facial expressions, gestures, and body language.
- **Sound:** Tone of voice, pitch, and verbal cues.
- **Smell:** Environmental cues and scents that influence interaction.
- **Touch:** Physical connection, like a handshake.
- **Taste:** Symbolic in some cultural and social communication settings.

CHAPTER III

Effective Communication

Effective Communication:

Effective communication involves exchanging ideas, thoughts, opinions, knowledge, and data so that the message is understood clearly and with purpose. Effective communication culminates in both sender and receiver feeling satisfied.

There are many forms of communication, including verbal, non-verbal, written, visual, and listening. Communication can take place in person, over the internet (on forums, social media, and websites), by phone (through apps, voice calls, and video), or by mail.

For communication to be effective, it must be **clear**, **correct**, **complete**, **concise**, and **compassionate**. The seven C's of communication are a list of principles for written and spoken communications to ensure they are effective. The seven C's are:

1. **Clarity:** Clarity ensures that what is being said is communicated clearly without miscommunication.
2. **Correctness: T**he most appropriate language for a specific message is the best form of communication. Maintaining correctness also involves avoiding grammatical, spelling, or other errors in a language.
3. **Conciseness:** Convey the points briefly and concisely. When communicating a message, use as few words as possible to keep the listener's attention.
4. **Courtesy:** Treat the audience politely and respectfully. Communicating effectively requires being friendly, considerate, and professional.
5. **Concreteness:** A concrete message is precise and backed by confidence and the use of supporting facts and figures.
6. **Coherent/Consideration:** A coherent conversation makes sense and follows a logical progression. A communicator has to think carefully about the order of his points and how he can make them come across in an easy-to-understand way.

7. **Completeness:** Make sure nothing is missing. Complete communication ensures the audience has all the information they need and can quickly reach the desired conclusion.

The 4's of communication are:

1. **Shortness:** It is said that "brevity is the spirit of wit." The same applies to the communication.
2. **Strength:** The power of the message is determined by the trustworthiness of the messenger.
3. **Simplicity:** Using simple words and concepts indicates clarity of thought.
4. **Sincerity:** The recipient can detect a genuine approach to a problem. Whenever the sender is sincere, it will be evident in their communication.

Benefits of effective communication

Communication effectiveness can be seen as a benefit in the workplace, an educational setting, and in an individual's personal life. These areas can benefit from the development of effective communication skills.

Effective communication in the workplace:

- Manages **employees** and strengthens teamwork.
- Boosts organizational **growth** and retention.
- Encourages **creativity** and innovation.
- Expands **opportunities** within the organization.
- Builds strong **relationships** professionally.

Effective communication in personal life:

- Effective **communication** improves social and mental health.
- Establishes **deeper** connections with others.
- Builds **trust** and transparency in relationships.
- Enhances **problem-solving** and conflict resolution.
- Strengthens **bonds** in personal interactions.

Question

To gain a good vocabulary for effective communication, learners should depend upon-

1. Teachers
2. Backbenchers
3. Their own initiatives
4. Outside tutors

Explanations
Answer: 3. Their own initiatives

To build a **strong vocabulary for effective communication**, learners must take **personal responsibility and initiative.** Self-driven efforts such as **reading extensively, practicing writing, engaging in conversations, and using new words in context** are key to vocabulary development.

Why not the other options?

Teachers: While teachers can guide and support, they cannot single-handedly build a learner's vocabulary.

Backbenchers: They are not typically a reliable source for structured vocabulary learning.

Outside tutors: Tutors can help, but consistent self-initiative remains essential for long-term vocabulary growth.

Question

Development of communication skills among learners involves:

A. Vertical flow of information
B. Restricted expression of views
C. Logical argumentation
D. Sharing of doubts
E. Understanding human psychology

1. ABC
2. BCD
3. CDE
4. ADE

Explanations

Answer: 3. CDE

The **development of communication skills** among learners requires fostering key abilities that encourage clarity, reasoning, and emotional intelligence. These include:

C. Logical argumentation: Encourages learners to **present their ideas clearly and defend them with reasoning and evidence.**

D. Sharing of doubts: Creates an **open environment for clarification and deeper understanding.**

E. Understanding human psychology: Helps learners **adapt their communication style based on audience emotions, reactions, and perspectives.**

Why not the other options?

A. Vertical flow of information: One-way communication from top to bottom **limits interaction and active engagement.**

B. Restricted expression of views: This stifles creativity, confidence, and open discussion in the classroom.

Question

Match the column:

A. Public speaking	(I) To gain information
B. Leadership	(II) Confidence
C. Self-presentation	(III) Problem-solving
D. Interviewing	(IV) Represents a credible person

1. A-I B-II C-III D-IV
2. A-III B-IV C-I D-II
3. A-IV B-I C-II D-III
4. A-ll B-III C-IV D-I

Explanations

Answer: 4. A-ll B-III C-IV D-I

A. Public speaking → II. Confidence: Public speaking **builds confidence by helping individuals express their ideas clearly and assertively** in front of an audience.

B. Leadership → III. Problem-solving: Effective leadership often involves **analyzing issues, making decisions, and guiding teams to solutions.**

C. Self-presentation → IV. Represents a credible person: Self-presentation is about **creating a strong impression, showcasing credibility, and building trust.**

D. Interviewing → I. To gain information: Interviews are primarily conducted to **extract valuable information or insights from individuals.**

Question

Which of the following are myths about communication?

A. Good communicators are born, not made
B. Stage fright is not a communication apprehension
C. Communication skills have nothing to do with relationships
D. Communication has its own barriers
E. Practice leads to the right habits of communication

1. A, B and C only
2. B, C and D only
3. C, D and E only
4. A, C and D only

Explanations
Answer: 1. A, B and C only

A. Good communicators are born, not made: This is a myth. **Communication skills can be learned, practiced, and improved** over time through training and experience.

B. Stage fright is not a communication apprehension: This is false. **Stage fright is a recognized form of communication apprehension**, often caused by anxiety about public speaking.

C. Communication skills have nothing to do with relationships: This is incorrect. **Effective communication is essential for building and maintaining healthy relationships**, whether personal or professional.

Why not the other options?

D. Communication has its own barriers: This is true. Communication often faces **barriers like noise, misunderstanding, or cultural differences.**

E. Practice leads to the right habits of communication: This is true. **Consistent practice helps develop effective communication habits.**

Question

Statement I: One's perceptions and beliefs are the basis of generalization in communication
Statement II: Generalisations of the environment develop through experiences.

1. Both Statement I and Statement Il are true
2. Both Statement I and Statement Il are false
3. Statement I is true but Statement ll is false
4. Statement I is false but Statement Il is true

Explanations
Answer: 1. Both Statement I and Statement Il are true

Statement I is true: In communication, **one's perceptions and beliefs shape how information is interpreted and generalized.** These mental frameworks act as filters, influencing how messages are received and understood.

Statement II is true: Generalizations about the environment are often formed through experiences. Repeated exposure to certain patterns, behaviors, or outcomes creates mental shortcuts or assumptions that guide communication.

Question

Identify the sequence of human communication skills.

A. Public speaking
B. Group interaction
C. Relationship
D. Feed forward
E. Self - presentation

1. B, D, E, C, A
2. A, C, D, B, E
3. G, E, A, D, B
4. E, C, B, A, D

Explanations
Answer: 4. E, C, B, A, D

The **sequence of human communication skills** follows a natural progression from individual interaction to more complex group dynamics:

E. Self-presentation: Communication begins with how individuals **present themselves and create first impressions.**

C. Relationship: Building **one-on-one relationships** comes next, focusing on interpersonal communication.

B. Group interaction: Communication expands to **small group settings**, requiring collaboration and active listening.

A. Public speaking: The next stage involves **addressing larger audiences confidently and effectively.**

D. Feed forward: Finally, advanced communication includes **anticipating and adjusting messages** based on audience reactions and feedback.

Question

Which of the following help in improving communication?

A. Non-consideration of others' views
B. Intelligible encoding
C. Clarifying the purpose of message
D. Identification of receivers' needs
E. Ignoring receivers' emotions

1. ABC
2. BCD
3. CDE
4. ADE

Explanations
Answer: 2. BCD

B (Correct): **Intelligible encoding** ensures clear and understandable communication.
C (Correct): **Clarifying the purpose** makes the message more effective.
D (Correct): **Identifying receivers' needs** helps tailor communication.
A (Incorrect): **Ignoring others' views** hinders effective communication.
E (Incorrect): **Ignoring emotions** reduces message impact and understanding.

Question

Identify the correct statements about effective communication.

A. Non-verbal Communication includes written words.
B. Cultural differences can affect the interpretation of a message.
C. Interpersonal communication involves direct interaction.
D. Effective communication ensures clarity and mutual understanding.

1. AB
2. ABC
3. BCD
4. CD

Explanations
Answer: 3. BCD

A (Incorrect): Non-verbal communication does not include written words; it involves gestures, facial expressions, and body language.

B (Correct): Cultural differences influence how messages are interpreted.

C (Correct): Interpersonal communication involves direct interaction between people.

D (Correct): Effective communication ensures clarity and mutual understanding.

I. Verbal communication

- **Verbal** communication includes oral and written messages.
- **Language** is a symbolic medium for communication.
- The Triangle of **Meaning** explains symbols.
- **Words** shape how messages are interpreted.
- **Phonology** and syntax influence language structure.
- **Semantics** and pragmatics define meaning use.
- Effective **interpretation** depends on language rules.
    - Phonology is sounds that typically appear in a language.
    - Morphology counts as a word.
    - The syntax is word order.
    - Semantics is a conventional meaning of words.
    - Pragmatic meanings are conventional in contexts.

Written Communication:

- **Written** communication involves exchanging messages.
- Typically more **formal** but less efficient.
- Requires clear **articulation** of thoughts.
- Involves multiple **audiences** and listening skills.
- Examples include **emails**, letters, and contracts.
- Used in **advertisements**, brochures, and proposals.
- Ensures **clarity** and documentation of messages.

Verbal Communication:

- **Oral** communication uses spoken words.
- **Verbal** communication conveys messages through sound.
- Includes **face-to-face** talks and presentations.
- Used in **phone calls**, speeches, and interviews.
- Supports **radio**, video chats, and intercoms.
- Helps in **expressing** ideas effectively.

- Essential for **daily** and professional interactions.

Factors of Effective Verbal communication:

- **Active** listening fosters openness and honesty.
- Being a **good** listener improves interactions.
- Shows the **speaker** values ideas and needs.
- **Clarification** prevents misunderstandings in conversations.
- Ask **open-ended** questions for deeper insights.
- **Nonverbal** cues reflect listening and engagement.
- **Clear** and concise speech enhances communication.
- Speaking **confidently** builds trust and respect.
- **Humour** helps engage and connect audiences.
- **Thinking** before speaking prevents awkward pauses.
- **Body language** influences message interpretation.
- **Gestures** and expressions should match speech.
- Consider the **listener's** perspective when speaking.
- **Knowledge** gaps affect understanding and response.
- **Vocal** tone impacts audience engagement levels.

Question

'Mind to mind' communication involves the communication of meanings through:

A. Physical settings
B. Shared beliefs
C. Values
D. Noise manipulation
E. Context

Choose the correct answer from the options given below:

1. ABD
2. BCD
3. ABCE
4. CDE

Explanations
Answer: 3. ABCE

A. Physical settings: The **environment or setting** influences how messages are perceived and interpreted.

B. Shared beliefs: Common beliefs act as a foundation for mutual understanding and interpretation of meanings.

C. Values: Shared values guide the interpretation and response to messages, forming a cultural or moral backdrop for communication.

E. Context: The situational context shapes meaning, intention, and interpretation in communication.

Question

All forms of communication are evaluated in relation to :

1. Face to face communication
2. Radio transmission
3. Television entertainment
4. Internet usage

Explanations
Answer: 1. Face to face communication

Face-to-face communication serves as the **benchmark for evaluating all other forms of communication** because it represents the **most direct, immediate, and interactive mode of human interaction.** It involves not only verbal exchanges but also **non-verbal cues such as facial expressions, body language, and tone of voice.**

Face-to-face communication provides:

Instant feedback from both parties.

Rich context through physical presence and gestures.

Clarity and emotional connection due to direct interaction.

Why not the other options?

Radio transmission: Limited to **audio-only communication**, lacking non-verbal elements.

Television entertainment: Primarily a **one-way communication medium** with limited interaction.

Internet usage: While interactive, it **lacks the immediacy and emotional depth** of face-to-face communication.

Question

Statement I: Verbal communication becomes more powerful if accompanied by non-verbal messages.
Statement II: Non-verbal communication does not reflect personal feelings. emotions and attitudes.

1. Both Statement I and Statement Il are true
2. Both Statement I and Statement Il are false
3. Statement I is true but Statement Il is false
4. Statement I is false but Statement Il is true

Explanations
Answer: 3. Statement I is true but Statement Il is false

Statement I is true: Verbal communication becomes more powerful when supported by non-verbal cues. Facial expressions, gestures, tone of voice, and body language enhance clarity, emphasize key points, and convey emotions that words alone might fail to express.

Statement II is false: Non-verbal communication **does reflect personal feelings, emotions, and attitudes.** For example, a smile can express happiness, crossed arms might indicate defensiveness, and a trembling voice can reveal nervousness.

Question

When people metacommunication, they are sending messages about:

1. senders
2. receivers
3. channels

4. messages

Explanations
Answer: 4. Messages

Metacommunication refers to sending messages about messages. It involves **providing additional information or context about how to interpret the primary message being communicated.**

For example:

Saying, *"I'm just joking!"* after a sarcastic comment helps clarify the intended meaning.

A raised eyebrow while saying *"That's interesting"* adds a layer of meaning to the verbal message.

Why not the other options?

Senders: Metacommunication is not about the sender's identity but about clarifying the message.

Receivers: While receivers interpret metacommunication, the focus is on the message itself.

Channels: Channels refer to the medium (e.g., speech, text), not the meta-layer of meaning in the message.

Question

When a communicated message is based on reference to another, it is called-

1. Meta message
2. Sourced message
3. Referential message
4. Ancillary message

Explanations
Answer: 1. Meta message

A **meta message** is a **message about another message.** It provides **additional context, clarification, or commentary on the primary message** being communicated. Meta messages often help the receiver understand the **intended meaning, tone, or emotional nuance** of the main message.

Example:

Saying, *"Don't take this personally, but..."* is a **meta message** because it sets the stage for how the following message should be interpreted.

Rolling eyes while saying, *"That's a great idea!"* adds a **meta layer** indicating sarcasm.

Why not the other options?

Sourced message: Refers to a message's **origin or source**, not its reference to another message.

Referential message: Refers to a message that **points to external information or context, not another message.**

Ancillary message: Implies a **supporting or secondary message**, not one referring to another.

Question

Communication apprehension is often described as:

1. Social relativity
2. Psycho-social barrier
3. Social anxiety
4. Social ambiguity

Explanations
Answer: 3. Social anxiety

Communication apprehension refers to the **fear or anxiety associated with real or anticipated communication with others.** It is commonly described as a form of **social anxiety**, where individuals feel nervous, self-conscious, or fearful about being judged or negatively evaluated during communication.

Key Characteristics of Communication Apprehension:

- Fear of public speaking or participating in group discussions.
- Nervousness during conversations with strangers or authority figures.
- Physical symptoms like sweating, trembling, or a racing heart.

Why not the other options?

Social relativity: Refers to how people perceive social norms and values, not fear in communication.

Psycho-social barrier: Refers to emotional or mental blocks affecting communication but is not specific to communication apprehension.

Social ambiguity: Refers to **uncertainty in social interactions**, not the fear associated with communication.

II. Non-verbal communication:

- Nonverbal communication (NVC) involves the exchange of messages or signals using nonverbal means such as eye contact, gestures, facial expressions, posture, and body language.
- Nonverbal communication was **first studied in 1872** with the publication of ***The Expression of the Emotions in Man and Animals*** by Charles Darwin.
- Encoding and decoding are conscious and unconscious processes involved in nonverbal communication.
  i. **Encoding** is described as the ability to express emotions in a way that can be accurately interpreted by the receiver(s).
  ii. **Decoding** is called "*nonverbal sensitivity*", the ability to take this encoded emotion and interpret its meanings accurately to what the sender intended.
- Among the factors that influence how learning activities are organized is culture, which plays a vital role in nonverbal communication.
- While the other person or group is absorbing the message, they are focused on the entire environment around them, which means they use all five senses in the interaction:

i. 83% sight,
ii. 11% hearing,
iii. 3% smell,
iv. 2% touch,
v. 1% taste.

Question

The non-verbal communication is studied across which of the following disciplines?

A. Physics
B. Chemistry
C. Linguistics
D. Social psychology
E. Anthropology

1. (A), (B) and (C) only.
2. (B), (C) and (D) only.
3. (C), (D), and (E).
4. (A), (B) and (E) only.

Explanations
Answer: 3. (C), (D), and (E).

Non-verbal communication is studied across disciplines that focus on **human interaction, language, society, and culture**. These include:

(C) Linguistics: Examines how **non-verbal cues (e.g., gestures, facial expressions, tone of voice)** complement or replace verbal language.

(D) Social psychology: Studies **how non-verbal behaviors influence relationships, emotions, and social interactions** among individuals.

(E) Anthropology: Explores **non-verbal communication across cultures, traditions, and societies**, highlighting cultural variations in gestures and body language.

Why not the other options?

(A) Physics: Deals with **natural laws and physical phenomena**, unrelated to human communication.

(B) Chemistry: Focuses on **chemical reactions and matter**, with no connection to non-verbal communication.

Social cues:

- **Social cues** include verbal and nonverbal signals.
- **Expressed** through face, body, and voice.
- **Guide** conversations and social interactions.
- **Convey** contextual and social information.
- **Facilitate** understanding and communication effectiveness.
- A few examples of social cues include:
  - Eye gaze
  - Facial expression
  - Vocal tone
  - Body language

Kinesics:

- **Kinesics** studies body movements and gestures.
- **Includes** facial expressions and nonverbal behavior.
- **Ray Birdwhistell** pioneered kinesics research.
- **Body language** differs from spoken language.
- **Cultural** differences affect movement interpretation.
- **Gestures** and motions convey social meaning.

Question

Which of the following are true of kinesics, a type of non-verbal communication?

A. Kinesics does not convey any meaning.
B. Kinesics does not reflect the social system of an individual.
C. Body movements of an individual have potential meanings.
D. Kinesics can be subject to systematic analysis.
E. A person's body language is part of his social system shared with others.

1. ABC
2. BCD
3. CDE
4. ADE

Explanations
Answer: 3. CDE

The **visual dimension of non-verbal communication** focuses on **what can be seen or observed** about an individual during interaction. It includes:

A. Physique: The **physical appearance and body structure** of a person contribute to first impressions and perceptions.

B. Gender: Visual cues associated with **gender identity and expression** influence communication and interpretation.

C. Skin colour: Skin colour can **affect cultural perceptions and non-verbal interpretations** in communication contexts.

Why not the other options?

D. Soft voice: This relates to **paralinguistic (vocal) aspects of non-verbal communication**, not the visual dimension.

E. Simple language: This pertains to **verbal communication**, not non-verbal or visual cues.

Question

Kinesics. when used, will communicate a person's-

A. Social status
B. Level of involvement
C. Emotional quotient
D. Political mobility
E. Language ambiguity

1. ABC
2. BCD
3. DCE

4. ADE

Explanations
Answer: 1. ABC

Kinesics refers to the **study of body movements, gestures, facial expressions, and posture** in communication. It plays a significant role in conveying non-verbal messages and can reveal the following about a person:

A. Social status: Body language, posture, and gestures often **reflect confidence, authority, or submissiveness**, which can indicate a person's social status.

B. Level of involvement: Active engagement through **eye contact, nodding, and open body posture** can show involvement, while crossed arms or lack of eye contact may indicate disengagement.

C. Emotional quotient: Facial expressions, micro-expressions, and body posture are **strong indicators of emotional intelligence**, showing how someone understands and manages their emotions.

Why not the other options?

D. Political mobility: Kinesics does not directly communicate political mobility, which is more about influence and strategy.

E. Language ambiguity: Ambiguity in language relates to **verbal communication, not body language.**

Facial Expression:

- **Facial expressions** convey emotions nonverbally.
- **Accurate interpretation** requires multiple cues.
- **Includes** eyes, eyebrows, lips, and cheeks.
- **Reveals** mood and state of mind.
    - **Happiness**
    - **Sadness**
    - **Focused**
    - **Unfocused**
    - **Confident**

- **Afraid**

Body Posture:

- **Posture** reflects comfort and professionalism.
- **Sitting** or standing conveys attitude.
- **Body language** reveals emotions subtly.
- **Posture** influences communication perception.
    - Sitting Erect (Confidence)
    - Slouching (Lack of Confidence)
    - Sitting with crossed legs and folded arms (Defensive mode)
    - Feeling angry
    - Feeling fearful
    - Relaxed posture (trust and confidence)
- How a person sits or stands can also be interpreted as an indication of his emotional state.

Gesture:

Gestures are movements made with body parts, for example, hands, arms, fingers, head, and legs which could be voluntary or involuntary.

- There are several ways in which arm gestures can be interpreted.
- The shrug shows that a person does not understand what is being said.
- The Head Nod is used to signify 'Yes'.
- The thumbs-up gesture could be interpreted as "OK" or "good".
- Handshakes for a meeting, greeting, offering congratulations.

Question

"Thums up is a kind of

1. Verbal
2. Non-Verbal
3. Transpersonal
4. Intrapersonal

Explanations

Answer: 2. Non-Verbal

"Thumbs up" is a kind of **Non-Verbal communication.**

Eye Contact:

Strategically using eye content (or lack of eye contact) is a highly effective way to communicate attention and interest.

Oculesics (Blink Rate):

- **A** subcategory of kinesics and body language.
- It is a kind of eye movement, eye behaviour, gaze, and eye-related nonverbal communication.
- Focuses on interpreting eye behaviour as a form of nonverbal communication.
- **Dimension 1: Eye Contact:**
    - Direct assessment
    - Indirect assessment
- **Dimension 2: Eye Movement:**
    - There are two types of eye movements: voluntary and involuntary.
    - It can be accomplished by changing eye direction, focusing, or following objects with the eyes.
- **Dimension 3: Pupil Dilation:**
    - The pupillary response is a change in pupil size, voluntarily or involuntarily.
    - A change in focus occurs when a new object of focus appears or is perceived, even when the indication of such an appearance is real or perceived.
- **Dimension 4: Gaze Direction:** Gazing deals with communicating and feeling intense desire with the eye, voluntarily or involuntarily.

Question

Statement (I): Every communication contains elements of both content and relationships.
Statement (II): Eye behaviour provides metacommunicative cues.

1. Both Statement (I) and Statement (II) are correct.
2. Both Statement (I) and Statement (II) are incorrect.
3. Statement (I) is correct but Statement (II) is incorrect
4. Statement (I) is incorrect but Statement (II) is correct

Explanations

Answer: 1. Both Statement (I) and Statement (II) are correct.
Statement (I) is correct: Every communication contains **two fundamental dimensions: content and relationship.**

Content: Refers to the **actual message or information being conveyed.**

Relationship: Refers to **how the participants relate to each other, including tone, power dynamics, and emotional context.**
Both aspects are present in every communication exchange, whether verbal or non-verbal.

Statement (II) is correct: Eye behavior serves as a metacommunicative cue, providing additional meaning beyond spoken words.

Eye contact, gaze direction, and blinking **can signal attention, honesty, confidence, discomfort, or avoidance.**

These cues are often unspoken yet powerful in regulating interaction and expressing emotions.

Question

Which of the following are part of the visual dimension of non-verbal communication?

A. Physique
B. Gender
C. Skin color
D. Soft voice
E. Simple language

1. ABC
2. BCD
3. CDE
4. ADE

Explanations
Answer: 1. ABC

The **visual dimension of non-verbal communication** focuses on **what can be seen or observed** about an individual during interaction. It includes:

A. Physique: The **physical appearance and body structure** of a person contribute to first impressions and perceptions.

B. Gender: Visual cues associated with **gender identity and expression** influence communication and interpretation.

C. Skin color: Skin color can **affect cultural perceptions and non-verbal interpretations** in communication contexts.

Why not the other options?

D. Soft voice: This relates to **paralinguistic (vocal) aspects of non-verbal communication**, not the visual dimension.

E. Simple language: This pertains to **verbal communication**, not non-verbal or visual cues.

Question

Match the column:

A. Paralanguage	(I) Objects and images with cultural context
B. Proxemics	(II) Hesitation noise
C. Colour	(III) Personal space
D. Artifact	(IV) Different moods

1. A-II B-III C-IV D-I
2. A-III B-IV C-I D-II
3. A-IV B-I C-II D-III
4. A-I B-II C-IV D-III

Explanations
Answer: 1. A-II B-III C-IV D-I

A. Paralanguage → II. Hesitation noise: Paralanguage refers to the **vocal aspects of communication**, such as **tone, pitch, volume, pauses, and hesitation sounds ("uh," "um")**, which add meaning to spoken words.

B. Proxemics → III. Personal space: Proxemics deals with **how people use physical space** during interactions, reflecting comfort, intimacy, or authority.

C. Colour → IV. Different moods: Colors are often associated with **emotions and moods.** For example, red signifies passion or urgency, while blue signifies calmness.

D. Artifact → I. Objects and images with cultural context: Artifacts refer to **physical objects, clothing, accessories, or decorations** that carry cultural or symbolic meaning in communication.

Proxemics (Distance and physical environments/appearance):

- **Edward T. Hall i**ntroduced Proxemics in 1966.
- It studies measurable distances between people as they interact with one another.
- **Intimate Distance: It occurs when** embracing, touching or whispering.
  - Close Phase (less than 6 inches or 15 cm).
  - Far Phase (6 to 18 inches or 15 to 46 cm).
- **Personal Distance:** It occurs when interacting among good friends or family members.
  - Close Phase (1.5 to 2.5 feet or 46 to 76 cm).
  - Far Phase (2.5 to 4 feet or 76 to 122 cm).
- **Social Distance:** It occurs when interacting among acquaintances.
  - Close Phase (4 to 7 feet or 1.2 to 2.1 m).
  - Far Phase (7 to 12 feet or 2.1 to 3.7 m).
- **Public Distance:** It occurs during public speaking.
  - Close Phase (12 to 25 feet or 3.7 to 7.6 m).
  - Far Phase (25 feet or 7.6 m or more).

Question

Which of the following belong to the field of proxemics in communication?

A. Facial expressions
B. Crowding
C. Territoriality
D. Personal space
E. Eye contact

1. (A), (B) and (C) Only
2. (B), (C) and (D) Only
3. (C), (D) and (E) Only
4. (A), (D) and (E) Only

Explanations
Answer: 2. (B), (C) and (D) Only

Proxemics is the study of **how people use space and distance in communication** to convey meaning, establish boundaries, and express comfort or discomfort. The following fall under proxemics:

(B) Crowding: Refers to the **perception of space and how people react to limited personal space** in crowded situations.

(C) Territoriality: Involves **claiming and defending personal or group space** to establish ownership or boundaries.

(D) Personal space: Refers to the **physical space individuals maintain around themselves** during interaction, which varies based on relationships, culture, and context.

Why not the other options?

(A) Facial expressions: These are part of **kinesics**, not proxemics, as they deal with facial gestures and emotional expression.

(E) Eye contact: This is part of **oculesics**, a subfield of non-verbal communication focused specifically on eye behavior.

Paralanguage (Of Voice):

- Includes voice quality, rate, pitch, loudness, and speaking style.
- It also has prosodic features such as rhythm, intonation, and stress.
- **Paralanguage**, also known as **vocalics.**
- Regarded as relating to nonphonemic properties only.
- Expressed consciously or unconsciously.

Question

Statement (I): Paralinguistic features express emotions and communicate personality traits.
Statement (II): The subtle use of vocal inflections can provide special significance to verbal messages.

1. Both Statement I and Statement Il are correct
2. Both Statement I and Statement Il are incorrect
3. Statement I is correct but Statement Il is incorrect
4. Statement I is incorrect but Statement Il is correct

Explanations
Answer: 1. Both Statement I and Statement Il are correct

Statement I is correct: Paralinguistic features refer to the **non-verbal elements of speech** such as tone, pitch, volume, rate of speech, and pauses. These features **express emotions, attitudes, and personality traits**, helping listeners interpret the speaker's emotional state and personality.

Statement II is correct: Subtle **vocal inflections**—changes in pitch, tone, or emphasis—can add **special significance to verbal messages.** For example, stressing a particular word can change the entire meaning of a sentence or convey sarcasm, urgency, or reassurance.

Why not the other options?

Both statements align with the principles of **paralinguistics**, which emphasize the role of vocal elements in communication beyond words.

Question

Which of the following are examples of paralanguage?

A. Tone of voice
B. Volume
C. Personal space
D. Eye contact
E. Pitch

1. ABE

2. ACD
3. ABD
4. BCE

Explanations
Answer: 1. ABE

Paralanguage refers to the **non-verbal elements of speech** that modify meaning, including:

- **A (Correct) - Tone of voice**: Expresses emotions and intent.
- **B (Correct) - Volume**: Loudness or softness of speech.
- **E (Correct) - Pitch**: Highness or lowness of voice.

C & D (Incorrect): **Personal space and eye contact** relate to **non-verbal communication**, not paralanguage.

Haptics (Touch):

- **Haptics** refers to communication through touch.
- **Derived** from the Greek word *haptikos*.
- **Essential** for both communication and survival.
- **Includes** handshakes, high fives, and pats.
- **Haptics** conveys emotions and social connections.
- Heslin outlines five haptic categories:
    i. **Functional/professional:** It expresses task orientation.
    ii. **Social/polite:** It expresses ritual interaction.
    iii. **Friendship/warmth:** It expresses the idiosyncratic relationship.
    iv. **Love/intimacy:** It expresses emotional attachment.
    v. **Sexual/arousal:** It expresses sexual intent.

Chronemics (the use of time):

- **Chronemics** studies time in communication.
- **Time usage** sends nonverbal messages.
- **Giving time** shows value and importance.
- **Time management** reflects social status.
- **Chronology** conveys power and priorities.

Question

Mirroring another person's non-verbal behaviour facilitates

1. Resistance
2. Restriction
3. Regression
4. Compliance

Explanations
Answer: 4. Compliance

Mirroring another person's non-verbal behavior involves subtly imitating their **gestures, body language, facial expressions, or tone of voice.** This technique creates a sense of **rapport, trust, and connection** between individuals, making the other person feel understood and comfortable.

When people see their non-verbal cues mirrored, they **subconsciously feel a sense of alignment and familiarity**, increasing their willingness to cooperate or comply with suggestions or requests.

Why not the other options?

Resistance: Mirroring reduces resistance by creating a sense of harmony.

Restriction: Mirroring promotes openness, not limitations or restrictions.

Regression: It does not cause emotional or behavioral backward movement.

Question

Statement (I): Non-verbal emotional expression precedes verbal communication in human life.
Statement (II): Socialisation inculcates display norms for appropriate emotional communication.

1. Both Statement I and Statement II are correct
2. Both Statement I and Statement II are incorrect
3. Statement I is correct but Statement II is incorrect
4. Statement I is incorrect but Statement II is correct

Explanations
Answer: 1. Both Statement I and Statement Il are correct

Statement I is correct: Non-verbal emotional expression precedes verbal communication in human development. Infants, for example, rely on facial expressions, crying, gestures, and body language to express emotions long before they acquire verbal language skills.

Statement II is correct: Socialization teaches individuals the norms and rules for expressing emotions appropriately. Through cultural and social interactions, people learn when, where, and how to display emotions in acceptable ways (e.g., not laughing during a serious situation).

Question

Which of the following are identified as non-verbal practices of communication?

A. Mimicking Speeches
B. Accent
C. Posture
D. Gait
E. Dress

1. A, B and C only
2. B, C and D only
3. C, D and E only
4. A, D and E only

Explanations
Answer: 3. C, D and E only

Non-verbal communication refers to the **use of body language, physical appearance, and other non-linguistic cues** to convey messages. The following are identified as non-verbal practices:

C. Posture: The way a person **stands, sits, or positions their body** communicates confidence, openness, or defensiveness.

D. Gait: A person's **style of walking** can convey confidence, nervousness, or urgency.

E. Dress: Clothing and appearance **communicate social status, professionalism, personality, and cultural identity.**

Why not the other options?

A. Mimicking Speeches: Mimicking involves **verbal imitation,** which is not purely non-verbal.

B. Accent: An accent is **related to speech patterns, tone, and pronunciation,** making it verbal rather than non-verbal.

III. Inter-Cultural Communication:

- **Intercultural communication** studies cross-cultural interactions.
- **Examines** how culture shapes communication.
- **Analyzes** behavior, perception, and language.
- **Addresses** communication issues in diverse settings.
- **Involves** religious, social, and ethnic differences.
- **Encourages** cultural awareness and respect.
- **Promotes** understanding between different cultures.
- **Develops** sensitivity to cultural variations.
- **Enhances** empathy in cross-cultural interactions.
- **Bridges** communication gaps across societies.

Factors in Effective Inter-Cultural Communication

- **Display of interest** shows respect and regard.
- **Orientation to knowledge** shapes self-expression.
- **Empathy** acknowledges others' perspectives.
- **Relational role behavior** fosters harmony.
- **Tolerance for ambiguity** eases new situations.
- **Interaction posture** avoids judgmental responses.
- **Sensitivity** enhances nonverbal awareness.
- **Self-reflection** prevents cultural misunderstandings.
- **Open-mindedness** respects diverse communication styles.
- **Mutual understanding** strengthens cultural appreciation.

IV. Group Communication:

- **Group communication** shares messages with multiple members.
- **Businesses** use it for ideas and motivation.
- **Occurs** when three or more collaborate.
- **Small groups** analyze and solve problems.
- **Includes** primary and secondary groups.
- **Exchanges** information, feelings, and feedback.
- **Online** tools like email and forums help.
- **Four types**: Verbal, Non-Verbal, In-Person, Virtual.

V. Classroom Communication:

Communication within the classroom is essential for students to learn effectively and should be implemented from an early stage of learning. Three fundamental elements must be noted before effective communication can occur in the classroom. The elements are:

i. **The communicator (teacher)**
ii. **The message (the impacted knowledge),**
iii. **The receiver (the pupils)**.

There are three types of classroom communication: verbal, nonverbal, and written.

Verbal Classroom Communication:

- **Verbal communication** uses sounds and language.
- **Teachers** convey messages orally to students.
- **Can address** individuals or the entire class.
- **Enhances** understanding through spoken words.
- **Example**: Asking students to sit or stand.

Non-Verbal Classroom Communication:

- **Nonverbal communication** conveys messages without words.
- **Includes** body language, gestures, and expressions.
- **Tone** and pitch influence message delivery.
- **Posture** reflects emotions and engagement.
- **Example**: Nodding shows agreement or encouragement.

Written Classroom Communication:

- **Written communication** shares information through text.
- **Involves** notes, assignments, and documents.
- **Used** for detailed explanations and instructions.
- **Enhances** clarity and record-keeping.
- **Example**: Lecture slides and written tests.

Question

Employment of classroom technology needs clarity regarding:

A. Instructional messages
B. Course objectives
C. Technological competencies
D. Experience of failures
E. Institutional indolence

Choose the correct answer from the options given below:

1. ABC
2. BCD
3. CDE
4. ADE

Explanations
Answer: 1. ABC

For **effective employment of classroom technology**, clarity is essential in the following areas:

A. Instructional messages: Clear communication of **what is being taught and how technology supports it** ensures students understand instructional goals.

B. Course objectives: Technology must **align with the overall learning goals and outcomes** of the course to remain purposeful.

C. Technological competencies: Both **teachers and students need the necessary skills and knowledge** to operate and utilize the technology effectively.

Why not the other options?

D. Experience of failures: While learning from failures is valuable, it is not a prerequisite for employing technology effectively.

E. Institutional indolence: This term refers to laziness or inaction within institutions and is unrelated to clarity in employing technology.

Question

Statement I: Through feedback, students can later critique their own communication competence outside the classroom.
Statement II: Motivational orientation towards communication should be identified by teachers to better the communication competence of the students.

1. Both Statement (I) and Statement (II) are correct.
2. Both Statement (I) and Statement (II) are incorrect.
3. Statement (I) is correct but Statement (II) is incorrect
4. Statement (I) is incorrect but Statement (II) is correct

Explanations
Answer: 1. Both Statement (I) and Statement (II) are correct.

Statement I is correct: Feedback serves as a **critical tool for self-improvement in communication skills**. When students receive constructive feedback, they can later **reflect on their communication strengths and weaknesses** and make necessary improvements in real-world scenarios.

Statement II is correct: Teachers play a crucial role in identifying **students' motivational orientation towards communication**. Understanding what drives or hinders a student's willingness to communicate helps **tailor teaching strategies** to enhance their communication competence effectively.

Barriers to Effective Classroom Communication:

Noise: Noise can interrupt the entire teaching-learning process in the classroom.

Lack of listening: A lack of effective listening can also hinder the learning process. Various students perceive the student differently and interpret it differently, which results in inappropriate information being conveyed to them.

Language: In the teaching-learning process, it isn't easy if the teacher and student speak different languages.

Medical or psychological issues: Ineffective communication may be influenced by medical or psychological problems. If the child is not mentally healthy due to medical or psychological reasons, it creates a barrier or disturbance in the teaching-learning process.

Emotional states: Depression, mood swings, anxiety, low self-esteem, effects of a traumatic event, etc., can also create a barrier to communication.

Effective Communication in the Classroom:

Safe environment: Ensure that a safe and supportive learning environment is created. Supportive relationships between students and teachers have been shown to positively affect student engagement, participation, and achievement in class.

Teamwork and Group Discussion: Teamwork and group discussions contribute to making the classroom a more comfortable environment. Working in small groups allows students to share their ideas more efficiently and improve their communication skills.

Body language: Communication is verbal and non-verbal: A teacher should ensure that the signals he gives out through his body language are positive, confident, and engaging.

Feedback: Teachers often neglect to mention when students have performed well, focusing instead on the negative aspects, such as bad behaviour. This can have significant effects and can demoralize students.

- **Positive feedback** (i.e. praise) builds students' confidence.
- **Negative feedback** can help students to improve.

Use of Multimedia: Using multimedia in the classroom helps the teacher engage the students and helps the student be more involved and retain more information from the lesson.

Technical Skills: Another way to keep students engaged and reinforce their understanding is to use up-to-date teaching aids such as computers, videos, and online resources.

Sense of humour: Laughter in the classroom has increased learning, self-motivation, and positive relationships between students and teachers. It allows a teacher to establish a rapport with his class and keep his students interested in the lesson.

Know Your Students: Understanding students will help to provide them with quality learning opportunities.

Be Clear: A teacher should always be unambiguous and adapt his words to his audience.

Precise: Giving clear instructions to students can ensure that they fully comprehend what they need to do to achieve in the classroom. In short, KISS (Keep it simple and short).

Take Artful Pause: The pause procedure is a technique in which the teacher uses strategic pauses to provide students with time during which they can review their notes, discuss among their pairs or undertake any similar activity that allows them to clarify, assimilate and retain the material.

Empathy: Demonstrating empathy in the classroom allows teachers to recognize the feelings of their students and themselves without lowering expectations.

Create Curiosity: Encouraging students to embrace their curiosity is essential to education. Curiosity is key to learning. Studies show that when we're curious about a subject, we are much more likely to remember the information we learned about that subject.

Equity: Equity in the classroom requires systems to ensure that every child has an equal chance for success.

Encourage Participation: A good question can pique their interest, make them wonder why, get them to think, and motivate them to connect with the content. Involving students in the classroom is an effective method of encouraging them and teaching them responsibility. Making participation fun by giving each student a job to do.

Motivate Students: Students look to teachers for approval and positive reinforcement and are more likely to be enthusiastic about learning if they feel their work is recognized and valued.

Respect: Respect in the classroom boosts teacher effectiveness and encourages active and appropriate participation in classroom activities. Positive, supportive, and respectful relationships between teachers and students increase students' odds of long-term academic and social success.

Bad behaviour should not be tolerated: Answering back, becoming confrontational, physically threatening a teacher or a pupil, or fighting in class is all examples. High-level disruptive behaviour cannot be ignored and must be dealt with immediately.

Effective Lesson Plan: A lesson plan describes a lesson's course of instruction or "learning trajectory". A teacher develops a daily lesson plan to guide class learning.

Classroom Management: It is the process by which teachers and schools create and maintain appropriate behaviour of students in classroom settings.

Question

A teacher to be an effective communicater should resort to-

A. Acquisition of elitist background
B. Natural flow of information
C. Voluntary support to learning
D. A system of immediate and regular feedback
E. Convoluted presentations

1. ABC
2. BCD

3. CDE
4. ADE

Explanations
Answer: 2. BCD

For a **teacher to be an effective communicator**, the focus should be on clarity, support, and feedback to ensure meaningful interaction and engagement in the classroom:

B. Natural flow of information: Communication should be **smooth, clear, and well-structured**, allowing ideas to be conveyed without confusion.

C. Voluntary support to learning: Teachers should **encourage students to participate willingly and create a supportive learning environment.**

D. A system of immediate and regular feedback: Providing **timely feedback ensures students understand their progress, correct mistakes, and improve effectively.**

Why not the other options?

A. Acquisition of elitist background: An elitist background does not guarantee effective communication and may create unnecessary barriers.

E. Convoluted presentations: Complex and unclear presentations **hinder understanding and engagement.**

Question

Match the column:

A. Effective verbal communication	(I) Knowledge and skills
B. Effective communication	(Il) Insufficient knowledge
C. Effective non-verbal communication	(III) Effective speaking
D. Barrier of communication	(IV) Body language

1. A-I B-Il C-IV D-III
2. A-Il B-III C-I D-IV
3. A-Il B-I C-III D-IV
4. A-III B-I C-IV D-II

Explanations
Answer: 4. A-III B-I C-IV D-II

A. Effective verbal communication → III. Effective speaking: Verbal communication focuses on **clear articulation, tone, and choice of words** to ensure messages are understood.

B. Effective communication → I. Knowledge and skills: Effective communication requires a **combination of knowledge and communication skills** to deliver messages accurately and appropriately.

C. Effective non-verbal communication → IV. Body language: Non-verbal communication involves **facial expressions, gestures, eye contact, and posture** to support or clarify verbal messages.

D. Barrier of communication → II. Insufficient knowledge: A lack of adequate knowledge can act as a **significant barrier, causing misunderstandings and poor communication outcomes.**

Question

Assertion A: Two fundamental features of classroom communication are classroom instruction and classroom management.
Reason R: The classroom communication of teachers rests on the principle of edutainment.

1. Both A and R are correct and R is the correct explanation of A
2. Both A and R are correct but R is NOT the correct explanation of A
3. A is correct but R is not correct
4. A is not correct but R is correct

Explanations
Answer: 2. Both A and R are correct but R is NOT the correct explanation of A

Assertion (A) is correct: Classroom communication involves two primary features—classroom instruction and classroom management. Instruction focuses on delivering knowledge effectively, while management ensures discipline, order, and an environment conducive to learning.

Reason (R) is correct: The **principle of edutainment (education + entertainment)** suggests that teaching should be engaging and enjoyable to enhance learning outcomes.

R is NOT the correct explanation of A: While **edutainment contributes to effective classroom communication**, it does not directly explain why **instruction and management are considered the fundamental features of classroom communication.**

Question

The sequence of elements in a classroom speech is:

A. Introduction
B. Description
C. Feedback
D. Clarification
E. Conclusion

1. (A), (B), (C), (D), (E)
2. (B), (A), (C), (E), (D)
3. (C), (D), (A), (B), (E)
4. (A), (B), (E), (C), (D)

Explanations
Answer: 4. (A), (B), (E), (C), (D)
(A) Introduction: The speech begins with an **attention-grabbing introduction** to set the context and outline objectives.

(B) Description: This is followed by a **detailed explanation of the topic**, providing necessary facts, examples, and elaboration.

(E) Conclusion: The key points are **summarized, and final thoughts are shared** to reinforce learning.

(C) Feedback: The teacher gathers **student responses, clarifying doubts or addressing concerns.**

(D) Clarification: Final **clarifications are made based on feedback** to ensure students have a clear understanding of the content.

Question

Structured classroom communication can be categorized as-

1. Inter-personal communication
2. Vertical communication
3. Group communication
4. Cross-purpose communication

Explanations
Answer: 3. Group communication

Structured classroom communication falls under **group communication** because: It involves **one teacher communicating with a group of students** in a classroom setting. There is **interaction, discussion, and shared learning objectives** among the group. Group communication in classrooms is **structured and goal-oriented**, focusing on delivering knowledge and facilitating dialogue.

Question

Effective classroom communication will enable

A. Efficient teaching
B. Interest in learning
C. Minimal assessment
D. Interaction between teachers and students
E. Teacher-centric behaviour

1. A, B and C only
2. B, C, D and E only
3. C, D and E only
4. A, B and D only

Explanations
Answer: 4. A, B and D only

Effective classroom communication focuses on creating an engaging, interactive, and supportive learning environment. It enables:

A. Efficient teaching: Clear communication helps **teachers deliver lessons effectively, ensuring students understand the content.**

B. Interest in learning: Engaging communication **encourages curiosity and enthusiasm among students.**

D. Interaction between teachers and students: Open communication fosters **dialogue, active participation, and better understanding.**

Why not the other options?

C. Minimal assessment: Effective communication encourages **continuous and meaningful assessment**, not minimal.

E. Teacher-centric behavior: Effective communication promotes **student engagement and collaboration**, not a teacher-dominated approach.

Question

Assertion (A): Communication competence is related to the power of knowledge in a classroom.
Reasons (R): Communication competence permits choices of communicating as required in the classroom context.

1. Both (A) and (R) are true and (R) s the correct explanation of (A)
2. Both (A) and (R) are true and (R) is NOT the correct explanation of (A)
3. (A) is true but (R) is not false
4. (A) is false but (R) is true

Explanations
Answer: 1. Both (A) and (R) are true and (R) s the correct explanation of (A)

Assertion (A) is true: Communication competence is closely tied to knowledge power in a classroom. A teacher's ability to convey knowledge effectively and meaningfully depends on their communication skills.

Reason (R) is true: Communication competence allows flexibility in choosing the appropriate communication style, tone, and method depending on the classroom context, audience, and purpose.

R explains A: The **ability to adapt communication styles and strategies enhances the effectiveness of knowledge sharing**, ensuring that students receive, understand, and engage with the content better.

Question

What are the relevant strategies of effective communication in a classroom?

A. Understanding the cultural background of students
B. Clarity in speech
C. Focused listening on both sides - teacher and students
D. Inventing cultural labels
E. Disdain for collective efforts

1. ABC
2. BCD
3. CDE
4. DEA

Explanations
Answer: 1. ABC

Effective **classroom communication** relies on strategies that **ensure clarity, inclusivity, and engagement**. These include:

A. Understanding the cultural background of students: Being aware of students' cultural contexts helps **tailor communication to be inclusive and respectful.**

B. Clarity in speech: Clear articulation and **well-structured speech enhance understanding** and minimize confusion.

C. Focused listening on both sides: Active listening by both teachers and students ensures mutual understanding and effective feedback.

Why not the other options?

D. Inventing cultural labels: This can lead to **misunderstandings, stereotypes, and unnecessary barriers** in communication.

E. Disdain for collective efforts: Collective participation is **crucial for fostering collaboration and engagement** in classroom communication.

Question

A class conducted on Google Meet in which students and teachers are engaged in discussion in an instance of:

1. Intrapersonal communication
2. Group communication
3. Mass communication
4. Downward communication

Explanations
Answer: 2. Group communication

A **class conducted on Google Meet** where students and teachers are actively engaged in **discussion** qualifies as **group communication** because:

Group Setting: The interaction occurs in a **small to medium-sized group**, where a teacher communicates with multiple students.

Interactive Exchange: Students and teachers can **share ideas, ask questions, and provide feedback** in real-time.

Collaborative Environment: The communication is **focused on shared goals**, such as learning, discussion, and problem-solving.

Question

Assertion A: In classroom communication, teachers should acknowledge and take into account students' views.
Reason R: In a classroom, the probability of message reception can be enhanced by establishing a viewpoint.

1. Both A and R are true and R is the correct explanation of A
2. Both A and R are true but R is NOT the correct explanation of A
3. A is true but R is false
4. A is false but R is true

Explanations

Answer: 1. Both A and R are true and R is the correct explanation of A

Assertion (A) is true: In **classroom communication**, it is essential for teachers to **acknowledge and value students' views.** This builds trust, encourages participation, and creates an inclusive learning environment.

Reason (R) is true: The **probability of effective message reception increases** when a common viewpoint or shared perspective is established. This ensures that students feel heard, understood, and more engaged with the communication process.

R explains A: Acknowledging students' views helps **establish a shared perspective**, making the communication more relatable and improving message reception.

Question

Assertion A: The classroom communication is a transactional process.
Reason R: Quality of questions asked determines the quality of learning.

1. Both A and R are true and R is the correct explanation of A
2. Both A and R are true but R is NOT the correct explanation of A
3. A is true but R is false
4. A is false but R is true

Explanations
Answer: 2. Both A and R are true but R is NOT the correct explanation of A

Assertion (A) is true: Classroom communication is a transactional process because it involves a two-way interaction between teachers and students. Both parties actively send, receive, and interpret messages, making communication dynamic and collaborative.

Reason (R) is true: The quality of questions asked significantly impacts the quality of learning, as thoughtful and well-structured questions stimulate critical thinking, engagement, and deeper understanding among students.

R is not the correct explanation of A: While both statements are true, the reason does not directly explain why classroom communication is transactional. Transactional communication emphasizes the continuous exchange of feedback and interaction, whereas the quality of questions focuses on content delivery and student engagement.

Question

Which of the following make classroom communication interesting?

A. Many asides while speaking
B. Fruitful discussions
C. Use of relevant transitions
D. Finding out the correct context
E. Pressurising the students with authoritarian commands.

1. ABC
2. BCD
3. CDE
4. ADE

Explanations
Answer: 2. BCD

To make **classroom communication engaging and effective**, the following elements are essential:

B. Fruitful discussions: Interactive and meaningful discussions **encourage student participation and critical thinking**, making lessons engaging.

C. Use of relevant transitions: Smooth transitions between topics **maintain clarity and flow**, keeping students focused and interested.

D. Finding out the correct context: Understanding and addressing the **relevant context ensures the message is relatable** and meaningful to students.

Why not the other options?

A. Many asides while speaking: Frequent asides can **distract from the main topic** and reduce clarity.

E. Pressurising the students with authoritarian commands: This approach creates a **tense environment** and hinders open communication and engagement.

Question

Effective classroom communication is intended to make learners acquire new:

A. Knowledge
B. Behaviours
C. Soft skills
D. Ways of aggressive attitude
E. Hyper-reaction

1. ABC
2. BCD
3. CDE
4. ADE

Explanations
Answer: 1. ABC

Effective **classroom communication** aims to **enhance learning outcomes** by focusing on the following areas:

A. Knowledge: Communication helps **impart new information, concepts, and ideas** effectively.

B. Behaviours: It encourages learners to **develop positive habits, attitudes, and actions.**

C. Soft skills: Effective classroom communication fosters **skills like teamwork, leadership, and critical thinking.**

Why not the other options?

D. Ways of aggressive attitude: Aggression is counterproductive in a learning environment.

E. Hyper-reaction: Overreacting disrupts the learning process and creates unnecessary tension.

Question

The dimensions of classroom communication are :

A. Level of obscurity
B. Level of Observation
C. Level of intrusion
D. Intentionality
E. Normative judgement

1. (A), (B), (C) only
2. (B), (C), (D) only
3. (C), (D), (E) only
4. (B), (D), (E) only

Explanations
Answer: 4. (B), (D), (E) only

The **dimensions of classroom communication** focus on how communication is observed, intentional, and judged within the classroom environment. These include:

(B) Level of Observation: Refers to **how communication behaviors, interactions, and patterns are observed and interpreted** within the classroom setting.

(D) Intentionality: Highlights whether communication is **deliberate and purposeful**, aiming to achieve specific educational objectives.

(E) Normative Judgment: Involves evaluating communication based on **established norms, values, and expectations** in the classroom context.

CHAPTER IV

Barriers to Effective Communication

Barriers to Effective Communication

Communication is an integral part of our daily lives. Communication occurs through conversation, expressions and body language, social media outlets, telephone calls, email, etc. Communicating allows us to deepen our friendships, repair marriages, order dinner, do shopping, express our opinions, ask for help, negotiate deals, accept job offers, etc. Communicating effectively can be hindered by barriers that distort the message or intention. This may fail in the communication process or cause an undesirable effect. There are many types of bias, including filtering, language, silence, communication apprehension, selective perception, information overload, emotions, gender differences, and political correctness.

The problem may also include the absence of "knowledge-appropriate" communication, which occurs when the message is conveyed using ambiguous or complex legal terms, medical jargon, or descriptions of situations or environments that the recipient does not understand.

I. Physical Barriers:

It often occurs due to the nature of the environment. For instance, it exists when workers are located in different buildings or on different sites—likewise, defective or outdated technical equipment. Another factor that frequently causes communication difficulties in an organization is a staff shortage.

Noise

- **Disrupts Information Flow** – Affects clear conversation.
- **Includes Sound & Technical Malfunctions** – Causes miscommunication.
- **Affects Technology Performance** – Leads to buffering issues.

Message Distortion

- **Receiver Misinterprets Message** – Alters intended meaning.
- **Leads to Incorrect Conclusions** – Misunderstanding occurs.
- **Varies Based on Perception** – Interpretation differs.

Architecture

- **Work Layout Affects Communication** – Distance impacts interaction.
- **Closed Offices Limit Collaboration** – Reduces engagement.
- **Lack of Meeting Spaces** – Restricts discussions.

Technical Difficulties

- **Equipment Malfunctions** – Interrupts communication flow.
- **Outdated Technology Fails** – Reduces efficiency.
- **Software & Hardware Glitches** – Cause work delays.

Time & Distance

- **Time Zone Differences** – Cause scheduling issues.
- **Physical Distance Restricts Interaction** – Limits engagement.
- **Hinders Face-to-Face Communication** – Affects personal connection.

Information Overload

- **Excessive Data Causes Confusion** – Delays response.
- **Leads to Mistakes** – Reduces clarity.
- **Overwhelms the Receiver** – Slows processing.

Environment

- **Weather Disrupts Communication** – Affects clarity.
- **Extreme Conditions Reduce Safety** – Hinders operations.
- **Noise from Surroundings Interferes** – Causes distractions.

Question

Match the column:

A. Physical	I. Different understanding
B. psychological	II. Stereotypes
C. Language	III. pre-disposed notions
D. Cultural	IV. Inaudible voice

1. A-IV B-III C-I D-II
2. A-III B-II C-IV D-1
3. A-II B-I C-III D-IV
4. A-I B-II C-III D-IV

Explanations
Answer: 1. A-IV B-III C-I D-II

Each **communication barrier type** corresponds to a specific characteristic:

A. Physical → IV. Inaudible voice: Physical barriers include **external, environmental factors** like noise, inaudible voice, or poor lighting that hinder communication.

B. Psychological → III. Pre-disposed notions: Psychological barriers stem from **biases, mental blocks, or pre-conceived ideas** affecting how messages are received or interpreted.

C. Language → I. Different understanding: Language barriers arise when **words, jargon, or accents are misunderstood**, leading to different interpretations.

D. Cultural → II. Stereotypes: Cultural barriers occur due to **stereotypes, biases, or cultural misinterpretations** between people from different cultural backgrounds.

Question

Information overload in a classroom environment by a teacher will lead to-

1. High level participation

2. Semantic precision
3. Effective impression
4. Delayed feedback

Explanations
Answer: 4. Delayed feedback

Information overload happens when a teacher provides **excessive information in a short time**, overwhelming students' capacity to process it.

This leads to **confusion, delayed understanding, and a slower response time**, resulting in **delayed feedback** from students.

II. Semantic Barriers:

The semantic barrier refers to the misunderstanding between the sender and receiver caused by the different meanings of words and other symbols. There are two types of semantic obstacles:

Denotative Barriers

- **Words Have Direct Meanings** – Can cause misunderstandings.
- **Meaning Varies by Generation** – Example: "Comment" on social media.
- **Different Interpretations Affect Communication** – Leads to confusion.

Connotative Barriers

- **Words Carry Implied Meanings** – Beyond dictionary definitions.
- **Different Contexts Change Meaning** – "Current" can mean time or water.
- **Misinterpretation Creates Confusion** – Affects message clarity.

Homophones

- **Same Pronunciation, Different Meanings** – Creates misunderstanding.
- **Different Spellings Cause Confusion** – Example: "Buy, by, bye."

- **Requires Context for Clarity** – Helps avoid mistakes.

Homonyms

- **Same Spelling & Pronunciation** – Different meanings exist.
- **Example: "Bear" (animal) vs. "Bear" (carry)** – Same form, distinct meanings.
- **Context Determines Meaning** – Essential for understanding.

Homographs

- **Same Spelling, Different Pronunciations** – Confuses readers.
- **Example: "Lead" (metal) vs. "Lead" (guide)** – Different sounds.
- **Context Affects Interpretation** – Ensures correct usage.

Differences in Dialects

- **Regional Variations Affect Understanding** – Words have different meanings.
- **Mother Tongue Influences Pronunciation** – Impacts speech clarity.
- **Semantic Differences Cause Barriers** – Alters intended message.

Bypassing

- **Different Symbolic Meanings Used** – Leads to miscommunication.
- **Example: "Restroom" vs. "Toilet"** – Varies by region.
- **Clarification is Needed** – Avoids ambiguity.

Individual Linguistic Ability

- **Jargon Can Confuse Listeners** – Hard to understand.
- **Difficult Words Reduce Clarity** – Prevents effective communication.
- **Poor Explanation Leads to Misinterpretation** – Message becomes unclear.

Question

Which one of the following is a communication barrier?

1. Communicatee attention
2. Semantic distortion
3. Amplified image
4. Infographic

Explanations
Answer: 2. Semantic distortion

Semantic distortion occurs when there is a **misinterpretation or misunderstanding of the meaning of words, symbols, or language** used in communication. It often arises from **ambiguous phrasing, cultural differences, or jargon.**

Why not the other options?

Communicatee attention: This refers to the **focus or engagement of the receiver**, which facilitates communication, not a barrier.

Amplified image: Refers to **enhanced visual clarity** and does not disrupt communication.

Infographic: A **visual communication tool** designed to simplify and clarify complex information.

Question

Which of the following is a semantic barrier?

1. Blurred image on television
2. Unclear printing in newspapers
3. Static broadeasting
4. Redundancy in writing

Explanations
Answer: 4. Redundancy in writing

A **semantic barrier** arises from issues related to the **meaning and interpretation of words, symbols, or language.**

Redundancy in writing occurs when **unnecessary repetition of words or phrases** makes the message **unclear or confusing**, leading to misinterpretation.

Why not the other options?

Blurred image on television: This is a **physical barrier** caused by technical faults.

Unclear printing in newspapers: This is also a **physical barrier**, affecting message visibility.

Static broadcasting: A **technical/physical barrier** disrupting audio or visual clarity.

Semantic barriers arise from language-related issues, and redundancy in writing directly impacts message clarity.

Question

Semantic noise in classroom communication can be limited by avoiding the use of

1. Dialogues
2. Cliched jargon
3. Non-verbal cues
4. Multi-media

Explanations
Answer: 2. Cliched jargon

Semantic noise refers to **misunderstandings caused by language, symbols, or unclear phrasing** in communication.

Clichéd jargon includes **overused, technical, or context-specific terms** that can confuse students and **hinder understanding**.

Avoiding jargon ensures **clear and simple communication**, minimizing semantic barriers.

Why not the other options?

Dialogues: Dialogues encourage **interaction and engagement** rather than creating barriers.

Non-verbal cues: These **enhance message clarity** through gestures, facial expressions, and tone.

Multi-media: Well-planned multimedia tools can **improve clarity and engagement** in teaching.

Question

In a classroom, delayed feedback can happen due to

1. Use of technology
2. Expanded communication
3. Semantic noise
4. Participatory environment

Explanations
Answer: 3. Semantic noise

Semantic noise arises from **misinterpretations, ambiguous language, jargon, or unclear phrasing** in communication.

In a classroom, if the **teacher's message is not clear or easily understood**, students may struggle to process it, leading to **delayed feedback.**

Why not the other options?

Use of technology: Technology often **enhances feedback mechanisms** rather than delaying them.

Expanded communication: Broader communication channels may **increase participation** but do not inherently delay feedback.

Participatory environment: An active and participatory environment **encourages quicker feedback**, not delays.

Question

Semantic barrier of communication is implied when the

1. signal is lost before reaching the receiver
2. message transmitted by the source is unclear
3. receiver's attention is diverted
4. receiver does not understand the meaning of the message

Explanations
Answer: 4. receiver does not understand the meaning of the message

A **semantic barrier** occurs when the **receiver cannot understand the intended meaning** of the message due to **language issues, jargon, symbols, or unclear phrasing**.

It focuses on the **interpretation of the message** rather than its transmission or reception.

Why not the other options?

Signal is lost before reaching the receiver: This is a **physical barrier**, not semantic.

Message transmitted by the source is unclear: This points to **encoding errors** but not specifically a semantic barrier.

Receiver's attention is diverted: This is a **psychological barrier** caused by distractions, not semantics.

III. Organizational Barriers:

Organizational barriers are those that prevent communication within an organization. Generally, this type of barrier refers to hindrances in the flow of information within an organization that could result in the organization's commercial failure.

System Design

- **Unclear Organizational Structure** – Causes communication confusion.
- **Lack of Supervision & Training** – Reduces role clarity.
- **Inefficient Information Systems** – Leads to uncertainty.

Negative Organizational Climate

- **Top Management Discourages Communication** – Limits transparency.
- **Reduces Employee Initiative** – Lowers engagement.
- **Creates a Toxic Work Environment** – Hinders openness.

Absence of Communication Policy

- **No Clear Guidelines for Communication** – Causes hesitation.
- **Employees Fail to Share Information** – Reduces collaboration.
- **Leads to Organizational Misunderstandings** – Creates inefficiency.

Excessive Authority Layers

- **Information Passes Through Many Levels** – Causes delays.
- **Data Gets Distorted or Lost** – Affects clarity.
- **Slows Down Decision-Making** – Reduces efficiency.

Filtering

- **Willful Distortion of Messages** – Alters original intent.
- **Common in Upward Communication** – Selective reporting occurs.
- **Employees Hide Negative Information** – Creates bias.

Attitudinal Barriers

- **Lack of Motivation Affects Communication** – Reduces engagement.
- **Personality Conflicts Create Resistance** – Hinders teamwork.
- **Poor Management Discourages Expression** – Suppresses employee voices.

VI. Psychological Barriers:

Psychological barriers are due to human beings' emotional character and mental limitations. These barriers can manifest in absent-mindedness, the fear of expressing one's ideas to others, excitement and emotional instability. These are all accounting for an overwhelming number of communication problems.

Fear of Being Criticized

- **Reduces Confidence in Speaking** – Causes hesitation.
- **Leads to Self-Doubt** – Lowers communication skills.
- **Practice Improves Confidence** – Reduces anxiety.

False Assumptions

- **Sender Assumes Receiver Understands** – Causes misinterpretation.
- **Partial Understanding Leads to Confusion** – Results in errors.
- **Clarification Prevents Miscommunication** – Ensures message accuracy.

Lack of Attention

- **Distractions Affect Message Processing** – Reduces focus.
- **Hinders Understanding & Response** – Causes confusion.
- **Active Listening Enhances Communication** – Improves clarity.

Poor Retention

- **Memory Fades Over Time** – Loses information.
- **Half of the Message is Forgotten** – Retention declines.
- **Reinforcement Improves Recall** – Enhances understanding.

Distrust & Defensiveness

- **Lack of Trust Blocks Communication** – Causes resistance.
- **Messages Are Misinterpreted Negatively** – Increases misunderstandings.
- **Trust Builds Effective Communication** – Encourages openness.

Perception

- **Judgments Are Based on Experiences** – Shapes understanding.
- **Different People See Reality Differently** – Alters meaning.
- **Perception Affects Message Interpretation** – Leads to bias.

Viewpoints

- **Different Perspectives Affect Meaning** – Causes misinterpretation.
- **Unexplained Viewpoints Create Barriers** – Message is unclear.
- **Clarification Ensures Proper Understanding** – Prevents confusion.

Attitudes & Opinions

- **Personal Beliefs Influence Understanding** – Shapes interpretation.
- **Preconceived Notions Block Communication** – Creates bias.
- **Open-Mindedness Reduces Barriers** – Encourages clarity.

Emotions

- **Negative Emotions Block Reasoning** – Distorts messages.
- **Anger & Fear Cause Miscommunication** – Creates misunderstanding.
- **Calm Communication Ensures Clarity** – Improves effectiveness

Question

How can psychological barrier affect classroom communication?

1. They facilitate mutual understanding
2. They create bias in the interpretation of the meaning of the message
3. They make messages clearer
4. They eliminate misunderstanding

Explanations

Answer: 2. They create bias in the interpretation of the meaning of the message

Psychological barriers in classroom communication arise from **emotions, attitudes, prejudices, or stress**, leading to **misinterpretation of messages**. These barriers create **biases**, affecting how students **perceive, process, and respond** to information.

Question

Match the column:

List I (Types of communication Barriers)	List II (Meaning)
A. Semantic Barrier	(I) Misunderstanding in words or phrases
B. Physical Barrier	(II) Noise or distance
C. Psychological Barrier	(III) Emotion or attitudes
D. Cultural Barrier	(IV) Differences in social norms

1. A-II B-I C-III D-IV
2. A-I B-II C-III D-IV
3. A-I B-II C-IV D-III
4. A-III B-II C-I D-IV

Explanations
Answer: 2. A-I B-II C-III D-IV

A. Semantic Barrier → I: Misunderstanding due to **words or phrases**.
B. Physical Barrier → II: **Noise or distance** affecting communication.
C. Psychological Barrier → III: Barriers caused by **emotions or attitudes**.
D. Cultural Barrier → IV: Differences in **social norms and values**

Question

How can psychological barriers affect classroom communication?

1. They facilitate mutual understanding
2. They create bias in the interpretation of the meaning of the message
3. They make messages clearer
4. They eliminate misunderstanding

Explanations
Answer: 2. They create bias in the interpretation of the meaning of the message

Question

Statement I: Personality conflicts in a classroom situation are a barrier to effective interaction
Statement II: Impersonal communication is invariably considered the best solution in a classroom environment

1. Both Statement I and Statement Il are true
2. Both Statement I and Statement Il are false
3. Statement I is correct but Statement Il is false
4. Statement I is incorrect but Statement Il is true

Explanations
Answer: 3. Statement I is correct but Statement Il is false

Statement I: Correct

Personality conflicts in a classroom (e.g., ego clashes, differing attitudes, or biases) **disrupt effective communication and interaction** between teachers and students or among peers.

Statement II: False

Impersonal communication (e.g., avoiding direct engagement or using standardized messages) **is not an ideal classroom solution** as it lacks personal connection, engagement, and empathy, which are essential for effective learning.

Question

Which of the following can be considered psychological barriers to effective communication?

A. Descriptive message
B. Inattentiveness
C. Too much reliance on the written word
D. Limited retention
E. Logical organization
F. Flow of thought

1. ABC

2. BCD
3. CDE
4. DEF

Explanations
Answer: 2. BCD

Psychological barriers arise from mental or emotional states that **hinder effective communication** and understanding.

B. Inattentiveness: A lack of focus or distraction **prevents proper message reception and understanding.**

C. Too much reliance on the written word: Over-dependence on written communication can **limit clarity and emotional engagement.**

D. Limited retention: The inability to **remember key details** affects how messages are processed and acted upon.

Why not the other options?

A. Descriptive message: A well-structured descriptive message **enhances clarity** and is not a barrier.

E. Logical organization: Proper organization of ideas **improves communication effectiveness.**

F. Flow of thought: A smooth flow of thought **enhances message delivery and understanding.**

V. Physiological Barriers:

Physiological barriers to communication are related to the limitations of the human body and mind **(memory, attention, and perception)**. Physiological barriers may result from personal discomfort caused by ill-health, poor eyesight, or hearing difficulties.

Question

Which of the following is an example of a physical barrier to communication?

1. Cultural disparity
2. Inattention
3. Verbalism
4. Ill health

Explanations
Answer: 4. Ill health

A **physical barrier** in communication refers to **tangible obstacles or conditions** that prevent effective message transmission or reception.

Ill health: Physical ailments like **fatigue, hearing loss, or illness** can impair a person's ability to **send, receive, or interpret messages effectively.**

Why not the other options?

Cultural disparity: This is a **cross-cultural barrier**, not physical.

Inattention: This is a **psychological barrier**, related to focus and mindset.

Verbalism: This refers to **overuse of words without clarity**, a **semantic barrier**.

VI. Social Barriers:

The social psychological phenomenon of conformity is one of the most prominent barriers to communication. Conformity occurs when those of a larger group influence an individual's norms, values, and behaviours. Communication may be hindered by social factors such as age, gender, socioeconomic status, and marital status.

Gender Barriers

- **Different Communication Styles Exist** – Varies by gender.
- **Women Focus on Conflict Resolution** – Prefer discussions.
- **Men Often Avoid Conflict** – May withdraw.

Poverty

- **Limits Social Participation** – Restricts engagement.
- **Creates Economic Communication Gaps** – Divides social groups.
- **Hinders Equal Access to Information** – Limits opportunities.

Conflict

- **Differences in Beliefs Create Barriers** – Causes division.
- **Opposing Views Prevent Understanding** – Increases tension.
- **Cultural Clashes Affect Communication** – Reduces cooperation.

Racism

- **Favors Certain Social Groups** – Causes inequality.
- **Prejudices Limit Open Communication** – Creates bias.
- **Discrimination Reduces Participation** – Affects engagement.

VII. Cultural Barriers:

Our culture shapes the way we think and behave. Our established communication patterns shape communication patterns. The cultural Barrier to communication often arises when individuals in one social group have developed different norms, values, or behaviours from individuals associated with another group. The cultural difference leads to a difference in interest, knowledge, value, and tradition. Therefore, people of different cultures will experience these cultural factors as a barrier to communicating with each other.

Language (Semantic)

- **Different Languages Create Barriers** – Limits understanding.
- **Dialects Affect Interpretation** – Meaning varies regionally.
- **Cross-Cultural Communication Is Challenging** – Requires adaptation.

Cultural Norms and Values

- **Each Culture Has Unique Norms** – Influences behavior.

- **Beliefs Shape Communication Styles** – Varies by society.
- **Different Truth Perceptions Exist** – Alters message meaning.

Stereotypes

- **Preconceived Notions Affect Perception** – Leads to bias.
- **Media Reinforces Stereotypes** – Shapes public opinion.
- **Transgender Identity Is Perceived Differently** – Varies by culture.

Values and Beliefs

- **Cultural Values Differ Globally** – Affects acceptance.
- **Religion Shapes Communication Practices** – Alters viewpoints.
- **Political Beliefs Create Barriers** – Influence interpretations.

Stereotypical Assumptions

- **Unintended Offense Can Occur** – Misunderstandings arise.
- **Assumptions Limit Open Communication** – Reinforces bias.
- **Cultural Sensitivity Is Essential** – Avoids miscommunication.

Question

In communication, cross-cultural barrier refers to:

1. Physical entities
2. Sincerity of speaker
3. Perceptions of people
4. General human values

Explanations
Answer: 3. Perceptions of people

Cross-cultural barriers arise from differences in **perceptions, interpretations, and understanding** shaped by cultural backgrounds. People from different cultures may **interpret gestures, words, or symbols differently**, leading to misunderstandings.

Perceptions of people: Cultural perceptions influence **how messages are sent, received, and interpreted.**

Question

Which one of the following is excluded from the list of communication barriers?

1. Physical
2. Semantic
3. Philosophical
4. Psychological

Explanations

Answer: 3. Philosophical

Communication barriers are factors that **hinder effective message transmission** between sender and receiver. The main barriers are:

- **Physical:** Environmental factors (e.g., noise, poor lighting).
- **Semantic:** Misinterpretation due to **language or symbol misunderstandings**.
- **Psychological:** Emotional states, biases, or mental distractions.

Question

Which of the following are barriers to acceptance of the communicated message:

A. Body language with positive vibes
B. Attitude of the listener
C. Values of the decoder
D. Status clash
E. Knowledge stimuli

1. ABC
2. BCD
3. CDE
4. ADE

Explanations

Answer: 2. BCD

Barriers to acceptance of a communicated message occur when **psychological, attitudinal, or social factors hinder understanding or agreement** with the message:

B. Attitude of the listener: A **negative or closed attitude** can prevent the listener from accepting the message.

C. Values of the decoder: If the message conflicts with the **listener's core values**, acceptance becomes difficult.

D. Status clash: Differences in **social or professional status** can create resistance or bias in accepting the message.

Why not the other options?

A. Body language with positive vibes: Positive body language **enhances communication**, not a barrier.

E. Knowledge stimuli: Knowledge **stimulates understanding** rather than acting as a barrier.

Question

Match the column:

A. Semantic	I. Exists outside of the receiver
B. Physical	II. communicator's prejudices and biases towards another person
C. Psychological	III. The biological influence on the communication process
D. Physiological	IV. Linguistic influence on message reception

1. A-II, B-III, C-IV, D-I
2. A-III, B-IV, C-I, D-II
3. A-IV, B-I, C-II, D-III
4. A-I, B-II, C-III, D-IV

Explanations
Answer: 3. A-IV, B-I, C-II, D-III

A. Semantic → IV. Linguistic influence on message reception:

Semantic barriers arise from **language-related issues**, such as the **use of jargon, ambiguous words, or misinterpretations.**

Example: A technical term not understood by the audience.

B. Physical → I. Exists outside of the receiver:

Physical barriers refer to **external environmental factors** that disrupt communication.

Example: Noise, poor lighting, or technical disruptions.

C. Psychological → II. Communicator's prejudices and biases towards another person:

Psychological barriers stem from **mental or emotional states, biases, or assumptions** that influence how messages are sent or received.

Example: A manager's bias affecting how they interpret an employee's suggestion.

D. Physiological → III. The biological influence on the communication process:

Physiological barriers are caused by **physical conditions or limitations** of the communicator or receiver.

Example: Hearing impairment, speech disorders, or illness affecting clarity.

Question

Which of the following are barriers to understand the communicated messages?

A. Emotional quotient
B. Jargon
C. Personal space
D. Pre-judgement
E. Cultural background

1. A, B and C only

2. B, D and E only
3. C, D and E only
4. B, C and D only

Explanations
Answer: 2. B, D and E only

Barriers to **understanding communicated messages** arise when factors **distort, misinterpret, or block clarity** during communication.

B. Jargon: Specialized or technical language can **confuse listeners unfamiliar with the terminology.**

D. Pre-judgement: Forming opinions **before fully understanding the message** hinders clarity.

E. Cultural background: Differences in **cultural norms, values, and interpretations** can lead to misunderstandings.

Why not the other options?

A. Emotional quotient: A **high emotional quotient (EQ)** enhances understanding and empathy, not a barrier.

C. Personal space: This is a **proxemic factor**, more about **physical interaction**, not directly affecting message understanding.

Question

Match the column:

A. Psychological barriers	I. use of technical language
B. Organisational	II. poor retention
C. Personal	III. functional specialization
D. Semantic	IV. fear of challenge to authority

1. A-I B-II C-III D-IV
2. A-II B-III C-IV D-I
3. A-III B-IV C-I D-II
4. A-IV B-I C-II D-III

Explanations
Answer: 2. A-Il B-III C-IV D-I

A. Psychological barriers → II. Poor retention: Psychological barriers include **stress, emotional instability, or poor memory**, leading to **difficulty retaining information.**

B. Organisational → III. Functional specialization: In organizational barriers, **functional silos or rigid structures** can restrict communication across departments.

C. Personal → IV. Fear of challenge to authority: Personal barriers stem from **individual insecurities or fear of authority figures**, limiting open communication.

D. Semantic → I. Use of technical language: Semantic barriers arise from **jargon, technical terms, or ambiguous language**, causing misunderstandings.

Question

Which one of the following is a strategy to overcome communication barriers?

1. Setting of ground rules
2. Aggression
3. Advance technology provision
4. Use of jargon

Explanations
Answer: 1. Setting of ground rules

Setting ground rules helps create **clarity, structure, and mutual understanding** in communication. It ensures everyone follows **agreed-upon norms and expectations**, reducing misunderstandings and barriers.

Why not the other options?

Aggression: Aggressive behavior creates **conflict and hinders open communication** rather than resolving barriers.

Advance technology provision: While useful, technology alone **cannot overcome all barriers**, especially emotional or semantic ones.

Use of jargon: Jargon **creates confusion** and acts as a **semantic barrier**, especially for unfamiliar audiences

Question

Which of the following are useful in overcoming the communication barriers in a classroom?

a. Identifying the level of redundancy
b. Use of unfamiliar words
c. Ignoring the students' vocabulary
d. Fragmented sentences
e. Voice inflexion
f. Contextualizing the speech

1. abc
2. bcd
3. cdf
4. aef

Explanations
Answer: 4. Aef

Overcoming **communication barriers in a classroom** requires clarity, adaptability, and alignment with the students' understanding level:

A. Identifying the level of redundancy: Reducing unnecessary repetition helps keep the **message clear and focused.**

E. Voice inflexion: Variation in tone and pitch maintains attention and emphasizes important points.

F. Contextualizing the speech: Adapting the message to fit the **students' background, examples, and context** improves understanding.

Why not the other options?

B. Use of unfamiliar words: Using complex or unfamiliar words **creates confusion** and acts as a **semantic barrier.**

C. Ignoring the students' vocabulary: Overlooking students' vocabulary **leads to miscommunication** and reduces engagement.

D. Fragmented sentences: Disjointed or incomplete sentences **obscure the message's clarity** and cause confusion.

Question

Match the column:

A. Semantic	I. Lack of physica clarity in channel
B. Psychological	II. Faulty message
C. Personal	III. Poor retention
D. Physical	IV. Lack of time

1. A-I B-II C-III D-IV
2. A-II B-III C-IV D-I
3. A-III B-IV C-I D-II
4. A-IV B-I C-II D-III

Explanations
Answer: 2. A-III B-IV C-I D-II

A. Semantic → II. Faulty message: Semantic barriers arise from **language-related issues, jargon, or unclear phrasing**, resulting in **faulty or misunderstood messages.**

B. Psychological → III. Poor retention: Psychological barriers, such as **stress, bias, or emotional disturbances**, affect a person's ability to **retain information effectively.**

C. Personal → IV. Lack of time: Personal barriers, like **time constraints or busy schedules**, prevent effective communication.

D. Physical → I. Lack of physical clarity in channel: Physical barriers include environmental factors like **noise, poor lighting, or weak audio clarity.**

Question

Removal of communication barriers in a classroom will result in

A. Clear enunciation of specific instructional behaviours
B. Climate of purposeful student interaction.
C. Promotion of personality cult.
D. The irrelevance of illustrative examples.

1. AB
2. BC
3. CD
4. AD

Explanations
Answer: 1. AB

The **removal of communication barriers** in a classroom ensures **clarity, engagement, and effective learning outcomes**:

A. Clear enunciation of specific instructional behaviours: When barriers are removed, **teachers can deliver instructions more clearly and precisely**, improving student understanding.

B. A climate of purposeful student interaction: Open communication **encourages meaningful discussions and active participation**, fostering a productive learning environment.

Why not the other options?

C. Promotion of personality cult: Effective communication **focuses on collective learning, not glorifying individual personalities.**

D. The irrelevance of illustrative examples: Illustrative examples **remain highly relevant** for better comprehension, even in barrier-free communication.

Question

Which of the following will help overcome communication barriers?

1. Focused listening
2. Neglecting semantic noise
3. Top-down command structure
4. Use of clichéd idioms

Explanations

Answer: 1. Focused listening

Focused listening involves **actively paying attention to the speaker's message**, understanding their intent, and minimizing distractions.

It ensures **clarity, reduces misunderstandings, and promotes effective two-way communication.**

Why not the other options?

Neglecting semantic noise: Ignoring semantic noise **worsens misunderstandings** caused by ambiguous language or jargon.

Top-down command structure: This style of communication **limits interaction and feedback**, often causing barriers.

Use of clichéd idioms: Overused idioms can **confuse listeners**, especially in diverse or non-native language contexts.

Question

Which of the following are barriers to effective communication?

a. Physical noise
b. Semantic noise
c. Psychological noise
d. Non-semantic noise

1. abd
2. abc
3. acd
4. ad

Explanations

Answer: 2. abc

Barriers to effective communication disrupt the **clarity, accuracy, and efficiency** of message delivery and understanding.

A. Physical noise: External disturbances (e.g., loud sounds, poor lighting) **hinder message transmission.**

B. Semantic noise: Misinterpretation caused by **jargon, ambiguous words, or unclear phrasing.**

C. Psychological noise: Emotional states (e.g., stress, anxiety, or bias) **affect message reception and interpretation.**

Why not the other option?

D. Non-semantic noise: This term is **not recognized in standard communication theory** and does not describe a valid communication barrier.

Question

Some of the barriers to effective communication are

a. Polysemy
b. Simple language
c. Use of Cliche's
d. Easy construction of sentences

1. ab
2. bc
3. cd
4. ac

Explanations
Answer: 4. Ac

Barriers to **effective communication** arise when the **message is unclear, ambiguous, or overly complex.**

A. Polysemy: Words with **multiple meanings** can create confusion if the context is unclear.

C. Use of clichés: Overused phrases or expressions **lose their impact and may confuse listeners**, especially in formal settings.

Why not the other options?

B. Simple language: Simple language **improves clarity** and reduces barriers.

D. Easy construction of sentences: Well-constructed sentences **enhance understanding**, not hinder it.

CHAPTER V

Mass Media and Society

Mass Media and Society

Introduction

Mass media can communicate instantly between a significant portion of a nation or the world. Mass media is considered any means by which a large number of people receive information. Mass media refers to a wide range of media technologies used in mass communication to reach a large audience. Technology includes a variety of outlets through which this communication occurs. A mass media outlet disseminates information to a large audience using media technologies. A critical function of mass media is to communicate various messages to the general public through television, movies, advertising, radio, the internet, magazines, and newspapers.

- **Inform** – Delivers news and updates.
- **Educate** – Provides knowledge through media.
- **Persuade** – Influences opinions and behaviors.
- **Entertain** – Offers films, music, shows.
- Media drives change.
- **Mobility** – Portable access to media.
- **Globalization** – Worldwide content availability.
- **Simulation** – Virtual content dominance.
- **Not Immobile** – Media is highly mobile.
- **Non-linear Content** – On-demand accessibility.
- **First Printing Press (1556)** – Introduced in Goa.
- **Spread Christian Literature** – Portuguese influence.

Question

Statement I: Persuasive communication does not blur the difference between truth and falsehood.
Statement II: Mass mediated communication never reflects truth.

1. Both Statement I and Statement Il are true
2. Both Statement I and Statement Il are false
3. Statement I is true but Statement ll is false
4. Statement I is false but Statement Il is true

Explanations
Answer: 2. Both Statement I and Statement Il are false

Statement I is false because persuasive communication often involves manipulating perceptions, and at times, it may blur the truth to persuade the audience.

Statement II is false because mass-mediated communication can reflect truth, but it can also distort it depending on the source and the context.

Question

When media create pictures in the head, they act as-

1. Corporate agendas-setters
2. Political representatives
3. Tools of dissonance
4. Agents of consonance

Explanations
Answer: 4. Agents of consonance

Explanation: When media create pictures in the head, they act as agents of consonance by aligning the audience's thoughts and perceptions in harmony with the media's portrayal, reinforcing the existing social and cultural norms or beliefs.

Question

Which of the following are the major criticisms of mass media as a cultural industry?

A. Mass media are pro-people.
B. Products of the culture industry are standardised.
C. The productions are devoid of aesthetic merit.
D. The culture industry does uniform mass production.

E. Avoids massification of culture.

1. A, B, C only
2. B, C, D only
3. C, D, E only
4. A, D, E only

Explanations
Answer: 2. B, C, D only

The **major criticisms of mass media as a cultural industry** focus on its role in standardizing and commodifying culture:

B. Products of the culture industry are standardized: Mass media tends to produce **uniform content** that lacks diversity and originality.

C. The productions are devoid of aesthetic merit: Cultural industry prioritizes **profit over artistic quality**, leading to **content with low aesthetic value.**

D. The culture industry does uniform mass production: It relies on **mass production techniques**, creating content for consumption on a large scale with minimal variation.

Why not the other options?

A. Mass media are pro-people: This is **not a criticism** but rather a positive aspect of media.

E. Avoids massification of culture: Mass media often **promotes massification**, not avoids it, homogenizing cultural experiences.

Question

The main functions of mass media are to:

A. Make a society static
B. Inform
C. Educate
D. Persuade
E. Entertain

1. A, B, C only
2. A, C, E only
3. B, C, D, E only
4. A, B, D only

Explanations
Answer: 3. B, C, D, E only

The **main functions of mass media** are:

B. Inform: Mass media provides **news and updates**, helping audiences stay informed.

C. Educate: Media educates through **documentaries, discussions, and informative content.**

D. Persuade: Media influences opinions through **advertising, campaigns, and propaganda.**

E. Entertain: Entertainment is a core function, offering **films, music, and shows** for leisure.

Why not the other options?

A. Make a society static: Media aims to **engage and transform society**, not make it static.

Question

Statement I: There is an argument that the emergence of cable and television audiences has brought in more personalized and interactive media culture.

Statement Il: Within an integrated communication system, messages do not acquire communicability and socialisation.

1. Both Statement I and Statement Il are true
2. Both Statement I and Statement Il are false
3. Statement I is true but Statement l is false
4. Statement I is false but Statement lI is true

Explanations

Answer: 3. Statement I is true but Statement l is false

Statement I is true: The emergence of cable and television audiences, particularly with interactive platforms and personalized content delivery (like streaming services), has fostered a **more personalized and interactive media culture**.

Statement II is false: Within an **integrated communication system**, messages gain **communicability** (the ability to be shared and understood) and **socialization** (promoting shared norms and connections). This system enhances, rather than diminishes, these elements.

Question

Statement I: The media of mass communication are in a continuous state of flux with many other elements of human experience.
Statement II: Such a state makes their operations and effects rich as well as elusive.

1. Both Statement I and Statement Il are true.
2. Both Statement I and Statement ll are false.
3. Statement I is true but Statement Il is false.
4. Statement I is false but Statement Il is true.

Explanations

Answer: 1. Both Statement I and Statement Il are true.

Statement I is true: Mass communication media are constantly changing due to technological, social, and cultural shifts. This state of flux ensures that media adapts to and reflects various aspects of human experience.

Statement II is true: The continuous evolution of media makes their operations rich with possibilities for engagement but also elusive, as the effects and implications can be complex and multifaceted.

Question

Statement I: Language and other symbolic means of mass communication are social products.

Statement II: Communication media always make their audiences feel comfortable.

1. Both Statement I and Statement Il are true
2. Both Statement I and Statement Il are false
3. Statement I is true but Statement Il is false
4. Statement I is false but Statement Il is true

Explanations
Answer: 3. Statement I is true but Statement Il is false

Statement I is true: Language and other symbolic means of mass communication are inherently social products, shaped and evolved within societal contexts and interactions.

Statement II is false: Communication media do not always make audiences feel comfortable; they often challenge, provoke, or disturb to inform, persuade, or engage.

Question

Media interactivity is experienced at different levels in different _ relations.

1. Political
2. Economic
3. Techno-social
4. Techno-ethical

Explanations
Answer: 3. Techno-social

Techno-social: Media interactivity varies based on how technology integrates with social behaviors and communication. It reflects the interplay of technological tools and social interactions.

Why not others?

Political: Focuses on governance and power structures, not primarily interactivity.

Economic: Relates to financial aspects, not interaction levels.

Techno-ethical: Involves moral considerations, not user interaction.

Mass Communication:

Communication through mass media is the process of imparting and exchanging information between large groups. It is generally understood as a term that refers to various media forms, as its technologies are used to disseminate information, including journalism and advertising. Information can be transmitted quickly through mass communication to large numbers of people who are typically far away from the sources of information. Various media are used in mass communication, including radio, television, social networking, billboards, newspapers, magazines, books, film, and the Internet.

- **Anthropology** – Analyzes culture's impact on communication.
- **Sociology** – Studies media influence on society.
- **Psychology** – Examines behavior and message reception.
- **Professional Communication** – Experts craft and deliver messages.
- **Use of Medium** – Uses TV, radio, internet.
- **Rapid Message Transmission** – Spreads information quickly.
- Audience is diverse.
- Feedback is delayed.
- Communication is regular.
- Heavily relies on the media.
- **Technological Medium** – Uses TV, radio, internet.
- **Large Audience** – Reaches diverse populations.
- **Professional Communicators** – Trained experts deliver messages.
- **Organizational Structure** – Media networks coordinate communication.
- **Continuous** – Provides constant information flow.
- **Scheduled** – Follows planned programming.
- **Media-Dependent** – Relies on technology.

Question

Which of the following social sciences have contributed much to the knowledge of mass communication?

A. Anthropology

B. Sociology
C. Psychology
D. Social medicine
E. Defence studies

1. A, D, E only
2. C, D, E only
3. B, C, D only
4. A, B, C only

Explanations
Answer: 4. A, B, C only

The fields of **Anthropology, Sociology, and Psychology** have significantly contributed to our understanding of **mass communication**:

Question

Mass Communication as a discipline has drawn ideas from-

1. Physics
2. Chemistry
3. Philosophy
4. Material Science

Explanations
Answer: 3. Philosophy

Philosophy has significantly influenced the **discipline of mass communication**, particularly in areas like **ethics, logic, critical thinking**, and understanding the **role of media in shaping human thought and society.**

Question

Which of the following are the characteristics of mass communication?

A. Homogeneous audience
B. Professional communication as a source
C. Immediate feedback
D. Use of medium

E. Rapid transmission of messages

Choose the most appropriate answer from the options given below :

1. ABC
2. BCD
3. CDE
4. BDE

Explanations
Answer: 4. BDE

The **characteristics of mass communication** include:

B. Professional communication as a source: Messages are crafted and delivered by **trained professionals** (e.g., journalists, broadcasters).

D. Use of medium: Mass communication utilizes **technological platforms** (e.g., TV, radio, internet) to reach audiences.

E. Rapid transmission of messages: It enables the **quick dissemination of information** across large geographical areas.

Why not the other options?

A. Homogeneous audience: Mass communication targets a **heterogeneous audience**, often diverse in nature.

C. Immediate feedback: Feedback in mass communication is **usually delayed** (e.g., through comments or audience surveys).

Question

Which of the following are features of mass communication?

A. Structured institutional system
B. Complex process of reproduction
C. Commodification of messages
D. Personalized way of communication
E. Space- time constraint

1. A, B, C only
2. B, C, D only
3. C, D, E only
4. B, D, E only

Explanations
Answer: 1. A, B, C only

The **features of mass communication** include:

A. Structured institutional system: Mass communication operates through **formal and organized structures**, such as media houses and broadcasting corporations.

B. Complex process of reproduction: It involves a **sophisticated process** to produce and distribute content across mediums.

C. Commodification of messages: Messages are often treated as **products for commercial purposes**, tailored to attract audiences and generate revenue.

Why not the other options?

D. Personalized way of communication: Mass communication is **not personalized**; it addresses a broad, generalized audience.

E. Space-time constraint: Mass communication **overcomes space and time barriers** using technology, allowing global reach.

Question

Which of the following are features of mass communication?

A. Face - to - face
B. Private
C. Public
D. Rapid
E. From a professional source

1. A, B, C only
2. B, C, D only

3. C, D, E only
4. A, B, E only

Explanations
Answer: 3. C, D, E only

The **features of mass communication** include:

C. Public: Mass communication is meant for a **broad public audience**, not private interactions.

D. Rapid: It ensures **quick dissemination of information** using technology.

E. From a professional source: Messages are crafted by **trained professionals** like journalists and broadcasters.

Why not the other options?

A. Face-to-face: Mass communication is **impersonal** and does not involve direct interaction like face-to-face communication.

B. Private: Mass communication targets a **public audience**, making it inherently non-private.

Question

Which of the following are true with regard to mass communication?

A. Messages are prepared by non-professionals
B. Messages are prepared by professionals
C. Messages are rapidly disseminated
D. Messages are supposed to be understood
E. Media audiences are homogenous

1. ABC
2. CDE
3. BCD
4. ADE

Explanations
Answer: 3. BCD

The following statements are true regarding **mass communication**:

B. Messages are prepared by professionals: Professional communicators, like journalists, broadcasters, or content creators, craft the messages.

C. Messages are rapidly disseminated: Mass communication ensures **quick transmission** of information using technology.

D. Messages are supposed to be understood: Messages are designed for **clarity and comprehensibility** to cater to a broad audience.

Why not the other options?

A. Messages are prepared by non-professionals: This is incorrect because mass communication relies on **trained professionals**.

E. Media audiences are homogenous: Audiences are **heterogeneous**, consisting of diverse individuals with varying backgrounds and interests.

Question

In which context, can the true effects of mass media communication on mass audiences be understood?

1. Economic
2. Social
3. Political
4. Spiritual

Explanations
Answer: 2. Social

Social context is crucial to understanding the **true effects of mass media communication** because it directly influences people's behaviors, attitudes, and cultural norms. Mass media shapes **public opinion, societal values, and interpersonal interactions**.

Why not the other options?

Economic: While media impacts economies (e.g., advertising, commerce), its **true effects are best observed in societal changes.**

Political: Media influences politics, but its **broader impact is visible in social structures.**

Spiritual: Spiritual contexts are limited and do not encompass the **full societal effects of mass communication.**

Question

Modern mass communication has the characteristics of being-

A. Sporadic
B. Continuous
C. Based on a schedule
D. Not much dependent on technology
E. Dependent on the use of media

1. ABC
2. BCE
3. CDE
4. ADE

Explanations
Answer: 2. BCE

Modern **mass communication** is characterized by:

B. Continuous: It provides a constant stream of information through various channels.

C. Based on a schedule: Programs and news broadcasts are planned and follow specific schedules.

E. Dependent on the use of media: Modern mass communication heavily relies on **media technologies** like TV, radio, and the internet.

Why not the other options?

A. Sporadic: Modern mass communication is **not sporadic**; it is regular and systematic.

D. Not much dependent on technology: Mass communication is **highly dependent on technology** to reach large audiences effectively.

Question

Which of the following are essential elements of mass communication?

A. Electronic observation
B. Technological medium
C. Large audience
D. Professional communicators
E. Organizational structure

1. ABE
2. ACD
3. ACDE
4. BCDE

Explanations
Answer: 4. BCDE

The **essential elements of mass communication** are:

B. Technological medium: Mass communication relies on technology (e.g., TV, radio, internet) for message delivery.

C. Large audience: Targets a **broad and often diverse audience**.

D. Professional communicators: Requires trained individuals (e.g., journalists, broadcasters) to craft and deliver messages.

E. Organizational structure: Involves a systematic framework, such as media companies or news networks, for effective communication.

Why not the other options?

A. Electronic observation: While observation plays a role, **it is not an essential element** in mass communication.

Question

Statement I: There is an argument that the emergence of television audiences has brought in more personalised and interactive communication and media culture
Statement II: Within an integrated communication system. messages do not acquire the elements of communicability and socialisation.

1. Both Statement I and Statement II are true.
2. Both Statement I and Statement II are false.
3. Statement I is true but Statement II is false.
4. Statement I is false but Statement II is true.

Explanations
Answer: 3. Statement I is true but Statement II is false.

Statement I is true: The emergence of television has indeed facilitated **personalized and interactive communication**, especially with advancements like smart TVs, on-demand content, and streaming services, fostering a more dynamic media culture.

Statement II is false: Within an integrated communication system, messages do acquire **communicability** (the ability to be understood and shared) and **socialization** (connecting individuals and promoting shared understanding). Integration enhances these elements rather than negates them.

Question

What are the characteristics of post-modern mass media?

A. immobility
B. mobility
C. Globalization
D. simulation
E. linearity

1. ABC
2. BCD
3. CDE
4. ACE

Explanations
Answer: 2. BCD

B. Mobility: Post-modern mass media thrives on mobile technologies, allowing access anywhere and anytime.

C. Globalization: Media connects audiences globally, erasing traditional geographic barriers.

D. Simulation: Simulated realities (e.g., virtual worlds, AI-generated content) are prominent features of post-modern media.

Why not other options?

A. Immobility: Contradicts mobility, as post-modern media emphasizes flexibility and portability.

E. Linearity: Modern media is non-linear, offering on-demand and interactive content.

Question

Statement (I): Media audiences are increasingly active in their communication with each other.
Statement (II): Media audiences are also active in communication with creators of mass communication contents.

1. Both Statement I and Statement Il are correct
2. Both Statement I and Statement Il are incorrect
3. Statement I is correct but Statement Il is incorrect
4. Statement I is incorrect but Statement Il is correct

Explanations
Answer: 1. Both Statement I and Statement Il are correct

Statement (I): Correct because media audiences interact with each other, particularly in digital and social media platforms.

Statement (II): Correct as audiences increasingly provide feedback and interact with creators through comments, reviews, and social media.

The History of Mass Media:

Communication has evolved from prehistoric forms of art and writing to modern methods such as the internet. The concept of mass communication began when humans were able to transmit messages to multiple recipients from a single source. **Downtime** refers to the period during which a communication network or system is **inoperative or unavailable**, often due to maintenance, technical issues, or failures. **Time fit:** This is unrelated to network operations; it implies scheduling. **Uptime:** Refers to the period when a system is **fully operational**. **Loadtime:** Refers to the time taken to load a program or webpage, not network inoperability. A number of theories regarding mass communication have evolved over the years, such as the hypodermic needle model (also known as the magic bullet theory) and more recent approaches, such as the computer-mediated communication theory. There were eight mass media industries in the late 20th century: books, the internet, magazines, movies, newspapers, radio, recordings, and television. In order of introduction, they are:

- **Print** includes books, pamphlets, periodicals, newspapers, magazines, and posters from the late 15th century.
- **Recordings** include gramophone records, magnetic tapes, cassettes, cartridges, CDs and DVDs from the late 19th century.
- **Cinema** from about 1900.
- **Radio** from about 1910.
- **Television** from about 1950.
- **Internet** from about 1990.
- **Mobile phones** from about 2000.

Question

Arrange the following events related to mass media in the correct chronological sequence.

A. Publication of early newspapers.
B. Development of Television Broadcasting.
C. Introduction of email.
D. Launch of online news websites.
E. Invention of Radio.

1. AEBDC

2. AEBCD
3. EACDB
4. ACBED

Explanations
Answer: 2. AEBCD

A - Publication of early newspapers (17th century) → **First newspapers emerged in the 1600s.**
E - Invention of Radio (Late 19th - Early 20th century) → **Radio broadcasting began in the early 1900s.**
B - Development of Television Broadcasting (1920s-1940s) → **TV broadcasting expanded globally in mid-20th century.**
C - Introduction of Email (1970s) → **Email was developed as part of ARPANET.**
D - Launch of online news websites (1990s) → **News moved to the internet with digital platforms.**

Question

The period of time when a communication network becomes inoperative, is referred to as:

1. Time fit
2. Uptime
3. Downtime
4. Loadtime

Explanations
Answer: 3. Downtime

Downtime refers to the period during which a communication network or system is **inoperative or unavailable**, often due to maintenance, technical issues, or failures.

Why not the other options?

Time fit: This is unrelated to network operations; it implies scheduling.

Uptime: Refers to the period when a system is **fully operational**.

Loadtime: Refers to the time taken to load a program or webpage, not network inoperability.

Question

Which of the following are traditional approaches to communication?

A. Machine-to-machine
B. Machine-to-man
C. Rhetorical
D. Semiotic
E. Phenomenological

1. A, B and C only
2. A, D and E only
3. B, C and D only
4. C, D and E only

Explanations
Answer: 4. C, D and E only

C. Rhetorical: A traditional approach focusing on persuasive speech and discourse.

D. Semiotic: Studies signs and symbols as a part of communication, a classic communication approach.

E. Phenomenological: Examines personal experiences and interpretation in communication, rooted in traditional communication theory.

Why not the other options?

A. Machine-to-machine: This is a modern approach related to digital communication technologies, not traditional.

B. Machine-to-man: While involving communication, this approach is linked to modern human-computer interaction, not traditional frameworks.

Question

Access to information through the invention of print was responsible for the emergence of

1. Mediated class distinction
2. Media monopoly
3. Mass media
4. Electronic device of interpersonal communication

Explanations
Answer: 3. Mass media

Mass media: The invention of the printing press enabled the mass production of books, pamphlets, and newspapers, making information accessible to a broader audience and laying the foundation for mass communication.

Why not other options?

Mediated class distinction: While print expanded access to information, it aimed to reduce, not create, class distinctions.

Media monopoly: Printing democratized access to information rather than creating monopolies.

Electronic device of interpersonal communication: Print technology is unrelated to electronic or interpersonal communication devices.

Question

List the following developments in chronological order:

(A) Invention of remote control of television
(B) daily publication
(C) Invention of camera
(D) Paperbacks coming into the market on a large scale
(E) Emergence of hieroglyphic writing system

1. ACEDB
2. BDCEA
3. CEDAB

4. EBCDA

Explanations
Answer: 4. EBCDA

E. Emergence of hieroglyphic writing system: The earliest form of writing, dating back to ancient Egypt (circa 3100 BCE).

B. Daily publication: Newspapers started publishing daily in the early 17th century (first in Germany in 1605).

C. Invention of camera: The first photographic camera was invented in the early 19th century (circa 1826).

D. Paperbacks coming into the market on a large scale: Mass-market paperbacks gained popularity in the mid-20th century (1930s-1940s).

A. Invention of remote control of television: Remote controls were introduced in the late 20th century (1950s).

Timeline of the Mass Media:

- The appearance of European popular prints in 1400.
- Johannes Gutenberg printed the Bible using his printing press, ushering in the Renaissance in 1453.
- **Printing Press (15th Century)** – Revolutionized mass communication.
- The first English-language newspaper (or coranto) appeared in 1620.
- Alexander Graham Bell made the first telephone call in 1876.
- The invention of tunable radios took place in 1916.
- BBC began broadcasting to London in 1922.
- Philo Taylor Farnsworth introduced the first electronic television system in 1927.
- The audio cassette was invented in the Netherlands in 1963.
- The Vietnam War became the first war to be televised in 1965.
- The ARPANET, the forerunner of the internet, was developed in the 1970s
- The first widely popular video game was Pong, released in 1972.
- Tim Berners-Lee publicly released world-Wide Web (WWW) at CERN in 1991.

- Japan introduced its first DVD player and disc in 1996. The first DVD release is Twister.
- **Mechanical Computer Plan (19th Century)** – Babbage's early computer concept.
- **Motion Picture Exhibition (19th Century)** – Birth of cinema.
- **Public TV Broadcast (20th Century)** – Mass media expansion.
- **Binary Computer (WWII Era)** – Digital computation emerged.

Question

Which of the following are the main functions of mass communication?

A. Detachment of individual from society
B. Indulge in message creation without worrying about moral consequences
C. Surveillance of environment
D. Transmission of social heritage
E. Correlating the parts of society in response to environment

1. ABC
2. CDE
3. ABD
4. ADE

Explanations
Answer: 2. CDE

The **main functions of mass communication** include:

C. Surveillance of environment: Monitors events and provides updates on surroundings.

D. Transmission of social heritage: Preserves and communicates cultural values and norms.

E. Correlating parts of society: Facilitates integration and adjustment in response to environmental changes.

Question

Arrange the following developments in mass communication in chronological sequence.

A. Invention of Printing Press
B. Launch of first Television network
C. Emergence of radio broadcasting
D. Creation of the internet
E. Introduction of social Media Platforms

1. A, C, D, B, E
2. A, B, D, C, E
3. A, B, C, D, E
4. A, C, B, D, E

Explanations
Answer: 4. A, C, B, D, E

- **A - Invention of Printing Press (1440s)** → Gutenberg's press enabled mass book production.
- **C - Emergence of Radio Broadcasting (1900s)** → First electronic medium for mass communication.
- **B - Launch of First TV Network (1920s-40s)** → Television became a dominant communication medium.
- **D - Creation of the Internet (1960s-80s)** → ARPANET evolved into the modern internet.
- **E - Social Media Platforms (2000s)** → Facebook, Twitter, YouTube transformed communication.

Question

Identify the correct sequence of the media production process.

A. Content Preparation
B. Planning
C. Production
D. Transmission
E. Feedback analysis

1. ABCDE
2. BCDAE
3. DCBEA
4. BACDE

Explanations
Answer: 4. BACDE

The correct sequence of the media production process involves:

1. **Planning** - Determining what content will be created and how.
2. **Content Preparation** - Developing the actual content, scripts, etc.
3. **Production** - The phase where the content is actually created.
4. **Transmission** - Distributing the content to the audience.
5. **Feedback analysis** - Evaluating how the content was received by the audience.

Question

Identify the correct chronological sequence of the following:

A. Launch of Twitter
B. Launch of Facebook
C. Appearance of social network sites
D. Launch of Sputnik
E. 'War of the worlds' broadcast

1. ACBED
2. EDCBA
3. BEDAC
4. CBADE

Explanations
Answer: 2. EDCBA

The correct chronological sequence is:

E. 'War of the Worlds' broadcast (1938): A famous radio drama by Orson Welles.

D. Launch of Sputnik (1957): The first artificial satellite by the Soviet Union.

C. Appearance of social network sites (1990s): Social networking began with platforms like Six Degrees.

B. Launch of Facebook (2004): A major milestone in social media.

A. Launch of Twitter (2006): Twitter followed Facebook and became a significant platform.

Question

Find out the correct chronological order of the following:

A. First binary computer by Britishers
B. Printing press
C. Plan for mechanical computer
D. Single-screen motion picture exhibition
E. First public broadcast of television

1. ACEDB
2. BCDEA
3. CEABD
4. DABCE

Explanations
Answer: 2. BCDEA

B. Printing press: Invented in the 15th century, it revolutionized communication by making mass production of written content possible.

C. Plan for mechanical computer: Charles Babbage proposed the design for a mechanical computer in the early 19th century.

D. Single-screen motion picture exhibition: The late 19th century saw the emergence of motion picture exhibitions, such as those by the Lumière brothers.

E. First public broadcast of television: Television broadcasts began in the early 20th century.

A. First binary computer by Britishers: The British Colossus computer, the first binary computer, was developed during World War II.

Question

Identify the correct chronological order of the following inventions related to communication:

A. Cable television
B. Telegraph
C. Telephone
D. MP3
E. Phonograph

1. A, C, D, B, E
2. B, C, E, A, D
3. C, A, B, D, E
4. E, A, C, B, D

Explanations
Answer: 2. B, C, E, A, D

B. Telegraph: Invented in the 1830s–1840s, it was the first long-distance communication technology.

C. Telephone: Invented by Alexander Graham Bell in 1876, it allowed direct voice communication over distances.

E. Phonograph: Invented by Thomas Edison in 1877, it was the first device to record and reproduce sound.

A. Cable television: Introduced in the 1940s–1950s, it provided enhanced TV reception.

D. MP3: Developed in the late 1980s and standardized in the early 1990s, it revolutionized digital audio compression.

Evolution of Mass Communication

- **Cave Paintings** – Early visual communication.
- **Language Emergence** – Structured human expression.
- **Interpersonal Communication** – Verbal interaction development.
- **Printing Technology** – Enabled mass literacy.
- **Telecommunication** – Digital evolution of communication.
- **Cave Paintings** – Primitive storytelling.
- **Language Development** – Structured expression.
- **Wooden Block Printing** – Early text duplication.
- **Acta Diurna** – First public news records.
- **Metal Printing** – Improved press efficiency.
- **Hieroglyphic Writing** – Ancient communication system.
- **Daily Publications (1605)** – First regular newspapers.
- **Invention of Camera (1826)** – Photography emergence.
- **Telegraph (1830s-1840s)** – Long-distance messaging.
- **Telephone (1876)** – Voice transmission innovation.
- **Phonograph (1877)** – First audio recording device.
- **Paperbacks (1930s-1940s)** – Affordable mass printing.
- **TV Remote Control (1950s)** – Enhancing convenience.
- **Cable TV (1940s-1950s)** – Improved television reception.
- **MP3 (1990s)** – Digital audio compression.

Traditional Media:

Dramas were probably the first mass media, dating back to ancient times in numerous cultures. When information was to be spread among a large number of people in the past, it was done through legends, folklore, riddles, and jokes. There was Nukad Natak or Nautanki and Khayal in India.

- **Legendary Tales:** A legend in literature is a traditional story or group of stories about a particular person or place. In the past, legends were stories about saints.
- **Folklore**: A community's traditional beliefs, customs, and stories passed through the generations by word of mouth.
    - **Jatra** – Bengali folk theatre.
    - **Puppetry** – Traditional storytelling method.
    - **Hari Katha** – Religious narrative art.
    - **Not Street Demonstrations** – Activism, not media.
    - **Not Filmy Dances** – Modern entertainment industry.
- **Riddles and Jokes:** Riddles are statements, questions, or phrases with a double or veiled meaning.

- **Drama and Theatre:** Drama refers almost exclusively to live performances in which the action is meticulously planned to create a coherent and meaningful effect. A written work that tells a story through action and speech is acted out.
- **Nukad Natak or Streat Theatre:** Street theatre is an outdoor theatrical performance without a paying audience.
- **Nautanki:** Nautanki is *one of South Asia's most famous folk performance forms*, particularly in northern India.
- **Puppetry**: This is a form of theatre that involves the manipulation of puppets – inanimate objects, often resembling some human or animal figure, that are animated or manipulated by a human called a puppeteer.

Question

Which of the following can not be treated as the folk tradition of communication in India?

1. Cinema
2. Jatra
3. Ramleela
4. Kumbh Mela

Explanations
Answer: 1. Cinema

Cinema: While cinema plays a significant role in modern communication and culture in India, it is not a folk tradition. It is a product of industrial and technological advancements.

Why not other options?

Jatra: A traditional folk theatre form in Bengal, deeply rooted in Indian culture.

Ramleela: A folk theatrical performance depicting the story of Ramayana, widely celebrated across India.

Kumbh Mela: A religious gathering and cultural tradition that has been practiced for centuries in India.

Question

Which of the following are forms of traditional media of communication?

A. Street demonstrations
B. Yakshagana
C. Puppetry
D. Hari Katha
E. Filmy dances

1. ABC
2. BCD
3. CDE
4. ADE

Explanations
Answer: 2. BCD

Yakshagana: A traditional Indian theatre form combining dance, music, and dialogue, popular in Karnataka.

Puppetry: A form of storytelling using puppets, rooted in Indian culture.

Hari Katha: A traditional form of narrative storytelling with a spiritual theme, prevalent in South India.

Why not other options?

Street demonstrations: While impactful, these are not considered traditional media of communication.

Filmy dances: These belong to modern mass media and entertainment, not traditional forms.

Question

The chronological sequence in the development of communication system is

A. Emergence of language
B. Cave paintings

C. Interpersonal communication (verbal)
D. Appearance of printing technology
E. Telecommunication system

1. ABCED
2. BEDCA
3. CDEAB
4. BACDE

Explanations
Answer: 4. BACDE

B: Cave paintings – One of the earliest forms of visual communication, predating language.

A: Emergence of language – Followed cave paintings, allowing verbal interaction and more complex communication.

C: Interpersonal communication (verbal) – Built upon language, enabling direct human interaction.

D: Appearance of printing technology – Revolutionized communication by mass-producing written content.

E: Telecommunication system – Represents modern advancements like telegraphy, telephony, and internet-based communication.

Question

Identify the correct sequence of phases in communication development:

A. Acta Diurna
B. Cave paintings
C. Wooden blocks for printing
D. Development of languages
E. Metal printing

1. ABDCE
2. BDCAE
3. CDEAB

4. DEABC

Explanations
Answer: 2. BDCAE

B: Cave paintings – Earliest form of visual communication, predating organized language.

D: Development of languages – Enabled more sophisticated and direct communication.

C: Wooden blocks for printing – Early printing method that allowed limited reproduction of texts.

A: Acta Diurna – Considered the first "newspaper" in ancient Rome, marking organized public communication.

E: Metal printing – Advanced the printing process, leading to mass communication through printed books.

Print Media and Electronic Media:

China invented the movable clay type in 1041. Johannes Gutenberg published the first book printed on a printing press with movable type in 1453. It was in 1620 that the first English newspaper was published. Newspapers developed around 1605. Direct access to a mass audience did not occur until the nineteenth century. Print media is **one of mass communication's oldest and most basic forms**. It includes newspapers, weeklies, magazines, monthlies and other printed journals.

- **Johannes Gutenberg** – Invented printing press.
- **Not G. Marconi** – Radio technology pioneer.
- **Not Tang Dynasty** – Early Chinese block printing.
- **Not William Caxton** – England's first printer.
- **Revolutionized Mass Communication** – Books became accessible.
- **Second Media Age** – Defined by interactivity.
- **Not First Media Age** – Focused on one-way.
- **Not Post-Media Age** – Concept not established.
- **Not Post-Technology Age** – Still tech-driven.

- **Internet & Social Media** – Key digital tools.
- **Enabled Mass Media** – Widespread information access.
- **Not Class Distinction** – Reduced knowledge gaps.
- **Not Media Monopoly** – Increased accessibility.
- **Not Electronic Media** – Pre-internet era.
- **Paved Way for Journalism** – Birth of newspapers.

Question

Media literacy is considered as a:

1. Corporate campaign
2. Limited objective
3. Temporary fad
4. Continuous process

Explanations
Answer: 4. Continuous process

Continuous process: Media literacy involves an ongoing effort to understand, evaluate, and use media effectively as it evolves over time with new technologies and platforms.

Why not others?

Corporate campaign: Media literacy isn't a promotional activity by corporations.

Limited objective: It has a broad and long-term educational goal, not confined to a single objective.

Temporary fad: Media literacy is enduring and grows with technological advancements, unlike trends that fade away.

Magazine

- **Periodical Publication** – Released weekly, monthly, or quarterly.
- **Covers Various Topics** – General and special interests.
- **Funded by Advertisements** – Revenue from sponsors.
- **Printed & Digital Formats** – Available physically and online.

- **Examples Include** – *India Today, Frontline, The Week.*

Newspaper

- **Daily or Weekly Publication** – Regular news updates.
- **Printed on Newsprint** – Cost-effective production.
- **Covers Various Topics** – General and specific interests.
- **First Published in 1605** – Long history of journalism.
- **Called 'One-Day Best Sellers'** – Short-lived relevance.
- **Hickey's Bengal Gazette (1780)** – First modern newspaper.
- **Not India Gazette** – Launched after Hickey's.
- **Not Samvad Kaumudi** – Started in 1821.
- **Not Udant Martand** – First Hindi newspaper.
- **British Colonial Influence** – Controlled press growth.

Question

First printing press in India was established at:

1. Goa
2. Kerala
3. Tamil Nadu
4. Bengal

Explanations
Answer: 1. Goa

Goa: The first printing press in India was established by Jesuit missionaries in 1556 in Goa. It was introduced by the Portuguese to promote Christian literature.

Question

Which is the first newspaper published in India in modern times?

1. Hickey's Bengal Gazzette
2. India Gazette
3. Samvad Kaumudi
4. Udant Martand

Explanations

Answer: 1. Hickey's Bengal Gazzette

Hickey's Bengal Gazette: Published in 1780 by James Augustus Hickey, it is recognized as the first newspaper in India in modern times. It was an English-language weekly newspaper.

Why not other options?

India Gazette: It was another English newspaper launched shortly after Hickey's Bengal Gazette but not the first.

Samvad Kaumudi: A Bengali newspaper started by Raja Ram Mohan Roy in 1821, much later than Hickey's Bengal Gazette.

Udant Martand: The first Hindi newspaper, published in 1826, also much later than Hickey's Bengal Gazette.

Question

Who invented the Printing process?

1. G.Marconi
2. Tang Dynasty
3. William Caxton
4. Johannes Gutenberg

Explanations

Answer: 4. Johannes Gutenberg

Hickey's Bengal Gazette: Published in 1780 by James Augustus Hickey, it is recognized as the first newspaper in India in modern times. It was an English-language weekly newspaper.

Why not other options?

India Gazette: It was another English newspaper launched shortly after Hickey's Bengal Gazette but not the first.

Samvad Kaumudi: A Bengali newspaper started by Raja Ram Mohan Roy in 1821, much later than Hickey's Bengal Gazette.

Udant Martand: The first Hindi newspaper, published in 1826, also much later than Hickey's Bengal Gazette.

Outdoor Media

- **Includes Billboards & Signs** – Public advertising tools.
- **Uses Skywriting & Blimps** – Aerial marketing techniques.
- **Captures Public Attention** – Placed in high-traffic areas.
- **Non-Digital Communication** – Traditional mass media.
- **Effective for Brand Visibility** – Reaches large audiences.

Book

- **Collection of Bound Pages** – Physical or digital format.
- **Includes Literary Works** – Fiction and non-fiction.
- **E-books Are Digital Versions** – Accessible online.
- **Used for Education & Entertainment** – Knowledge resource.
- **Mass Printing Enabled Wide Distribution** – Low-cost production.

Broadcasting

- **Includes Radio & Television** – Audio-visual communication.
- **Requires Licensing & Regulation** – Controlled by authorities.
- **Uses Electromagnetic Waves** – Transmits over airwaves.
- **Reaches Large Audiences** – Popular mass media form.
- **Delivers News & Entertainment** – Informative and engaging.
- **One-way Communication** – No audience interaction.
- **Not Positive or Negative** – Subjective impact.
- **Not Two-way Communication** – Lacked real engagement.
- **Centralized Message Delivery** – State or corporate control.
- **Limited Audience Participation** – No instant feedback.
- **One-way Communication** – No audience interaction.
- **State-Controlled Media** – Government oversight existed.
- **Means of Inequality** – Limited access to media.
- **Not Decentralized** – Highly centralized system.
- **No Multi-way Communication** – Lacked audience participation.

Question

Which of the following are characteristics of the broadcast (first media) era?

A. Decentralized
B. one-way communication
C. Multi-way communication
D. Control of the state from pre-prone
E. a means of inequality

1. ABC
2. BDE
3. CDE
4. ACD

Explanations
Answer: 2. BDE

B. One-way communication: Broadcast media primarily involved one-way communication where the audience could not interact with the content creators.

D. Control of the state from pre-prone: State-controlled broadcast media was common, especially in its early stages.

E. A means of inequality: Limited access to broadcast media created inequalities in information dissemination.

Why not other options?

A. Decentralized: Broadcast media was initially highly centralized, not decentralized.

C. Multi-way communication: Multi-way communication became possible with digital and interactive media, not in the broadcast era.

Question

In the early stages of development, broadcast media were marked by-

1. Positive communication
2. Negative communication
3. One-way communication
4. Two-way communication

Explanations
Answer: 3. One-way communication

One-way communication: Early broadcast media, like radio and television, primarily delivered information from a single source to a passive audience without opportunities for interaction or feedback.

Why not other options?

Positive communication: This is a subjective quality, not a defining characteristic of early broadcast media.

Negative communication: Early broadcast media were not inherently negative; they aimed to inform and entertain.

Two-way communication: Interactivity became possible only with the advent of new media and digital technologies.

Question

One of the features of broadcast communication is that it is

1. Static for the audience
2. Hidden from the audience
3. High- brow for the audience
4. Live for the audience

Explanations
Answer: 4. Live for the audience

Broadcast communication refers to the **transmission of information through mass media platforms like radio, television, or live-streaming services** to a large audience. One of its defining features is that it is often **live**, allowing audiences to experience events in **real-time.**

Question

Statement I: In terms of communication, the dominant interests of a larger culture will form the image of minority audiences.
Statement II: The medium of television is often considered as a new religion.

1. Both Statement I and Statement II are correct.
2. Both Statement I and Statement II are incorrect.
3. Statement I is correct but Statement II is incorrect.
4. Statement I is incorrect but Statement II is correct.

Explanations
Answer: 1. Both Statement I and Statement II are correct.

Statement I is correct: Larger cultural dominance often shapes the portrayal and perception of minority audiences, aligning with media studies on cultural hegemony.

Statement II is correct: Television, due to its pervasive influence and role in shaping societal norms and beliefs, is metaphorically referred to as a "new religion."

Audio Recording & Reproduction

- **Captures & Reproduces Sound** – Electrical or mechanical.
- **Used for Music & Speech** – Primary audio medium.
- **Includes Tapes & Discs** – Physical storage formats.
- **20th Century Dominance** – Key entertainment industry.
- **Evolved to Digital Formats** – MP3, streaming services.

Film

- **Motion Picture Entertainment** – Visual storytelling medium.
- **Used for Documentaries & Fiction** – Informative or creative.
- **Known as 'Cinema' & 'Movies'** – Various terminologies.
- **Silver Screen Representation** – Historical film medium.
- **Mass Audience Appeal** – Global industry impact.
- **Enabled Silent Film Era** – Early movie screenings.
- **Not Video Ads** – No advertising impact.
- **Not TV Networks** – Television emerged later.

- **Not Computers** – Unrelated to digital age.
- **Pioneered Film Projection** – Key cinema innovation.

Question

The development of vitascope led to:

1. The silent film era
2. Video advertisements
3. The television network system
4. The arrival of computers

Explanations
Answer: 1. The silent film era

The silent film era: The Vitascope, an early film projector developed in 1896, marked the beginning of large-scale public film screenings, which were silent films at the time.

Internet

- **Global Communication Network** – Connects users worldwide.
- **Hosts Blogs & Podcasts** – Interactive content.
- **Used in Education & Work** – Digital learning tools.
- **Facilitates Instant Information Sharing** – Real-time updates.
- **Web-Based Media Platform** – Video, news, and communication.

Computer & Video Games

- **Computer-Controlled Gaming** – Digital interactive experiences.
- **Uses Screens for Feedback** – Visual gameplay elements.
- **Expanded Mass Media Influence** – Mainstream entertainment.
- **Popular Gaming Consoles** – PlayStation, Xbox, GameCube.
- **Evolved with Online Play** – Multiplayer digital interaction.

Question

Match the column:

A. FM	I. The Tribune
B. Newspaper	II. Rediff.com

C. TV Channel	III. Radio Mirchee
D. Internet	IV. CNBC

1. A-III, B-II, C-I, D-IV
2. A-III, B-I, C-IV, D-II
3. A-I,B-II, C-IV, D-III
4. A-II, B-I, C-III, D-IV

Explanations
Answer: 2. A-III, B-I, C-IV, D-I

A. FM → III. Radio Mirchi: FM refers to **frequency modulation**, and Radio Mirchi is a popular FM radio station.

B. Newspaper → I. The Tribune: The Tribune is a well-known **newspaper** in India.

C. TV Channel → IV. CNBC: CNBC is a **television channel**, primarily focused on business and financial news.

D. Internet → II. Rediff.com: Rediff.com is a prominent **internet-based platform** for news and online content.

Question

Which of the following media is often described as 'one day best seller'?

1. Radio
2. Internet
3. Novel
4. Newspaper

Explanations
Answer: 4. Newspaper

Newspapers are often described as **'one day best sellers'** because their content is relevant and sought after only for a single day. Readers typically consume them for daily updates, after which they lose relevance.

Question

The chronological sequence of the media starring the place marked by Harold Innis is:

A. Radio
B. Television
C. Bhojpatra (Papyrus)
D. paper
E. Newspaper

1. ACDEB
2. CDEAB
3. DEBAC
4. EBADC

Explanations
Answer: 2. CDEAB

The chronological sequence of media as identified by **Harold Innis** reflects the progression of communication technologies over time:

C. Bhojpatra (Papyrus): Among the earliest media, **Papyrus** was used in ancient civilizations for writing.

D. Paper: Paper followed as a medium for documentation and communication after Papyrus.

E. Newspaper: With the invention of the printing press, **newspapers** became a significant medium for mass communication.

A. Radio: The 20th century saw the rise of **radio**, enabling wireless communication and broadcasting.

B. Television: Television emerged as a powerful visual medium later in the 20th century.

Question

Vladimir Zworykin was associated with the invention of

1. Colour printing
2. Radio
3. Television
4. Internet

Explanations
Answer: 3. Television

Vladimir Zworykin was a pioneering inventor associated with the development of **television technology**. He invented the **iconoscope** (an early television camera tube) and the **kinescope** (a cathode-ray tube used for displaying images), which were crucial to the evolution of television.

Why not the other options?

Colour printing: This is unrelated to Zworykin's work, which focused on electronic imaging systems.

Radio: While similar in timeline, Zworykin was not involved in the invention of radio technology.

Internet: The internet emerged much later and involved different technologies and inventors.

Question

In mass communication print is considered as a/an

1. Folk medium
2. Electronic medium
3. Mechanical medium
4. Ordinary medium

Explanations
Answer: 3. Mechanical medium

Print is considered a **mechanical medium** because it involves **mechanical processes** such as typesetting, printing, and binding to produce newspapers, magazines, and books. It relies on machines like printing presses for mass production.

Question

Match the List

A. Newspaper	I. Networking
B. Radio and television	Il. Audio, Video and graphics
C. Social Media	III. Broadsheet
D. Multi-media	IV. Broadcasting

1. A-IlI B-IV C-I D-II
2. A-IV B-I C-II D-III
3. A-I B-II C-III D-IV
4. A-II B-III C-IV D-I

Explanations
Answer: 1. A-IlI B-IV C-I D-II

A. Newspaper → III. Broadsheet: Newspapers are typically associated with the **broadsheet format**, a traditional print medium.

B. Radio and television → IV. Broadcasting: Both radio and television are categorized as **broadcasting media**, delivering content to large audiences.

C. Social Media → I. Networking: Social media platforms focus on **networking**, enabling users to connect, share, and interact globally.

D. Multi-media → II. Audio, Video and Graphics: Multi-media combines **audio, video, and graphics**, offering a rich, interactive experience.

Question

Statement I: Digital technology has enabled an increase in media consumption.
Statement Il: Analog media are superior in quality. but do not have popular demand.

1. Both Statement I and Statement Il are true
2. Both Statement I and Statement Il are false
3. Statement I is true but Statement Il is false
4. Statement I is false but Statement Il is true

Explanations
Answer: 3. Statement I is true but Statement II is false

Statement I is true: Digital technology has significantly increased **media consumption** by making content easily accessible, portable, and affordable across various platforms.

Statement II is false: Analog media, while often nostalgic or valued for specific qualities (like vinyl records), is generally not considered **superior in quality** compared to digital media, which offers better clarity, durability, and accessibility. Analog media also lacks popular demand due to its limitations and the convenience of digital formats.

Old Media:

Old media, or legacy media, are the mass media institutions that predominated before the Information Age, particularly print media, film studios, music studios, advertising agencies, radio broadcasting, and television.

Old media institutions are centralized and communicate with one-way technologies to a (generally anonymous) mass audience. New media computer technologies are interactive and comparatively decentralized; they enable people to telecommunicate with one another. The defining telecommunications network of the Information Age is the internet.

Question

Which technology was first marked as a separation between transportation and communication?

1. Telegraph
2. Projection
3. Printing
4. Photography

Explanations
Answer: 1. Telegraph

The **telegraph** was the first technology to **separate communication from physical transportation.** Before its invention, messages were physically carried by messengers, ships, or pigeons. With the telegraph, information could be transmitted **instantaneously over long distances**, independent of physical movement.

Question

Statement I: Photographs, graphs, films and other art works do not clarify and enhance the visual value of the written messages much.

Statement II: Bar graphs, pie charts and other infographic devices cannot replace the mass of numbers in print.

1. Both Statement I and Statement Il are correct.
2. Both Statement I and Statement II are incorrect.
3. Statement I is correct but Statement Il is incorrect.
4. Statement I is incorrect but Statement Il is correct.

Explanations
Answer: 2. Both Statement I and Statement II are incorrect.

Statement I is incorrect: Photographs, graphs, films, and other artworks **greatly enhance and clarify the visual value** of written messages, making them more engaging and easier to understand.

Statement II is incorrect: Bar graphs, pie charts, and infographics are highly effective at **replacing complex numerical data** by presenting it in a visual, easily digestible format.

Question

Which of the following mass media is considered less expensive and more effective than others for educational communication of non-literates?

1. Television
2. Radio
3. News papers
4. Films

Explanations
Answer: 2. Radio

Radio is considered **less expensive and more effective** for educational communication, especially for non-literates, because:

- It is an **audio medium**, eliminating the need for literacy.
- It is **cost-effective** to produce and broadcast programs.
- It has a **wide reach**, even in remote areas with limited infrastructure.

Why not the other options?

Television: While effective, it is **more expensive** to produce content and requires visual literacy.

Newspapers: Requires **reading skills**, making it unsuitable for non-literates.

Films: Effective but **costly** to produce and distribute, and may require some level of literacy for full comprehension.

Question

Statement I: Personal conversation is more effective than a broadcast speech.
Statement II: The factor of personalization makes the radio a more effective means of communication than a newspaper.

1. Both Statement I and Statement Il are true
2. Both Statement I and Statement Il are false
3. Statement l is true but Statement Il is false
4. Statement I is false but Statement Il is true

Explanations
Answer: 1. Both Statement I and Statement Il are true

Statement I: Personal conversation is more effective than a broadcast speech because it allows for **direct interaction, immediate feedback, and personalization**, making communication more engaging and impactful.

Statement II: The **personalization factor of radio** (e.g., conversational tone of radio hosts or targeted programming) makes it more effective than newspapers, which are static and lack the dynamic personal touch.

New Media:

New media are forms of computational media that rely on computers and the internet for redistribution. Some examples of new media are computer 3D animations, video games, human-computer interfaces, interactive computer installations, websites, and virtual worlds. **Instagram** is an example of **New Media** as it represents a **digital and interactive platform** that allows users to create, share, and interact with content in real-time. New media, such as online platforms and digital tools, indeed expand learning environments, providing **unprecedented access to resources, collaboration, and interactivity**. Learners can **design their own learning processes** using new media by selecting personalized content, pacing their learning, and utilizing interactive tools.

Question

Which one of the following is an example of form of New Media?

1. Newspapers
2. TV
3. Radio
4. Instagram

Explanations
Answer: 4. Instagram

Instagram is an example of **New Media** as it represents a **digital and interactive platform** that allows users to create, share, and interact with content in real-time. It is a hallmark of the internet-driven era of communication.

Why not the other options?

Newspapers: Classified as **traditional media** because they rely on print and static content.

TV: Also part of **traditional media**, focusing on one-way communication.

Radio: Though effective, it is a **traditional broadcast medium** and lacks the interactivity associated with New Media.

Question

Assertion A: New media enhance the opportunities to expand the learning environment unheard of before
Reason R: Learners can design their own learning process

1. Both A and R are correct and Rs the correct explanation of A
2. Both A and R are correct but R is NOT the correct explanation of A
3. A is correct but R is not correct
4. A is not correct but R is correct

Explanations
Answer: 1. Both A and R are correct and Rs the correct explanation of A

Assertion (A): New media, such as online platforms and digital tools, indeed expand learning environments, providing **unprecedented access to resources, collaboration, and interactivity**.

Reason (R): Learners can **design their own learning processes** using new media by selecting personalized content, pacing their learning, and utilizing interactive tools. This ability is a direct reason for the expanded learning opportunities mentioned in the assertion.

Question

In the post-information age, information is highly-

1. Homogeneous
2. Communitarian
3. Personalised
4. Impersonal

Explanations
Answer: 3. Personalised

Personalised: In the post-information age, technologies like AI and big data enable tailored content delivery based on user preferences, habits, and behavior.

Question

The interactive technologies are responsible for the appearance of:

1. Traditional media age
2. Broadcast media age
3. Market media age
4. Second media age

Explanations
Answer: 4. Second media age

Second media age: Interactive technologies, such as the internet, social media, and mobile platforms, define the second media age by enabling two-way communication and interactivity.

Why not other options?

Traditional media age: Associated with print and early broadcast media, focused on one-way communication.

Broadcast media age: Involves mass communication through radio and television, with limited interactivity.

Market media age: Focuses on commercialization but does not specifically emphasize interactivity.

Question

The 'Second media age' is characterised by the rise of:

1. Print media
2. Radio
3. Television
4. Interactive media

Explanations

Answer: 4. Interactive media

The **Second Media Age** refers to the transition from **traditional mass media (one-way communication)** to **interactive, digital, and networked media**. It emphasizes **user participation, decentralization, and interactivity**.

First Media Age → Dominated by **print, radio, and television** (one-way communication).

Second Media Age → Rise of **interactive media** such as the **internet, social media, and digital platforms** (two-way communication).

Social Media:

A social media platform is an interactive technology that facilitates creating and sharing of information, ideas, opinions, interests, and other forms of expression through virtual communities and networks. Some common characteristics of social media make it difficult to define due to the variety of stand-alone and built-in services currently available:

- Internet-based social media applications are interactive Web 2.0 applications.
- The backbone of social media is user-generated content, which includes text posts, stories, reels or comments, digital photos or videos, gifs and data generated through all online interactions.
- The social media organization designs and maintains service-specific profiles for the website or app.
- A social media website facilitates the development of online social networks by connecting the profiles of individuals or groups. Some of the most popular social media are:
    - Facebook or Meta,
    - TikTok,
    - WeChat,
    - Instagram,
    - Twitter,
    - Tumblr,
    - LinkedIn,
    - YouTube,
    - Telegram,
    - WhatsApp,

- LINE,
- Snapchat,
- Pinterest,

Question

The emergence of media of communication, in chronological sequence, is

A. Radio
B. Newspaper
C. Film
D. Television
E. Internet

1. ACDEB
2. BCADE
3. CDEAB
4. DECBA

Explanations
Answer: 2. BCADE

The chronological sequence of media of communication reflects the timeline of their invention and adoption:

B. Newspaper: Emerged first in the **17th century**, providing printed communication.

C. Radio: Invented in the late **19th century**, enabling audio communication.

A. Film: Developed in the late **19th and early 20th centuries** as a visual medium.

D. Television: Became popular in the **mid-20th century** for audiovisual communication.

E. Internet: Emerged in the **late 20th century**, revolutionizing communication with interactivity and connectivity.

Question

Identify the correct sequence of the following modes of communication:

A. Written
B. Face-to-face
C. Print
D. Broadcasting
E. Datacasting

1. ACBED
2. BACDE
3. CDEAB
4. DEABC

Explanations
Answer: 2. BACDE

The correct chronological sequence of communication modes is:

B. Face-to-face: The earliest and most basic form of communication.

A. Written: Introduced later as a means of recording and sharing information.

C. Print: Emerged with the invention of the printing press, enabling mass communication.

D. Broadcasting: Introduced in the 20th century with radio and television.

E. Datacasting: A modern form of communication using digital technology for data transmission.

Question

Internet portals work-

A. Like a public entertainer
B. Similar to magazines circulated in large numbers
C. Similar to TV network
D. Similar to sites of accumulated text material
E. Similar to the users' home page

1. ABC
2. ABCD
3. ACD
4. BCDE

Explanations
Answer: 4. BCDE

Internet portals function in various ways:

B. Similar to magazines circulated in large numbers: Portals aggregate and present diverse content for wide consumption.

C. Similar to TV network: They offer multimedia content, including videos and live streaming.

D. Similar to sites of accumulated text material: Portals serve as repositories of textual information.

E. Similar to the users' home page: Portals often serve as customizable gateways for user interaction and access to multiple resources.

Question

Which of the following are associated with heavy use of the Internet?

A. Internet addiction
B. Depression
C. Distraction
D. Atomization
E. Media Literacy

1. A, B, C, D
2. B, C,D, E
3. A, B, E
4. A, B, C, E

Explanations
Answer: 1. A, B, C, D

Heavy use of the internet is associated with:

A. Internet addiction: Excessive use leading to dependency and behavioral issues.

B. Depression: Overuse may result in isolation, reduced social interaction, and mental health challenges.

C. Distraction: Heavy internet use often reduces focus and productivity.

D. Atomization: Overreliance on the internet can cause fragmentation of social relationships and individual isolation.

Why not the other options?

E. Media Literacy: This is a skill or knowledge area, not a consequence of heavy internet use.

Question

A Substitute for the gestural communication over the Internet is the use of:

1. Emoticons
2. Infographics
3. Photographs
4. Anonymous attachments

Explanations
Answer: 1. Emoticons

Emoticons are used as substitutes for **gestural communication** over the Internet. They convey emotions, expressions, and non-verbal cues in textual communication, mimicking facial expressions and gestures.

Why not the other options?

Infographics: These are visual representations of data or information, not substitutes for gestures.

Photographs: While visual, they do not serve as a direct substitute for gestures in communication.

Anonymous attachments: These are unrelated to conveying non-verbal expressions.

Analogue and Digital Media

- **Analogue Media Uses Physical Formats** – Includes tapes, vinyl, and film.
- **Digital Media Stores Data Electronically** – Uses binary code for storage.
- **Analogue Signals Are Continuous** – Transmit information in waveforms.
- **Digital Signals Are Discrete** – Use 0s and 1s for precision.
- **Modes of data transmission** that define how information flows between **sender and receiver** in a communication system:
    - **Simplex Communication**: **One-way communication**, where data flows in a **single direction only**. **No feedback** from the receiver. **Examples**: Radio broadcasts, television, keyboards to computers.
    - **Half-Duplex Communication: Two-way communication**, but only **one direction at a time**. Sender and receiver must **take turns** to transmit. **Examples**: Walkie-talkies, police radios, push-to-talk systems.
    - **Full-Duplex Communication**: **Two-way communication happening simultaneously**. Sender and receiver can **both transmit and receive at the same time**. **Examples**: Telephone calls, video calls, fiber-optic internet.
- **Analogue Media Degrades Over Time** – Quality reduces with repeated use.
- **Digital Media Maintains Quality** – Data remains unchanged over time.
- **Analogue Devices Require Physical Interaction** – Manual operation needed.
- **Digital Media Allows Instant Access** – Enables quick retrieval and sharing.
- **Analogue Media Offers Warm Sound** – Preferred for natural audio quality.

- **Digital Media Enables Easy Editing** – Supports modifications and enhancements.

Question

The term 'analogue media' was originally derived from:

1. Folk performances
2. Satellite communication
3. Internet
4. Audio recordings

Explanations
Answer: 4. Audio recordings

The term **"analog media"** originated from **audio recordings**, where analog signals represent continuous variations of sound waves. Early technologies like vinyl records and cassette tapes are examples of analog audio media.

Why not the other options?

Folk performances: These are traditional, cultural expressions but not related to the origin of the term "analog media."

Satellite communication: Satellite technologies involve digital and analog signals but are not the origin of the term.

Internet: The internet is a digital medium, distinct from analog technologies.

Question

What are the advantages of digital media?

A. Network communication is avoided.
B. People can create and distribute media content.
C. The end-product can be delivered in real-time.
D. Reproduction and distribution of information products are less expensive.
E. Online political involvement is of no importance.

1. A, B, C only

2. B, C, D only
3. C, D, E only
4. A, B, E only

Explanations
Answer: 2. B, C, D only

The advantages of digital media include:

B. People can create and distribute media content: Digital platforms empower users to produce and share content globally.

C. The end-product can be delivered in real-time: Digital media facilitates instant sharing and access to information.

D. Reproduction and distribution of information products are less expensive: Digital distribution reduces costs compared to traditional media formats.

Why not the other options?

A. Network communication is avoided: Digital media relies heavily on networks for connectivity and distribution.

E. Online political involvement is of no importance: Online political engagement is significant and increasingly impactful in digital spaces.

Question

With reference to digital communication, which of the following are examples of simplex type of communication?

A. Radio broadcasting
B. Television broadcasting
C. Computer to Printer communication
D. Keyboard to computer communication
E. Walkie-Talkie communication

1. E
2. ABCD
3. ACE

4. DE

Explanations
Answer: 2. ABCD

Simplex communication is a **one-way** communication system where information flows in **only one direction**, with no feedback from the receiver.

- **A (Correct) - Radio broadcasting**: Information flows one way (station to listener).
- **B (Correct) - Television broadcasting**: Signals are sent, but viewers cannot respond.
- **C (Correct) - Computer to Printer communication**: The printer only **receives** data from the computer.
- **D (Correct) - Keyboard to computer communication**: The computer receives input but does not send feedback to the keyboard.

E (Incorrect) - Walkie-Talkie communication: This is **half-duplex**, allowing two-way communication but one direction at a time.

Question

In digital communication, a Television broadcast and a Radio broadcast are examples of type of transmission.

1. Automatic
2. Half-duplex
3. Simplex
4. Full duplex

Explanations
Answer: 3. Simplex

Simplex transmission is a **one-way communication** where data flows in **only one direction** without any return communication.

- **Television broadcast** → Signal flows from the station to viewers.
- **Radio broadcast** → Signal flows from the radio station to listeners.
- **No feedback or two-way interaction occurs.**

Question

With reference to digital communication, which of the following statements A-D are true?

A. A Radio broadcast is an example of automatic type of transmission mode.
B. A Keyboard communicating with a computer is an example of simplex type of transmission mode.
C. Walkie-Talkies operate on half-duplex transmission mode.
D. Telephone calls are an example of full-duplex transmission mode.

1. AB
2. BC
3. AC
4. BCD

Explanations
Answer: 4. BCD

A (Incorrect): **Radio broadcast is simplex**, not automatic. It is a **one-way transmission** with no return communication.
B (Correct): **Keyboard to computer is simplex**, as data flows **one-way** from the keyboard to the computer.
C (Correct): **Walkie-Talkies use half-duplex**, meaning data flows in **both directions, but one at a time**.
D (Correct): **Telephone calls use full duplex**, allowing **simultaneous two-way communication**.

Question

Statement I: Due to technological developments, communication has become mass communication.
Statement II: With the arrival of satellites and computers, communication has become more efficient and complex than ever before.

1. Both Statement I and Statement II are correct
2. Both Statement I and Statement Il are incorrect
3. Statement I is correct but Statement Il is incorrect
4. Statement I is incorrect but Statement Il is correct

Explanations
Answer: 1. Both Statement I and Statement II are correct

Statement I: Technological advancements such as radio, television, and the internet have enabled communication to reach **mass audiences**, making communication more widespread and impactful.

Statement II: The introduction of **satellites and computers** has revolutionized communication, making it **faster, more efficient, and interconnected**, while also increasing complexity due to advanced technologies and global reach.

Question

In analog media, contents are:

1. Non-linear
2. Linear
3. Interactive
4. Customised

Explanations
Answer: 2. Linear

Analog media refers to traditional forms of media (e.g., radio, television, print) where content is delivered in a **linear sequence**, meaning the audience receives information in the order it is presented, without the ability to rearrange or interact with it.

Why not the other options?

Non-linear: Non-linear content allows audiences to navigate freely, a feature of digital media, not analog.

Interactive: Interaction is a characteristic of digital media, where users can engage with the content.

Customised: Customization is not inherent in analog media; it is a feature of digital platforms tailored to individual preferences.

Question

The automation element of online media has enabled the generation of:

1. Limited quantity of quality information
2. User specific information
3. Complex philosophical information
4. Non-specific general information

Explanations
Answer: 2. User specific information

Automation in online media uses algorithms and data analytics to provide **user-specific information**, tailoring content based on individual preferences, behaviors, and search history.

Why not the other options?

Limited quantity of quality information: Automation increases the volume of available information rather than limiting it.

Complex philosophical information: Automation focuses on relevance and user behavior, not on generating philosophical content.

Non-specific general information: Automation aims to personalize, not generalize, the information provided.

Question

Which of the following are true in the case of the audience for analog media? They are:

A. Personally addressable
B. Active campaigners
C. large
D. Heterogeneous
E. Anonymous

1. A, B, only
2. B, C, only
3. A, B, E only

4. C, D, E only

Explanations
Answer: 4. C, D, E only

C. Large: Analog media, like radio and television, caters to **large audiences** simultaneously.

D. Heterogeneous: Analog media audiences are diverse, encompassing people from various demographics and backgrounds.

E. Anonymous: Audiences of analog media are often **anonymous**, as there is no direct feedback mechanism to identify individuals.

Why not the other options?

A. Personally addressable: Analog media does not have the capability to target specific individuals; it addresses audiences collectively.

B. Active campaigners: Analog audiences are typically **passive consumers**, not actively involved in content creation or dissemination.

Question

Statement I: The centralised control of signs and symbols of mediated communication may affect plurality of opinions on the Internet.
Statement II: The global corporate owners of internet companies aim only at profits. not the existence of the pluriverse.
In the light of the above statements. choose the correct answer from the options given below

1. Both Statement I and Statement Il are true
2. Both Statement I and Statement Il are false
3. Statement I is true but Statement Il is false
4. Statement I is false but Statement II is true

Explanations
Answer: 1. Both Statement I and Statement Il are true

Statement I is true: Centralized control over **signs and symbols in mediated communication** (e.g., algorithms, content moderation) can **limit plurality of opinions** by prioritizing certain voices or perspectives over others.

Statement II is true: Many global corporate owners of internet companies prioritize **profit-making** through targeted advertising and data monetization, often disregarding the need for a **pluriverse** (diverse world of opinions and cultures).

Question

Which of the following are the features of narrowcasting?

A. Large area of reach
B. Weak reception
C. Limited reach in terms of geographical area
D. Noise free
E. Appropriate for specialised media channels

1. A, B, C only
2. B, C, D only
3. A, C, D only
4. C, D, E only

Explanations
Answer: 4. C, D, E only

C. Limited reach in terms of geographical area: Narrowcasting targets a **specific and limited audience** or geographical region, unlike broadcasting, which has a wide reach.

D. Noise free: Narrowcasting often uses advanced technologies, leading to **clear signal quality** and minimal interference.

E. Appropriate for specialised media channels: Narrowcasting is ideal for **targeted content delivery**, such as niche channels or specific interest groups.

Question

Which of the following are the characteristics of virtual interaction?

A. Time-zone constraints are abundant within a small country.
B. Itis aspatial.
C. It is spatial.
D. Mutual presence is redundant.
E. Virtual interaction through some system is asynchronous.

1. ABC
2. BCD
3. CDE
4. BDE

Explanations
Answer: 4. BDE

B. It is aspatial: Virtual interaction eliminates physical constraints, allowing communication across locations without geographical limitations.

D. Mutual presence is redundant: Virtual interaction does not require both parties to be present simultaneously, especially in asynchronous systems like email.

E. Virtual interaction through some system is asynchronous: Many virtual interactions, such as emails and forums, allow communication at different times, making them asynchronous.

Why not the other options?

A. Time-zone constraints are abundant within a small country: Time-zone constraints are less relevant, especially for asynchronous communication.

C. It is spatial: Virtual interaction transcends spatial boundaries, making "spatial" an incorrect characteristic.

Question

The major characteristics of digital media are:

A. Interactivity
B. Automation

C. Cheaper cost
D. Higher cost
E. Not different from analog technology

1. ABC
2. BCD
3. CDE
4. ADE

Explanations
Answer: 1. ABC

A. Interactivity: Digital media allows users to interact with content, such as commenting, sharing, or choosing what to consume.

B. Automation: Digital media often involves automated processes, such as content recommendations and data-driven personalization.

C. Cheaper cost: Digital media is generally more cost-effective compared to traditional analog technologies, particularly in distribution and reproduction.

Why not the other options?

D. Higher cost: Digital media is typically less expensive than analog technology in terms of scalability and delivery.

E. Not different from analog technology: Digital media is significantly different from analog technology, offering features like interactivity, automation, and better quality.

Question

The term 'analog media' is primarily derived from-

1. Newspaper reading
2. Audio recording
3. Computer printing
4. Multi-media production

Explanations

Answer: 2. Audio recording

Audio recording gave rise to the term "analog media" because analog signals are used to store and reproduce sound as continuous waveforms, such as in vinyl records and magnetic tapes. These recordings represent the original sound waveforms in a continuous format, which is a hallmark of analog media.

Why not the other options?

Newspaper reading: While traditional, newspapers are not directly related to the origin of the term "analog."

Computer printing: Printing involves digital processes and is unrelated to analog waveforms.

Multi-media production: Multimedia is more aligned with digital formats and not relevant to the analog concept.

Question

Statement I: Communication technology has made revisiting of ideas impossible.
Statement II: Technology has redefined the elements of time and distance in favour of communication managers.

1. Both Statement I and Statement Il are true
2. Both Statement I and Statement Il are false
3. Statement I is true but Statement Il is false
4. Statement I is false but Statement Il is true

Explanations
Answer: 4. Statement I is false but Statement Il is true

Statement I is false: Communication technology has made **revisiting ideas easier**, not impossible. Digital platforms allow for archiving, retrieving, and revising content anytime, enhancing accessibility.

Statement II is true: Technology has indeed **redefined time and distance**, enabling instantaneous communication across vast distances, which benefits communication managers by streamlining operations and decision-making.

Question

Assertion (A): The new system of digital communication has made the emergence of an interactive society possible.
Reasons (R): The new system is based on 'digitized and networked integration of multiple communication modes".

1. Both A and R are true and R is the correct explanation of A
2. Both A and R are true but R is NOT the correct explanation of A
3. A is true but R is false
4. A is false but R is true

Explanations
Answer: 1. Both A and R are true and R is the correct explanation of A

Assertion (A) is true: The **new system of digital communication** enables interactivity, allowing individuals to connect, share, and engage in ways that foster an **interactive society**.

Reason (R) is true: The **digitized and networked integration** of various communication modes (e.g., text, audio, video) forms the foundation of this interactivity, making the emergence of an interactive society possible.

R explains A: The reason directly explains why digital communication leads to an interactive society, as the integrated nature of digital platforms facilitates seamless, multidimensional communication.

Question

Statement I: The new system of communication has facilitated the emergence of an Interactive society.
Statement II: The new system of communication is digital and has integrated multiple modes of communication through networks

1. Both Statement I and Statement II are true
2. Both Statement I and Statement II are false
3. Statement I is true but Statement II is false
4. Statement I is false but Statement II is true

Explanations
Answer: 1. Both Statement I and Statement II are true

Statement I is true: The **new system of communication** has enabled an **interactive society** by facilitating two-way communication through digital platforms, encouraging engagement, and fostering collaboration.

Statement II is true: The **digital communication system** integrates multiple modes (e.g., text, audio, video, and images) via networks, allowing for seamless and efficient communication across various platforms.

Question

The modern communication revolution is propelled by

1. Cold war propaganda
2. International commerce
3. Technological convergence
4. Change in political systems

Explanations
Answer: 3. Technological convergence

Technological convergence drives the modern communication revolution by integrating multiple communication technologies (e.g., internet, television, radio, and mobile) into unified platforms. This convergence enhances accessibility, interactivity, and efficiency in global communication systems.

Why not the other options?

Cold war propaganda: While communication systems played a role during the Cold War, they were not the primary driver of the modern communication revolution.

International commerce: Commerce benefits from the revolution but is not its primary cause.

Change in political systems: Political changes influence communication but are not the key propelling factor.

Purpose and Function of Mass Media:

Mass media can serve various purposes and functions:

Advocacy

- **Supports Business & Social Causes** – Promotes change effectively.
- **Uses Media for Awareness** – Spreads key messages.
- **Influences Public Perception** – Shapes opinions widely.
- **Aims for Policy Change** – Drives social reforms.
- **Encourages Action Through Media** – Mobilizes audiences.

Advertising

- **Promotes Products or Services** – Attracts consumers.
- **Targets Mass Media Markets** – Reaches large audiences.
- **Uses Persuasive Techniques** – Influences buying behavior.
- **Involves Paid Media Placement** – Ensures visibility.
- **Enhances Brand Recognition** – Builds public awareness.
- **Driven by New Technologies** – Custom audience targeting.
- **Second Media Age Impact** – Changed media landscape.
- **Not Generalized Content** – Personalized information flow.
- **Data-Driven Strategies** – AI-based audience segmentation.
- **User Participation Increased** – Engaged media consumers.

Publicity

- **Increases Public Awareness** – Expands recognition.
- **Can Be Controlled or Uncontrolled** – Varies by source.
- **Uses Media for Exposure** – Gains attention.
- **Benefits Products, Services, Organizations** – Boosts visibility.
- **Often Earned, Not Paid** – Grows organically.

Marketing

- **Creates & Communicates Value** – Benefits customers.
- **Uses Various Media Channels** – Expands outreach.
- **Drives Customer Engagement** – Enhances brand loyalty.
- **Employs Strategic Campaigns** – Targets specific markets.

- **Focuses on Customer Needs** – Satisfies demand.

Question

The arrival of interactive communication technologies has been described as

1. The first media age
2. The second media age
3. Post-media age
4. Post-technology age

Explanations
Answer: 2. The second media age

The second media age: Refers to the era characterized by interactive communication technologies, such as the internet and social media, enabling two-way communication and user-generated content. It followed the one-way communication of the "first media age," marked by broadcast media like radio and television.

Why not other options?

The first media age: Associated with traditional, one-way communication media like print, radio, and television.

Post-media age: This term is not commonly used in describing media eras.

Post-technology age: This concept does not align with interactive communication technologies, as they depend heavily on technological advancements.

Question

Statement I: The new technologies have brought in 'Market Specific Communication'.
Statement II: The second media age has made the interactive technologies of communication to change the mediascape.

1. Both Statement I and Statement II are true.
2. Both Statement I and Statement II are false.

3. Statement I is true but Statement Il is false.
4. Statement I is false but Statement Il is true.

Explanations
Answer: 1. Both Statement I and Statement II are true.

Statement I is true: New technologies have enabled "Market Specific Communication," targeting specific audiences with tailored messages using data-driven insights and segmentation strategies.

Statement II is true: The second media age, characterized by interactive communication technologies such as social media and digital platforms, has significantly transformed the mediascape by enabling personalized and participatory media experiences.

Question

Which of the following are objectives in marketing communication?

A. Belittling competitive brands
B. Category need
C. Brand awareness
D. Brand attitude
E. Brand purchase intention

1. ABCD
2. BCDE
3. ACDE
4. ABDE

Explanations
Answer: 2. BCDE

Category need: The objective to create awareness that a product or service category is required in the market.

Brand awareness: The goal of making consumers aware of the brand, ensuring that it is recognized.

Brand attitude: Shaping the consumer's positive perceptions and feelings toward the brand.

Brand purchase intention: Encouraging consumers to develop the intention to purchase the brand.

Why not others?

Belittling competitive brands is typically not an objective in marketing communication, as it can lead to negative advertising, which is generally less effective in the long term and can backfire.

Question

Identify the correct sequence of the following types of visual communication.

A. Objects
B. Maps
C. Graphs
D. Photographs.
E. Models

1. A, B, D, C, E
2. A, E, C, B, D
3. B, D, E, C, A
4. C, A, D, B, E

Explanations
Answer: 2. A, E, C, B, D

A. Objects: Real-world physical objects serve as the **most direct and tangible form of visual communication.**

E. Models: Models are **scaled representations of real objects,** providing a clearer perspective.

C. Graphs: Graphs present **quantitative data visually, making complex information understandable.**

B. Maps: Maps visually represent **geographical or spatial relationships,** combining abstraction and clarity.

D. Photographs: Photographs **capture real-life scenarios or subjects** visually and accurately.

Propaganda

- **Persuades for Specific Agendas** – Shapes opinions.
- **Uses Selective Facts & Bias** – Controls narratives.
- **Appeals to Emotions Over Logic** – Influences deeply.
- **Loaded Language Creates Impact** – Evokes strong reactions.
- **Can Be Positive or Negative** – Varies in intent.

Question

Assertion (A): Communication has the power to inform, persuade and misinform.
Reason (R): Propaganda blurs the thin line between truth and falsehood to be persuasive.

1. Both (A) and (R) are true and (R) is the correct explanation of (A)
2. Both (A) and (R) are true, but (R) is not the correct explanation of (A)
3. (A) is true, but (R) is false
4. (A) is false, but (R) is true

Explanations
Answer: 1. Both (A) and (R) are true and (R) is the correct explanation of (A)

Assertion (A) is correct because communication has the power to **inform**, **persuade**, and **misinform**. This highlights the dual role of communication, as it can convey accurate or misleading information.

Reason (R) is also correct because **propaganda** often involves blurring the lines between **truth** and **falsehood** to make a message more persuasive. This is how propaganda manipulates information for persuasive purposes.

Question

Which of the following is considered unethical communication?

1. Use of alternative source of information
2. Not revealing the source of information
3. Propaganda
4. Non-commercial publicity

Explanations
Answer: 3. Propaganda

Propaganda is often considered unethical because it involves manipulating information, distorting facts, or using biased or misleading messaging to influence public opinion or promote a specific agenda. It typically lacks transparency and can mislead people intentionally.

Question

Assertion (A): Communication has the power to persuade. inform and misinform.
Reasons (R): The process of propaganda makes the line of distinction transparent between its elements for being persuasive.

1. Both A and R are true and R is the correct explanation of A
2. Both A and R are true but R is NOT the correct explanation of A
3. A is true but R is false
4. A is false but R is true

Explanations
Answer: 3. A is true but R is false

A is true: Communication indeed has the power to persuade, inform, and disinform, as it shapes perceptions and actions.

R is false: Propaganda does not necessarily make the distinction between elements (truth and falsehood) clear for persuasion. In fact, it often blurs those lines to manipulate opinions, which makes the reasoning incorrect.

Question

Subliminal communication is part of-

1. Government notification
2. Political propaganda

3. Legal documentation
4. Research reports

Explanations
Answer: 2. Political propaganda

Explanation: Subliminal communication is often associated with political propaganda, as it involves messages that are designed to influence the audience on a subconscious level. These messages may be hidden or subtly embedded in media to shape opinions without the audience being fully aware of the influence.

Question

Condensation symbols in political communication are -

1. Dormant
2. Evocative
3. Weak assumptions
4. Escapist

Explanations
Answer: 2. Evocative

Explanation: Condensation symbols in political communication are evocative because they carry a wealth of emotional and symbolic meaning, often triggering strong feelings or associations in the audience. These symbols help simplify complex political messages and make them more relatable or impactful.

Question

Statement I: Propagandic communication at the National level is supposed to recognize the fact that truth need not be separated from falsehood.
Statement II: The mediated propaganda process blurs truth and falsehood in order to be persuasive.

1. Both Statement I and Statement II are true
2. Both Statement I and Statement II are false
3. Statement I is true but Statement II is false

4. Statement I is false but Statement I is true

Explanations
Answer: 1. Both Statement I and Statement II are true

Explanation: Both statements are correct. Propagandic communication often blurs the line between truth and falsehood to persuade and manipulate audiences at the national level. This helps in shaping opinions without clear separation of facts from misinformation, making it more effective for mass persuasion.

Question

Statement I: By supplying facts and opinions, mass media enable the audience to make decisions.
Statement II: Mass media should supress facts and opinions in order to influence the government decisions.

1. Both Statement I and Statement II are true.
2. Both Statement I and Statement II are false.
3. Statement I is true but Statement Il is false.
4. Statement I is false but Statement Il is true.

Explanations
Answer: 3. Statement I is true but Statement Il is false.

Statement I is true: Mass media provides facts and opinions, empowering audiences to make informed decisions.

Statement II is false: Suppressing facts and opinions contradicts the fundamental role of mass media, which is to promote transparency and informed public discourse rather than manipulate decisions.

Public Relations (PR)

- **Manages Public Image** – Shapes reputations.
- **Controls Internal Communication** – Maintains brand consistency.
- **Engages Media & Public** – Builds strong relations.
- **Influences Public Perception** – Enhances credibility.
- **Differs from Publicity** – Maintains control.

Enrichment & Education

- **Mass Media Expands Knowledge** – Enhances learning.
- **Simplifies Complex Concepts** – Improves understanding.
- **Stimulates Curiosity & Interest** – Engages learners.
- **Provides Visual & Audio Learning** – Enhances retention.
- **Supports Formal & Informal Education** – Broadens knowledge.

Entertainment

- **Includes Music, Films, & Games** – Engages audiences.
- **Provides Leisure & Enjoyment** – Relieves stress.
- **Influences Cultural Trends** – Shapes entertainment.
- **Evolves With Technology** – Expands accessibility.
- **SITE stands** for **"Satellite Instructional Television Experiment."**
- **Blends Art & Commercialization** – Drives industry growth.

Question

In the context of communication the acronym 'SITE' is

1. Satellite Instructional Television Education
2. Science Instructional Television Education
3. Science Instructional Television Experiment
4. Satellite Instructional Television Experiment

Explanations
Answer: 4. Satellite Instructional Television Experiment

In the context of communication, the acronym **'SITE'** stands for **"Satellite Instructional Television Experiment."**

Question

What does the acronym "TRP" mean?

1. Television Recording Parameter
2. Telephone Recording Points
3. Television Rating Parameter
4. Television Rating Points

Explanations
Answer: 4. Television Rating Points

TRP (Television Rating Points) measures the **popularity and viewership of television programs**. It helps advertisers and broadcasters **analyze audience preferences** and determine the **reach and impact** of TV shows.

Question

The domain of media appeal addresses the issues related to

1. Knowledge
2. Learning
3. Legality
4. Emotions

Explanations
Answer: 4. Emotions

The domain of media appeal is concerned with influencing emotions, as media often aims to evoke emotional responses from the audience to drive engagement or action. Other options like knowledge or legality are related to the content but not the core emotional appeal.

Question

The main purpose of establishing Television in India at the initial stage was:

1. News
2. Entertainment
3. Education and awareness among the rural population
4. Scientific development

Explanations
Answer: 3. Education and awareness among the rural population

The primary purpose of establishing **Television in India** during its initial stage (1959) was to **educate and create awareness among rural populations** about health, agriculture, and social development. This was evident in projects like **SITE (Satellite Instructional Television Experiment)** in the 1970s.

attention, making them newsworthy. Therefore, **(R)** correctly explains why **(A)** is newsworthy.

Question

Being a smart consumer of media means:

1. Following a few select TV channels one likes
2. Belief in a few mass media channels
3. Disbelief in messages received
4. Being adept at recognizing subtle and not subtle forms of messages

Explanations
Answer: 4. Being adept at recognizing subtle and not subtle forms of messages

Being a smart consumer of media means being able to critically assess and understand the messages conveyed by various media forms. This involves recognizing both obvious and subtle forms of communication, which includes identifying biases, motivations, and hidden messages. Simply following a few channels or believing media without scrutiny does not demonstrate media literacy. Therefore, **option 4** is the correct choice.

Journalism

- **Reports Events & News** – Informs society.
- **Distributes Reliable Information** – Ensures credibility.
- **Holds Authority Accountable** – Supports transparency.
- **Uses Investigative Techniques** – Exposes facts.
- **Adapts to Digital Evolution** – Expands reach.
- **Citizen journalism** refers to the **collection, reporting, and dissemination of news** by **ordinary individuals.**

Question

The production and distribution of news by ordinary people is referred to as:

1. Popular journalism
2. Common journalism
3. Citizen journalism
4. New journalism

Explanations
Answer: 3. Citizen journalism

Citizen journalism refers to the **collection, reporting, and dissemination of news** by **ordinary individuals** rather than professional journalists. It typically involves the use of digital platforms like blogs, social media, and independent websites.

Why not the other options?

Popular journalism: Focuses on content that appeals to mass audiences, not necessarily produced by ordinary people.

Common journalism: This term is **not widely recognized** in the field of journalism.

New journalism: Refers to a **writing style** that blends literary techniques with factual reporting, primarily by professionals.

Question

Assertion (A): A man pulls a loaded truck by his hair which becomes news.
Reasons (R): Unusual things make news called oddity and generate public interest.

1. Both (A) and (R) are correct and (R) is the correct explanation of (A).
2. Both (A) and (R) are correct but (R) is NOT the correct explanation of (A).
3. (A) is correct but (R) is not correct.
4. (A) is not correct but (R) is correct.

Explanations
Answer: 1. Both (A) and (R) are correct and (R) is the correct explanation of (A).

Assertion (A): The example of a man pulling a loaded truck by his hair is unusual and attention-grabbing, making it newsworthy.

Reason (R): Unusual events, known as oddities, are often deemed newsworthy because they generate public interest due to their rare or strange nature.

Question

Statement I: In mass communication, the news content includes social values also.
Statement Il: News also contains ideology that changes according to times.

1. Both Statement I and Statement Il are correct.
2. Both Statement I and Statement Il are incorrect.
3. Statement I is correct but Statement Il is incorrect.
4. Statement I is incorrect but Statement Il is correct.

Explanations
Answer: 1. Both Statement I and Statement Il are correct.

Statement I is correct: News content often reflects social values, as it is influenced by cultural, societal, and ethical standards. This makes news a mirror of the society it represents.

Statement II is correct: Ideologies embedded in news evolve with societal changes, reflecting shifts in political, cultural, and economic contexts over time.

Correlation

- **Determines Newsworthiness** – Filters information.
- **Shapes Media Interpretations** – Frames stories.
- **Guides Public Awareness** – Highlights key issues.
- **Connects Experts With Audiences** – Provides insights.
- **Influences News & Perceptions** – Affects perspectives.

Public Service Announcements (PSA)

- **Short Media Messages** – Spreads awareness.

- **Airs on Radio & TV** – Reaches public.
- **Encourages Social Awareness** – Educates society.
- **Promotes Public Safety & Health** – Guides citizens.
- **Government & NGOs Use PSA** – Drives initiatives.

Surveillance

- **Monitors Global Events** – Provides updates.
- **Delivers Real-Time News** – Informs audiences.
- **Tracks Political & Social Issues** – Ensures awareness.
- **Alerts Public in Crisis** – Provides warnings.
- **Supports Investigative Journalism** – Uncovers truth.

Question

Match the column:

A. Publicity	I. Reputation management
B. Propaganda	II. Paid message
C. Advertising	III. Non-commercial promotion
D. Public relations	IV. Communication with motives

1. A-I B-II C-III D-IV
2. A-II B-III C-IV D-I
3. A-IV B-I C-III D-II
4. A-III B-IV C-II D-I

Explanations
Answer: 4. A-III B-IV C-II D-I

A-III: Publicity - Non-commercial promotion: Publicity refers to efforts to promote something without direct payment, aiming to increase visibility without commercial objectives.
B-IV: Propaganda - Communication with motives: Propaganda involves spreading information or ideas to influence the audience, often with specific motives or agendas behind it.
C-II: Advertising - Paid message: Advertising is a paid communication aimed at promoting a product, service, or idea.

D-I: Public relations - Reputation management: Public relations is primarily focused on managing and enhancing the reputation of an individual or organization.

Question

Match the column:

A. surveillance	I. to influence public opinion
B. correlation	II. provide pleasure
C. propaganda	III. supply of information
D. cultural transmission	IV. interpretation

1. A-I, B-II, C-II, D-IV
2. A-II, B-I, C-IV, D-III
3. A-III, B-IV, C-I, D-II
4. A-IV, B-I, C-III, D-II

Explanations
Answer: 3. A-III, B-IV, C-I, D-II

A-III (Surveillance - Supply of information): Surveillance refers to providing the necessary information to keep people informed.

B-IV (Correlation - Interpretation): Correlation involves interpreting the information and forming conclusions.

C-I (Propaganda - To influence public opinion): Propaganda aims to shape and influence public opinion through selective information dissemination.

D-II (Cultural transmission - Provide pleasure): Cultural transmission involves sharing culture, traditions, and values, often for the enjoyment and learning of others.

Gatekeeping

- **Filters Information Flow** – Controls narratives.
- **Determines Media Content** – Selects news stories.
- **Limits or Expands Messages** – Influences perception.
- **Ensures News Accuracy** – Maintains credibility.

- **Shapes Public Knowledge** – Directs understanding.

Question

Gatekeeping by media to ensure what audiences consume is indicative of

1. The audiences' voice in media programming
2. Media's control on society
3. Feedback received by the media
4. Media's role in creating culture

Explanations
Answer: 2. Media's control on society

Gatekeeping refers to the process where media organizations decide what information is shared with the public and what is withheld. This process reflects the **media's control** over the flow of information, influencing how society views events, issues, and topics. It shows the influence of media in shaping public perception and societal values.

Question

In both mass communication and classroom communication, filtering of information and contents is referred to as

1. Rationalisation
2. Gate keeping
3. Content correction
4. One - way flow

Explanations
Answer: 2. Gate keeping

Question

Statement I: In a classroom, every teacher has to perform the gatekeeping function
Statement II: Every teacher in any higher educational institution should act as the moral custodian of students, both inside and outside it

1. Both Statement I and Statement II are true

2. Both Statement I and Statement Il are false
3. Statement I is correct but Statement Il is false
4. Statement I is incorrect but Statement Il is true

Explanations

Answer: 3. Statement I is correct but Statement Il is false

Statement I is correct because **gatekeeping** in a classroom refers to the teacher's role in controlling the flow of information, deciding what content is presented, and managing the educational environment. Teachers do, in fact, perform this function by selecting, prioritizing, and filtering the information they teach.

Statement II is false because while teachers do have ethical responsibilities, being the "moral custodian" of students **outside** the institution isn't typically part of their professional role. Teachers are responsible for guiding and mentoring students inside the classroom and ensuring a positive, respectful learning environment, but their responsibility doesn't extend to being moral custodians outside of academic settings.

Question

Match the column:

A. Gatekeeping	I. Time-binding capacity
B. Persuasion	II. News
C. Entropy	III. Advertising
D. Memory	IV. Chaos in communication

1. A-II B-III C-IV D-I
2. A-III B-IV C-II D-I
3. A-IV B-I C-II D-III
4. A-I B-II C-III D-IV

Explanations

Answer: 1. A-II B-III C-IV D-I

- **A. Gatekeeping → II. News**
- **B. Persuasion → III. Advertising**
- **C. Entropy → IV. Chaos in communication**

- **D. Memory → I. Time-binding capacity**

Question

Net neutrality is the principle that all internets be treated equally.

1. Users
2. Data
3. Servers
4. Routers

Explanations
Answer: 2. Data
Net neutrality is the principle that **all data on the internet should be treated equally**, without discrimination by **internet service providers (ISPs)**. This means **no preferential treatment, throttling, or blocking** based on content, user, or platform.

Influence on Democracy

- **Media as Fourth Estate** – Monitors power.
- **Frames Political Issues** – Shapes debates.
- **Supports Democratic Principles** – Ensures transparency.
- **Informs Citizens of Policies** – Educates voters.
- **Challenges Government Actions** – Promotes accountability.

Cultural Transmission

- **Spreads Cultural Norms** – Preserves traditions.
- **Uses Media as a Medium** – Transfers values.
- **Influences Social Behaviors** – Shapes practices.
- **Reflects Societal Changes** – Adapts over time.
- **Defines Collective Identity** – Strengthens heritage.

Question

Statement I: Knowledge is a form of cultural capital for all practical purposes
Statement II: Communication media make cultural capital a form of illimitable property.

1. Both Statement I and Statement II are correct
2. Both Statement I and Statement II are incorrect
3. Statement I is correct but Statement II is incorrect
4. Statement I is incorrect but Statement II is correct

Explanations
Answer: 1. Both Statement I and Statement II are correct

Statement I: Knowledge as a form of cultural capital refers to how knowledge is a valuable resource in society, contributing to an individual's or group's power, status, and ability to influence.

Statement II: Communication media amplify and democratize access to cultural capital, turning knowledge into an ever-expandable resource that can be accessed by a wider audience, making it "illimitable."

Social Influence

- **Shapes Public Norms** – Sets trends.
- **Encourages Social Acceptance** – Reinforces behaviors.
- **Creates Common Knowledge** – Builds awareness.
- **Media Strengthens Influence** – Expands reach.
- **Coordinates Collective Actions** – Drives movements.

Characteristics of a Mass Media:

According to sociologist John Thompson of Cambridge University, mass communication exhibits five characteristics:

1. Comprises both technical and institutional methods of production and distribution.
2. Involves the commodification of symbolic forms.
3. Separate contexts between the production and reception of information.
4. It reaches those far removed in time and space compared to the producers.
5. Information distribution.

Influence of Mass Media

Media influence and media effects are topics in media studies, media psychology, communication theory, and sociology related to how mass media and media culture affect individuals' thoughts, attitudes, and behaviours. Mass media reaches a wide audience, whether it be through written or televised content. The role and impact of mass media on modern culture are central concerns in the study of culture.

Mass media affects many aspects of human life, such as voting a certain way, individual beliefs, or skewing a person's knowledge of a particular topic due to false information. Mass media have gained significant influence over the past few decades and will continue to do so as the media develops.

There is a profound influence of the media on the psychosocial development of children. Media effects studies have a broad scope, which presents an organizational challenge. An effective method is to organize media effects based on their intended audience type, either on an individual level (micro) or on a macro level.

Micro-Level Media Effects:

There are six ways in which individuals can be affected on a micro level.

1. ***Cognitive or* Priming**: The concept derives from the notion of a network model of memory in cognitive psychology. In this context, it refers to any new information, meaning, or message acquired through media consumption. Patterns can be identified, information sources can be combined, and new behaviours can be inferred from the information.
2. ***Beliefs***: People cannot validate every single media message, but they may believe many messages, even those relating to events, people, places, and ideas they have never experienced personally.
3. ***Attitudes***: Regardless of their intentions, media messages often trigger judgments or attitudes.
4. ***Effect***: The emotional impact of media exposure on an individual, whether positive or negative.
5. ***Physiological***: Media content may cause an automatic physical reaction, such as a fight-or-flight response or dilated pupils.
6. ***Behaviours***: Researchers assess whether an individual's behaviour changes or is reinforced in response to media content.

Macro-level media effects

The following are some examples of media effects studies that examine media influence on an aggregate audience.

- **Cultivation**: Media effects are not always instantaneous or short-lived. As audiences become accustomed to repetitive themes and storylines, they may also begin to expect them to occur in the real world. In the context of media messages, particularly television, audiences can draw inferences about the world portrayed from the real world.
- **Agenda-setting theory:** It explains how topic selection and the frequency of coverage in the mass media affect the perceived salience of specific topics in the public sphere.
- **Framing:** Public opinion can be influenced by controlling information presentation variables. It is common for news gathering professionals to curate facts to emphasize a particular viewpoint. By carefully controlling angles, facts, opinions, and the amount of coverage of a media message, the media can manipulate audience interpretations of media messages.

Question

Statement I: In mass communication, the message is rapid and public
Statement II: New technology has blurred the distinction between inter-personal communication and mass

1. Both Statement (I) and Statement (II) are correct.
2. Both Statement I) and Statement (II) are incorrect.
3. Statement (I) is correct but Statement (II) is incorrect
4. Statement (I) is incorrect but Statement (II) is correct

Explanations
Answer: 1. Both Statement (I) and Statement (II) are correct.

Statement (I): Mass communication is characterized by rapid dissemination of information to a public audience, making it accurate.

Statement (II): Advancements in technology, such as social media, have indeed blurred the lines between interpersonal and mass communication, making this correct.

Question

Statement I: Communication media are neither neutral nor value free containers that carry information to different places
Statement II: No Communication technology has its own unique set of physical, technical, symbolic and environmental characteristics.

1. Both Statement (I) and Statement (II) are correct.
2. Both Statement (I) and Statement (II) are incorrect.
3. Statement (I) is correct but Statement (II) is incorrect.
4. Statement (I) is incorrect but Statement (II) is correct.

Explanations
Answer: 3. Statement (I) is correct but Statement (II) is incorrect.

Statement (I): Communication media are influenced by cultural, societal, and contextual values, making them neither neutral nor value-free containers. This is correct.

Statement (II): Every communication technology has unique characteristics that shape how it is used and perceived, making this statement incorrect.

Marshall McLuhan's Key Concepts

- **The Medium is the Message** – Medium shapes perception over content.
- **Hot and Cool Media** – Differ in audience engagement levels.
- **Global Village** – Media connects people worldwide instantly.
- **High-Definition vs. Low-Definition Media** – Varies in sensory detail and participation.
- **Retribalization** – Digital media revives oral culture.
- **Media as Extensions of Man** – Technology expands human capabilities.
- **Tetrad of Media Effects** – Enhances, obsolesces, retrieves, reverses impact.

- **Print Culture vs. Electronic Culture** – Print is linear; digital is dynamic.
- **Acoustic vs. Visual Space** – Oral traditions differ from literate culture.
- **Media Alters Social Structures** – Changes interaction and communication patterns.
- High-definition media provide detailed information clarity.
- Low-definition media require greater audience participation.
- Cartoons are considered low-definition media.
- Hot media supply large amounts of information.
- Hot media need little interpretation or effort.
- Radio is an acoustic and hot medium.
- Print media are asynchronous, delivering high information.
- Cool media encourage high audience participation.
- Television is a cool medium of communication.
- Cool media provide limited, low-definition information.
- Hot media include cinema, radio, and print.
- Cool media require user involvement to complete.
- Television fosters engagement and audience contribution.
- Marshall McLuhan distinguished hot and cool media types.
- Hot media envelopes a single sense experience.
- Cool media often supplement hot media forms.
- High participation defines the characteristics of cool media.
- "The medium is the message" by McLuhan emphasizes impact.
- Media shapes societal behavior beyond content delivered.
- McLuhan's work focuses on media influence dynamics.

High-Definition (HD) Media

- **Rich Sensory Detail** – Provides clear, detailed information.
- **Minimal Audience Participation** – Requires little interpretation.
- **Engages a Single Sense Deeply** – Focuses on one sensory channel.
- **Encourages Passive Consumption** – Audience absorbs content directly.
- **Examples: Radio, Film, Print Media** – Fully-formed message delivery.

Low-Definition (LD) Media

- **Limited Sensory Input** – Requires audience interpretation.
- **High Audience Engagement** – Encourages active participation.
- **Engages Multiple Senses** – Stimulates interaction.
- **Encourages Mental Effort** – Viewers fill in gaps.
- **Examples: TV, Speech, Cartoons** – Interactive meaning-making

Question

According to Marshal McLuhan, examples of high-definition media are:

A. Speech
B. Photograph
C. Radio
D. Cinema
E. Cartoon

1. ABC
2. BCD
3. CDE
4. ADE

Explanations
Answer: 2. BCD

Marshal McLuhan's concept of "high-definition" media refers to media that are rich in data and detail, requiring minimal effort from the audience to interpret.

Photograph: Highly detailed, presenting clear visual information.

Radio: Provides rich auditory information, engaging the listener directly.

Cinema: Combines detailed visual and auditory information, making it immersive.

Why not other options?

Speech (A): Considered "low-definition" as it requires active interpretation by the audience.

Cartoon (E): Simplified and abstract, requiring more audience involvement to interpret.

Question

A cartoon is of :

1. High definition
2. Low definition
3. Neutral definition
4. Negative definition

Explanations
Answer: 2. Low definition

Cartoons are considered "low-definition" media as per Marshal McLuhan's theory because they are abstract and simplified, leaving room for the audience to interpret and fill in the details.

Why not other options?

High definition: Cartoons lack the rich detail required to be considered high-definition.

Neutral definition: This is not a recognized category in McLuhan's framework.

Negative definition: This term is unrelated to the media classification.

Hot Media

- **High Definition Content** – Provides extensive sensory details.
- **Requires Less Audience Participation** – Passive consumption.
- **Examples Include Radio & Cinema** – Engages limited senses deeply.
- **Delivers Clear & Detailed Information** – Minimal user involvement.
- **Encourages Passive Engagement** – Little effort to interpret.

Question

A hot medium has the features of:

A. Pre-supposition of interaction
B. Providing large amounts of information
C. Little effort needed for interpretation
D. Less scope for participation
E. Immediate feedback

1. A, B, C
2. C, D, E
3. A, C, D
4. B, C, D

Explanations
Answer: 4. B, C, D

Hot medium: Marshal McLuhan's concept of a "hot medium" describes media that deliver detailed, high-definition content, engaging only one sense and requiring minimal audience involvement.

Providing large amounts of information (B): Hot media, such as films or books, are rich in detail and information.

Little effort needed for interpretation (C): They present information in a clear, self-sufficient manner.

Less scope for participation (D): The audience passively absorbs the content with limited interaction.

Why not other options?

Pre-supposition of interaction (A): This is a feature of "cool" media, which require audience involvement.

Immediate feedback (E): This is not a characteristic of hot media but rather of interactive communication.

Question

Match the column:

A. Radio	I. Asynchronous
B. Print	II. High intensity of information

C. Hot medium	Ill. Interactivity
D. Internet	IV. Only Acoustic medium

1. A-I, B-II, C-III, D-IV
2. A-II, B-III, C-IV, D-I
3. A-III, B-IV, C-I, D-II
4. A-IV, B-I, C-II, D-III

Explanations
Answer: 4. A-IV, B-I, C-II, D-III

Radio - Only Acoustic medium (A-IV): Radio relies solely on sound and is considered an acoustic medium.

Print - Asynchronous (B-I): Print media does not rely on real-time interaction and is consumed at the reader's convenience, making it asynchronous.

Hot medium - High intensity of information (C-II): Hot media, like print or film, provide detailed and high-definition content requiring minimal interpretation.

Internet - Interactivity (D-III): The internet is an interactive medium that allows users to engage actively with content and each other.

Question

Which of the following are considered hot media?

A. Telephone
B. Television
C. Radio
D. Cinema
E. Photographs

1. ABC
2. BCD
3. CDE
4. ADE

Explanations
Answer: 3. CDE

Radio, Cinema, Photographs (CDE): These are considered **hot media** as they provide high-definition content and require minimal audience participation. They convey a substantial amount of information in a straightforward manner.

Why not other options?

A (Telephone): Telephone is a **cool medium** because it involves high interaction and effort to interpret the conversation.

B (Television): Television is also a **cool medium** as it combines audio and visuals, requiring audience engagement and interpretation.

Question

According to some experts like Marshal McLuhan, the following are considered hot media:

A. Telephone
B. Television
C. Radio
D. Cinema
E. Print

1. A, B, C
2. B, C, D
3. C, D, E
4. A, C, E

Explanations
Answer: 3. C, D, E

Radio (C): Hot media provide extensive information with minimal audience participation, and radio fits this description as it delivers content with high detail.

Cinema (D): Cinema is a hot medium due to its high-definition visuals and rich audio, requiring little interpretation from the audience.

Print (E): Print is considered hot as it delivers detailed and structured information, requiring focus but minimal participation.

Question

A hot medium is characterised by-

A. Non mechanical components
B. Low Audience participation
C. It envelopes only one sense
D. Large amounts of information supplies
E. High audience participation

1. ABC
2. BCD
3. CDE
4. ADE

Explanations
Answer: 2. BCD

Low audience participation: Hot media provide detailed and high-definition content, requiring minimal interaction or engagement from the audience.

It envelops only one sense: Hot media often stimulate a single sense, such as sight (e.g., movies) or hearing (e.g., radio).

Large amounts of information supplies: Hot media deliver detailed and abundant information, leaving little to the audience's imagination.

Why not other options?

Non-mechanical components (A): Hot media can involve mechanical processes, like television and cinema, making this irrelevant.

High audience participation (E): High participation is a characteristic of cool media, not hot media.

Cool Media

- **Low Definition Content** – Requires audience interpretation.
- **Encourages High Participation** – Interactive engagement needed.
- **Examples Include TV & Telephone** – Users fill in missing details.
- **Delivers Fragmented Information** – Demands active involvement.
- **Stimulates Audience Imagination** – Encourages mental interaction.

Question

The characteristics of cool media are:

1. High participation
2. Low definition
3. High definition
4. Small amount of information
5. High amount of information

1. A, B, C
2. B, C, D
3. C, D, E
4. A, B, D

Explanations
Answer: 4. A, B, D

High Participation (A): Cool media demand significant audience engagement to fill in the gaps and interpret content.

Low Definition (B): They provide limited information, requiring the audience to actively contribute meaning.

Small Amount of Information (D): Cool media convey less detailed content, encouraging more interpretation and interaction.

Why not other options?

C (High Definition): High-definition content is a feature of **hot media**, not cool media.

E (High Amount of Information): This is also a characteristic of **hot media**, which provides extensive information with minimal audience effort.

Question

One of the cool media of communication is:

1. Print
2. Television
3. Photograph
4. Radio

Explanations
Answer: 2.

Television: It is a **cool medium** as it offers low definition and requires active participation and interpretation from the viewers. The combination of audio and visual elements engages the audience interactively.

Why not other options?

Print: A **hot medium** as it delivers detailed, high-definition content with little need for interpretation.

Photograph: A **hot medium** because it conveys high-definition visual information with minimal engagement required.

Radio: Another **hot medium** due to its high-definition audio content that delivers information directly, requiring less audience participation.

Question

A cool medium has the features of:

A. High definition
B. High participation
C. It provides small amount of information
D. Tends not to be supplemented by hot media
E. supplemented by hot media

1. ABC
2. CD
3. BCE
4. BDE

Explanations
Answer: 3. BCE

High participation: Cool media require audience engagement and active interpretation (e.g., television, cartoons).

It provides a small amount of information: Cool media offer low-definition content that leaves gaps for the audience to fill.

Supplemented by hot media: Cool media are often complemented by hot media for providing additional clarity or detail.

Why not other options?

High definition (A): Cool media are characterized by low definition, not high definition.

Tends not to be supplemented by hot media (D): Cool media often rely on hot media for support to increase clarity or reduce ambiguity.

Question

Marshall Mcluhan's name is associated with the assertion:

1. The message is the medium
2. The medium is the message
3. The message determines the medium accurately
4. A message is a message

Explanations
Answer: 2. The medium is the message

Marshall McLuhan famously coined the phrase *"The medium is the message."* This assertion highlights that the medium through which information is transmitted significantly influences how the message is perceived, shaping societal behaviors and thoughts more than the content itself.

Why not other options?

The message is the medium (1): This reverses McLuhan's concept and does not align with his views.

The message determines the medium accurately (3): McLuhan focused on the impact of the medium, not the message determining the medium.

A message is a message (4): This is oversimplified and ignores McLuhan's emphasis on the medium's impact.

Question

The media accountability system to improve media quality focuses on:

A. Evaluation
B. Audience control
C. Monitoring
D. Education
E. Feedback

Choose the correct answer from the options given below -

1. ABC
2. BCD
3. BDE
4. ACDE

Explanations
Answer: 4. ACDE

ACDE (Evaluation, Monitoring, Education, Feedback) are integral to improving media quality as they ensure accountability, learning, and corrective actions.

Audience control (B) is not a primary focus, as media accountability relies more on the systems and frameworks in place rather than the direct control of the audience.

Last Minute Revision

Key Concepts and Principles of Communication: A Comprehensive Overview:

- Communication is Inevitable – Happens in every interaction.
- Communication is Irreversible – Cannot undo delivered messages.
- Communication Reflects Culture – Mirrors societal values.
- Language is Social – Shaped by culture.
- Communication is Verbal & Non-Verbal – Uses words, gestures.
- Communication Shares Knowledge – Facilitates learning.
- Communication Defines Goals – Aligns objectives.
- Communication Supports Norms – Drives cultural acceptance.
- Communication Builds Relations – Strengthens connections.
- Communication Simplifies Tasks – Reduces confusion.
- Communication Manages Truth – Reveals or suppresses.
- Communication Affects Policy – Informs decisions.
- Popular Sources Improve Recall – Boosts retention.
- Communication Increases Awareness – Promotes knowledge.
- Communication is Cultural – Shares traditions.
- Communication Aids Socialization – Teaches norms.
- Communication Promotes Enculturation – Instills values.
- Family Builds Communication – First social learning.
- Motivation Drives Communication – Encourages engagement.
- Communication Builds Narratives – Shares stories.
- Personal Address Defines Roles – Builds relationships.
- Social Drama Reflects Culture – Shows values.
- Silence Holds Meaning – Context defines.
- Symbols Carry Meaning – Understood culturally.
- Communication is Emotional – Words convey feelings.
- Communication Shapes Reality – Alters perceptions.
- Communication is Social – Relies on understanding.
- Communication is Continuous – Adapts constantly.
- Language Frames Interaction – Guides understanding.
- Communication Builds Trust – Strengthens bonds.
- Narratives Share Perspectives – Express viewpoints.
- Communication Aids Leadership – Builds authority.
- Communication Aligns Goals – Ensures efficiency.
- Non-Verbal Cues Clarify – Enhance meaning.

- Communication Strengthens Communities – Builds identity.
- Social Interaction Fuels Communication – Drives exchange.
- Emotions Influence Communication – Shape interpretation.
- Communication Can Manipulate – Controls perceptions.
- Ethics Build Trust – Ensures honesty.
- Communication Enhances Education – Improves learning.
- Symbols are Culture-Specific – Vary globally.
- Communication Shapes Opinion – Influences society.
- Media Spreads Communication – Reaches globally.
- Communication Builds Connectivity – Breaks barriers.
- Feedback Completes Communication – Confirms understanding.
- Communication Structures Behavior – Defines norms.
- Credibility Strengthens Impact – Builds trust.
- Power Influences Communication – Shapes reception.
- Communication Sparks Change – Drives awareness.
- Communication is Context-Dependent – Meaning shifts.
- Primary Orality Relies on Spoken Traditions.
- Semiotics Analyzes Signs and Symbolic Meanings.
- Communication is Inter-subjective and Shared.
- Symbols Are Arbitrary and Culturally Conventional.
- Symbols Derive Meaning from Cultural Contexts.
- Symbolic Communication Reflects Socio-Cultural Values.
- Codes Are Never Neutral or Objective.
- Signs Form Meaning Through Relational Networks.
- Codes Represent Ideas in Communication Messages.
- Signs Gain Meaning from Inter-relationships.
- Symbolic Environments Build Community Connections.
- Social Interaction Strengthens Collective Bonds.
- Words Act as Symbols in Communication.
- Signs Are Tools for Conveying Messages.
- Communication Fosters Social Interaction and Unity.
- Symbols Are Context-Dependent for Meaning.
- Cultural Norms Shape Symbolic Communication Practices.
- Communication Builds Shared Social Realities.
- Channels Transmit Messages, Not Create Meaning.
- Codes Simplify Message Encoding and Decoding.
- Narratives Use Symbols to Share Stories.
- Symbols Carry Emotional and Cultural Weight.
- Meaning is Co-Constructed Between Participants.

- Symbols Reflect Cultural Identity and Values.
- Signs Rely on Context for Interpretation.
- Shared Understanding Ensures Effective Communication.
- Verbal Symbols Translate Thoughts into Words.
- Communication is a Two-Way Symbolic Process.
- Communication Shapes Social and Cultural Realities.
- Symbols Preserve and Express Cultural Values

Key Concepts in Communication Models and Processes

- Receiver completes the communication process cycle.
- Communication stages: Sender → Encoding → Transmission → Feedback.
- Semantic barriers arise from language issues.
- Physical context affects the communication environment directly.
- Psychological barriers include biases and assumptions.
- Physiological barriers stem from physical limitations.
- Communication situation defines overall interaction context.
- Feedback ensures clarity in communication cycles.
- Parsimony emphasizes simplicity in communication models.
- Schramm's model highlights interpreters' dual roles.
- Transactional model enables role interchanging.
- Linear communication is sender-centric and one-way.
- Linear model lacks interactive feedback loops.
- Transactional model emphasizes simultaneous feedback.
- Interactional model includes two-way communication.
- Physical, social, and cultural contexts matter.
- Social, cultural, relational contexts shape communication.
- Sender sends messages; receiver interprets meaning.
- Speech serves as a verbal communication channel.
- Decoding converts signals into meaningful messages.
- Communication follows: Encoding → Message → Medium → Decoding.
- Noise disrupts communication clarity during transmission.
- Linear model focuses on one-way message flow.
- Transactional model focuses on real-time interaction.
- Interactive model includes feedback and context.
- Aristotle's model focuses on speaker-centric communication.
- Shannon-Weaver emphasizes linear message transmission.
- Schramm highlights circular feedback interaction.

- David Berlo's model follows SMCR framework.
- Meaning emerges from internal message interpretation.
- Feedback completes the communication loop effectively.
- Context impacts message clarity and interpretation.
- Transactional model ensures dynamic role switching.
- Social norms influence effective communication exchanges.
- Psychological states impact message decoding clarity.
- Paralinguistic cues add emotional message context.
- Sender encodes messages for audience clarity.
- Speech acts as a rich communication channel.
- Communication focuses on sender-receiver interaction.
- Linear models prioritize sender over interaction.
- Transactional emphasizes active two-way exchanges.
- Noise interferes with message clarity and focus.
- Cultural norms shape message interpretation accuracy.
- Temporal context deals with message timing.
- Group discussions use transactional communication models.
- Aristotle highlights speaker-centered persuasive messages.
- Shannon-Weaver defines noise in linear communication.
- Schramm emphasizes continuous feedback interaction.
- David Berlo focuses on SMCR model elements.
- Effective communication depends on immediate feedback.
- Physical barriers disrupt message delivery accuracy.
- Transactional emphasizes simultaneous encoding and decoding.
- Feedback clarifies misunderstandings in communication.
- Encoding structures raw ideas into clear messages.
- Decoding ensures message understanding post-transmission.
- Transactional adapts to relational communication dynamics.
- Interactional emphasizes delayed but clear feedback.
- Linear lacks adaptability to immediate responses.
- Relational context shapes message tone and delivery.
- Social context adds layers to communication meaning.

Key Principles of Organizational and Classroom Communication

- Organizational communication is applied and practical.
- Grapevine reveals morale and employee concerns.
- Social networks drive grapevine communication flow.
- Diagonal communication crosses hierarchical boundaries.
- Diagonal communication boosts morale and coordination.

- Lateral communication occurs between team members.
- Lateral communication promotes collaboration and teamwork.
- Upward communication flows from subordinates to superiors.
- Downward communication flows from superiors to subordinates.
- Diagonal communication bypasses traditional reporting structures.
- Animated classroom discussions foster horizontal communication.
- Horizontal communication encourages mutual exchange of ideas.
- Linear communication involves one-way message flow.
- Mechanical communication relies on technology or automation.
- Grapevine spreads through informal social interactions.
- Classroom discussions support collaborative communication styles.
- Effective diagonal communication improves organizational efficiency.
- Lateral communication reduces misunderstandings and confusion.
- Feedback enhances clarity in communication exchanges.
- Communication fosters teamwork, morale, and productivity.

Key Insights into Lavels, Types, Stages, and Dynamics of Communication

- Communication types follow a logical progression.
- Mass communication targets large anonymous audiences.
- Intrapersonal communication involves self-reflection and dialogue.
- Group communication occurs in structured group settings.
- Interpersonal communication happens between two individuals.
- Mass communication relies on mediated channels.
- Horizontal communication fosters peer-level collaboration.
- Vertical communication follows hierarchical information flow.
- Transactional communication emphasizes mutual exchange.
- Circular communication relies on continuous feedback.
- Dyadic communication offers equal participation opportunities.
- Public communication occurs in formal settings.
- Network communication thrives on interdependent relationships.
- Group workshops encourage collaborative knowledge sharing.
- Intrapersonal reflection aids in personal insight.
- Google Meet classes represent group communication.
- Railway announcements are examples of public communication.
- Organizational communication follows structured message flow.
- Classroom teaching aligns with group communication.
- Self-reflection is key in intrapersonal communication.
- Communication apprehension arises from social anxiety.

- Mass communication struggles with delayed feedback.
- Interpersonal communication fosters homogeneity of opinion.
- Humans rely on five senses for communication.
- Writing letters is interpersonal verbal communication.
- Mass communication operates beyond interpersonal realms.
- Workplace gossip spreads through horizontal communication.
- Public communication addresses structured large audiences.
- Transactional communication focuses on interpersonal feedback.
- Self-awareness defines transcendental communication.
- Small groups foster unique communication dynamics.
- Internal conversations represent intrapersonal reflection.
- Dyadic communication involves two active participants.
- Workshops enable structured group interactions.
- Top-down messages characterize vertical communication.
- Rumor spreads through informal communication channels.
- Circular communication emphasizes ongoing feedback.
- Railway announcements exemplify structured public communication.
- Google Meet discussions facilitate group collaboration.
- Classroom communication blends structure with group interaction.
- Mass media enables large-scale message dissemination.
- Interpersonal discussions build strong relational dynamics.
- Network communication thrives on interconnected relationships.
- Self-talk shapes thoughts in intrapersonal dialogue.
- Social anxiety hinders effective communication interaction.
- Public speaking relies on formal communication structures.
- Horizontal communication improves team coordination.
- Vertical communication follows hierarchical command flow.
- Feedback improves communication clarity and understanding.
- Transcendental communication explores deeper self-awareness.

Key Concepts in Synchronous and Asynchronous Communication Technologies:

- Web conferencing enables real-time virtual interaction.
- Broadcast communication often happens live.
- Blogs allow delayed asynchronous communication.
- Podcasts enable flexible time-independent engagement.
- Emails facilitate delayed, asynchronous message exchange.
- Discussion boards support collaborative asynchronous interaction.
- Synchronous tools enable immediate real-time feedback.

- Video chat allows live face-to-face communication.
- Virtual classrooms foster dynamic live interaction.
- Audio conferencing supports real-time group discussions.
- Asynchronous tools include email and forums.
- Instant messaging typically enables synchronous communication.
- Forums support delayed, collaborative online discussions.
- Emails provide time-independent communication flexibility.
- Synchronous instructions enable live class participation.
- Teachers give real-time feedback in synchronous learning.
- Asynchronous instructions enable self-paced learning flexibility.
- Newspapers represent asynchronous communication channels.
- Video conferencing enables live virtual discussions.
- Instant messaging offers immediate real-time responses.
- Wikis support collaborative asynchronous document editing.
- Synchronous learning fosters active group participation.
- Asynchronous learning supports self-paced content access.
- Blogs offer delayed but interactive engagement.
- Email allows non-instant message delivery.
- Forums facilitate ongoing asynchronous topic discussions.
- Live sessions depend on synchronous platforms.
- Mass communication reaches large, diverse audiences.
- Online tools blend synchronous and asynchronous modes.
- Interaction style depends on communication technology.

Key Concepts and Principles of Communication (Latest Insights)

- Primary orality relies on spoken traditions.
- Semiotics studies meaning through signs.
- Communication is inter-subjective and shared.
- Symbols derive meaning from cultural context.
- Metacommunication conveys messages about messages.
- Non-verbal cues emphasize verbal communication.
- Non-verbal signals reflect emotions and attitudes.
- Proxemics focuses on spatial communication cues.
- Artifacts carry cultural and symbolic meaning.
- Paralinguistic features express tone and hesitation.
- Color communicates moods and emotional states.
- Feedback completes effective communication cycles.
- Context defines non-verbal communication meaning.
- Eye behavior offers metacommunicative cues.

- Personal space varies with cultural context.
- Shared beliefs influence communication effectiveness.
- Self-awareness enhances metacognitive communication.
- Effective communicators are culturally sensitive.
- Body language conveys emotional and social cues.
- Mirroring body language builds rapport.
- Non-verbal signals are mostly involuntary.
- Paralinguistics modifies verbal message interpretation.
- Smiles and laughter should match context.
- Non-verbal cues often outshine verbal messages.
- Territoriality defines personal communication spaces.
- Crowding affects non-verbal communication dynamics.
- Kinesics studies body movement and gestures.
- Effective speakers combine verbal and non-verbal cues.
- Teachers should adjust messages to student views.
- Communication competence enhances classroom outcomes.
- Edutainment combines education with entertainment.
- Non-verbal communication depends on shared contexts.
- Social norms influence emotional display rules.
- Non-verbal cues often substitute verbal messages.
- Symbols in communication are culturally defined.
- Metacommunication adds clarity to primary messages.
- Classroom communication includes instruction and management.
- Personal space varies based on cultural norms.
- Physical appearance affects communication impressions.
- Effective listening strengthens communication clarity.
- Feedback enhances message understanding and adjustment.
- Intentional gestures support verbal communication.
- Unintentional non-verbal cues reveal emotions.
- Cultural sensitivity prevents communication misunderstandings.
- Classroom communication builds trust and engagement.
- Non-verbal cues are often context-dependent.
- Proxemics defines interactional space boundaries.
- Metacommunication provides meaning beyond spoken words.
- Communication barriers include noise and ambiguity.
- Shared experiences shape communication interpretation.

Key Features and Insights of Modern Communication and Media

- Mass media informs, educates, and entertains audiences.

- Mass communication transmits cultural heritage and values.
- Anthropology, sociology, psychology enrich mass communication.
- Mass communication draws ideas from philosophy.
- Citizen journalism involves news by ordinary people.
- Mass communication requires a technological medium.
- Mass communication uses professionals for message creation.
- Features include rapid, structured, and public communication.
- Mass media employs institutional systems and reproduction.
- Mass media standardizes messages and commodifies culture.
- Mass communication uses space-time overcoming technology.
- Surveillance and correlation are mass media functions.
- Telegraph separated communication from transportation first.
- Newspapers are considered "one day best sellers."
- Radio is less expensive and effective educational media.
- Television initially focused on rural education awareness.
- Vladimir Zworykin invented the iconoscope for television.
- Print is categorized as a mechanical communication medium.
- Visual aids clarify and enhance written communication.
- Radio's personalization exceeds newspapers' static communication.
- Instagram exemplifies new interactive digital media.
- Chronological media evolution: Newspaper, radio, TV, internet.
- New media personalizes and expands learning environments.
- Harold Innis highlights papyrus as an early medium.
- FM is represented by stations like Radio Mirchi.
- Interactive communication is emphasized in learning design.
- Synchronous media includes video calls, live interactions.
- Asynchronous media includes email, forums, blogs, etc.
- Rich media integrates dynamic and interactive content.
- Hyper media combines text, visuals, and multimedia tools.
- Broadcasting involves audio-visual media like radio, TV.
- Infographics replace complex data with simple visuals.
- Barriers include semantic noise and cultural perceptions.
- Synchronous media requires real-time interaction.
- Mass media critiques include lack of aesthetics.
- Social contexts determine mass media's effects.
- Interactive models rely on feedback and adaptation.
- Transactional models include social, cultural contexts.
- Feedback in linear communication is delayed or absent.
- Email represents asynchronous communication effectively.

- Face-to-face media ensures immediate audience feedback.
- Mass communication targets heterogeneous global audiences.
- Infographics enhance comprehension in print communication.
- Semantic noise is reduced by avoiding jargon.
- Newspapers represent traditional static print media.
- Personalization boosts radio's engagement over newspapers.
- Educational radio aids non-literate population effectively.
- Internet allows asynchronous and multimedia communication.
- Hypermedia supports interactive educational environments.
- Telephone is an example of synchronous communication.
- Chronological sequence: Papyrus, paper, radio, internet.
- New media promotes self-designed learning processes.
- Transactional models feature role interchanging dynamics.
- Interactive learning thrives on real-time discussions.
- Mass media impacts societal and cultural integration.
- Photographs and visuals enhance textual communication.
- Citizen journalism democratizes news creation processes.
- Broadcast media includes structured, professional formats.
- Feedback improves communication efficiency and clarity.
- Mass communication relies on rapid message transmission.

Key Features and Insights on Modern Communication Systems

- Downtime refers to network inactivity periods.
- "War of the Worlds" preceded other media events.
- Chronological communication modes: Face-to-face to datacasting.
- Internet portals function like TV networks.
- Heavy internet use leads to addiction, depression.
- Emoticons replace gestures in digital communication.
- Technology enables efficient, complex communication systems.
- Analog media contents are linear in structure.
- Automation creates user-specific information online.
- Analog media term originates from audio recording.
- Digital media enables creation, distribution of content.
- Television fosters interactive, personalized media culture.
- Digital technology boosts media consumption significantly.
- Cable TV audiences introduced interactive media culture.
- Analog media audiences are large, heterogeneous, anonymous.
- Centralized signs control impacts internet plurality.
- Narrowcasting targets limited audiences with specific needs.

- Virtual interaction is aspatial and asynchronous.
- Digital communication creates interactive societies globally.
- Technological convergence drives the modern communication revolution.
- Rhetorical, semiotic, phenomenological are traditional approaches.
- Digital integration networks redefine communication frameworks.
- Interactive society emerges from digitized communication modes.
- Feedback delays due to semantic noise in classrooms.
- Narrowcasting uses noise-free, specialized media channels.
- Analog media lacks interactivity and customization.
- Digital media offers cheaper distribution alternatives.
- Linear communication models prioritize sender over receiver.
- Broadcast communication reaches large audiences quickly.
- Satellites redefined communication speed and efficiency globally.
- Integrated systems promote interactivity and socialization.
- Audience behavior influences modern media culture.
- Technological advancements redefine time-distance communication barriers.
- Television initially emphasized education, rural awareness.
- New media, like Instagram, revolutionize connectivity.

Key Barriers and Strategies in Effective Classroom Communication

- Philosophical barriers are not communication barriers.
- Semantic distortion causes unclear message meaning.
- Redundancy in writing creates semantic barriers.
- Attitude affects message acceptance significantly.
- Cultural values influence message interpretation.
- Status clash creates psychological communication barriers.
- Jargon confuses message meaning and clarity.
- Pre-judgment limits open communication understanding.
- Cultural background shapes message perception effectively.
- Semantic barriers arise from faulty messages.
- Psychological barriers include poor message retention.
- Personal barriers involve time management issues.
- Physical barriers include environmental disruptions.
- Low internet bandwidth is a technological barrier.
- Setting ground rules improves communication clarity.
- Perceptions create cross-cultural communication barriers.

- Ill health disrupts physical communication clarity.
- Psychological barriers include mental biases and stress.
- Clear enunciation improves instructional communication clarity.
- Purposeful interaction enhances classroom communication effectiveness.
- Focused listening ensures message clarity and retention.
- Information overload delays effective classroom feedback.
- Semantic noise arises from unclear message interpretation.
- Physical, semantic, and psychological noises disrupt communication.
- Semantic noise delays classroom communication feedback.
- Polysemy creates multiple interpretations and confusion.
- Clichés reduce clarity and effectiveness of communication.
- Simple language enhances message clarity and understanding.
- Effective communication avoids ambiguous or unclear phrases.
- Use of clichés reduces communication precision.
- Jargon adds unnecessary complexity to messages.
- Psychological noise hinders clarity and message focus.
- Physical noise disrupts auditory and visual clarity.
- Delayed feedback reduces classroom interaction efficiency.
- Polysemy increases confusion in message interpretation.
- Status clashes affect openness in communication.
- Participatory environments reduce feedback delays.
- Technology aids quick and precise communication feedback.
- Message clarity depends on reduced semantic barriers.
- Focused listening prevents misunderstandings in classrooms.

Key Points on Communication Systems and Media Development

- Broadcast era marked by one-way communication.
- Post-modern mass media emphasizes mobility, globalization.
- Personalized information dominates the post-information age.
- Interactive technologies led to second media age.
- First printing press in India at Goa.
- Vitascope development led to silent films.
- Broadcast media began with one-way communication.
- Printing access led to mass media emergence.
- Chronological order: hieroglyphics, daily publications, cameras.
- Cinema is not a traditional communication medium.
- Hickey's Bengal Gazette was India's first newspaper.
- Johannes Gutenberg invented the printing process.

- Interactive communication tech led to second media age.
- Market-specific communication is enabled by technology.
- Yakshagana, Puppetry, Hari Katha are traditional media.
- Correct sequence: cave paintings, language, printing, telecom.
- Chronological phases: cave paintings, Acta Diurna, metal printing.
- Telecommunication revolutionized communication technologies globally.
- Digital media promotes interactivity and automation.
- Analog media originated from audio recordings.
- Broadcast era controlled state communication heavily.
- Printing press democratized access to information.
- Post-modern media emphasizes simulation and mobility.
- Goa saw India's first printing press establishment.
- Development of vitascope led to silent film era.
- Cave paintings preceded language development chronologically.
- Emergence of printing led to mass communication.
- Cultural media forms include Yakshagana, Puppetry.
- Second media age emphasizes interactive media culture.
- Johannes Gutenberg revolutionized communication with printing.

Key Points on Media Communication, Marketing, and Consumer Awareness

- Smart consumers recognize subtle media messages.
- Unusual events generate public interest and news.
- Media knowledge is a form of cultural capital.
- Knowledge is considered cultural capital for society.
- Marketing communication objectives include brand awareness.
- Brand purchase intention influences marketing communication.
- Media continuously evolve with human experience.
- The flux of media operations and effects.
- Cultural capital becomes illimitable property via media.
- Media affect social values and ideologies.
- Public interest makes odd events newsworthy.
- Knowledge in media enhances cultural capital.
- Marketing communication emphasizes brand attitudes.
- Media's continuous change makes effects elusive.
- Competitive brands should not be belittled.
- Brand attitude influences consumer purchasing behavior.

- Consumer recognition of subtle message forms.
- Effective marketing communication drives category need.
- Feedback analysis follows media content transmission.
- Oddities in life generate media attention.
- Knowledge dissemination in media is important.
- Communication media facilitate cultural capital property.
- Communication media influence social structures and norms.
- Branding intentions affect consumer communication preferences.
- Feedback analysis optimizes media message effectiveness.

Key Points on Gatekeeping and Media Influence

- Gatekeeping controls media content consumption.
- Media can inform, persuade, and misinform.
- Propaganda blurs truth for persuasion purposes.
- Gatekeeping reflects the media's societal control power.
- Media's influence shapes public opinion.
- Media decides what content is shared.
- Gatekeeping ensures content consumption aligns with goals.
- Propaganda manipulates facts for persuasive communication.
- Media's control impacts audience perception significantly.
- Media influences culture through selective content sharing.
- The audience's voice isn't always heard in gatekeeping.
- Content filtering affects the public's worldview.
- Gatekeeping impacts societal norms and values.
- Media can both inform and mislead audiences.
- Media gatekeeping serves societal power structures.
- Propaganda plays a critical role in persuasion.
- Gatekeeping practices exclude certain voices from media.
- Information flow is regulated through media control.
- Propaganda blurs factual distinction for persuasive effect.
- Media control reflects broader societal influence mechanisms.

Unit III

Comprehension

Unit III

Comprehension

A passage of text be given. Questions be asked from the passage to be answered.

Table of Contents

Introduction to Reading Comprehension for UGC NET Paper 1

Reading Comprehension is an essential component of **UGC NET Paper 1**, designed to assess a candidate's ability to read, analyze, and interpret textual information effectively. This section evaluates not only one's understanding of written material but also their ability to **draw inferences, recognize arguments, and identify the tone and intent of the author**.

The passages in this section are drawn from diverse fields, including **education, science, technology, humanities, social sciences, and contemporary issues**, making it crucial for aspirants to develop strong reading and analytical skills. The ability to extract meaningful insights from the given text is critical, as the questions often test conceptual understanding rather than mere factual recall.

This chapter provides a **structured approach to mastering Reading Comprehension**, explaining the various types of questions that appear in the exam, strategies to improve accuracy, and techniques to enhance reading speed. With the right approach and regular practice, aspirants can efficiently tackle this section and improve their overall score in UGC NET Paper 1.

Types of Questions in Reading Comprehension

The **Reading Comprehension** section in UGC NET Paper 1 consists of different types of questions that assess a candidate's ability to **understand, interpret, and analyze** written content. Each type of question requires a specific approach for accurate answering. Below are the major types of questions that commonly appear in this section:

1. Main Idea-Based Questions

These questions assess a candidate's ability to identify the **central theme or main idea** of the passage. The main idea is the **core message or purpose** of the passage and is often stated in the introduction or conclusion. However, in some cases, it must be inferred from the supporting details throughout the passage.

Approach to Answering:

- Read the first and last sentences carefully, as they often contain the main idea.
- Identify the recurring theme across different paragraphs.
- Ignore unnecessary details and focus on the passage's **general purpose** rather than specific examples.

Example Question:
What is the main idea of the passage?
A) The role of education in social development
B) Challenges in modern education
C) The impact of technology on learning
D) The importance of traditional teaching methods

Tip: The main idea should summarize the **entire passage, not just a part of it**. If an option focuses only on a specific paragraph or example, it is **not** the correct answer.

2. Inference-Based Questions

These questions test the ability to **read between the lines** and draw conclusions based on the information provided in the passage. Unlike fact-based questions, inference-based questions require candidates to **interpret implicit meanings** rather than recall explicitly stated details.

Approach to Answering:

- Look for **clues** in the passage that indirectly support a conclusion.
- Avoid extreme assumptions—choose the **most logical inference** that aligns with the passage.
- Eliminate answers that introduce **new, unrelated information** not hinted at in the passage.

Example Question:
Which of the following can be inferred from the passage?
A) Education policies should prioritize digital learning.
B) Digital learning is the best method for all students.
C) The passage suggests that education is evolving with technology.
D) Online education will completely replace traditional teaching.

Tip: If an answer is **too absolute or extreme**, it is **likely incorrect**. The correct inference should be based on reasonable conclusions drawn from the passage.

3. Fact-Based or Detail-Based Questions

These questions are **direct and specific**, asking for factual details mentioned in the passage. Candidates must locate the information in the text and recall it accurately.

Approach to Answering:

- Scan the passage for **keywords** from the question.
- Read **before and after** the keyword to ensure context.
- Be careful of **trap options** that use similar words but change the meaning.

Example Question:
According to the passage, what is the impact of globalization on education?
A) It has improved access to educational resources.
B) It has led to the downfall of traditional education.
C) It has had no effect on education.
D) It has made education more expensive.

Tip: These questions **do not** require interpretation—stick to what is **explicitly stated** in the passage.

4. Tone and Style-Based Questions

These questions focus on identifying the **author's attitude, perspective, or emotional tone** in the passage. The tone reflects the **mood** in which the passage is written, and understanding it helps in grasping the underlying message.

Common Tones in Passages:

- **Critical** – Expressing disapproval or judgment
- **Optimistic** – Positive and hopeful
- **Pessimistic** – Negative and doubtful
- **Neutral** – Unbiased and factual

- **Sarcastic/Ironic** – Saying the opposite of what is meant in a humorous or mocking way
- **Persuasive** – Convincing the reader about a viewpoint

Approach to Answering:

- Focus on the **choice of words** (e.g., "unfortunately" suggests negativity, while "remarkable" suggests admiration).
- Determine whether the passage is **objective (neutral)** or **subjective (emotional/opinionated)**.

Example Question:
What is the tone of the passage?
A) Critical
B) Neutral
C) Optimistic
D) Sarcastic

Tip: If the passage contains **facts and explanations**, the tone is likely **neutral**. If it has strong **opinions**, look for words that indicate a positive or negative stance.

5. Logical Structure-Based Questions

These questions test the ability to recognize the **organization and structure** of the passage. They analyze how ideas are presented and developed within the text.

Common Structures in Passages:

- **Cause and Effect:** Discusses reasons and results of an issue.
- **Comparison and Contrast:** Compares two or more ideas.
- **Problem-Solution:** Describes a problem and its solution.
- **Chronological Order:** Follows a timeline or sequence.

Approach to Answering:

- Identify **transition words** (e.g., "therefore" for cause-effect, "similarly" for comparison).
- Analyze how ideas progress from **introduction to conclusion**.

Example Question:
Which of the following best describes the organization of the passage?
A) Cause and effect
B) Comparison and contrast
C) Problem-solution
D) Chronological order

Tip: Look at the **flow of ideas**—does the passage focus on causes, differences, a problem, or a timeline?

6. Synonyms and Antonyms-Based Questions

These questions assess **vocabulary knowledge**, requiring candidates to determine the meaning of words **in context**.

Approach to Answering:

- Read the **sentence containing the word** and analyze the surrounding words.
- Use **context clues** to guess the meaning if unfamiliar.
- Avoid literal dictionary meanings—focus on how the word is used in the passage.

Example Question:
What is the meaning of the word 'resilient' as used in the passage?
A) Weak
B) Strong and adaptable
C) Ignorant
D) Aggressive

Tip: If confused, replace the word with the answer choices and see which one fits best.

7. Title/Heading-Based Questions

These questions require selecting the **most suitable title** that summarizes the passage **as a whole**.

Approach to Answering:

- The title should reflect the **central theme**, not just a single detail.
- Avoid **too broad or too narrow** options.
- Eliminate options that are **factually correct but not representative** of the entire passage.

Example Question:
Which of the following is the most appropriate title for the passage?
A) The Role of Digital Learning in Education
B) The Rise of Online Teaching Platforms
C) Challenges and Opportunities in Modern Education
D) A History of Educational Technology

Tip: The **best title** is the one that captures the **essence of the entire passage** in **one phrase**.

Mastering Reading Comprehension requires **regular practice** and **strong analytical skills**. Understanding the different types of questions will help candidates **approach passages strategically** and improve their accuracy in answering. By following the techniques discussed, aspirants can significantly enhance their **reading speed, critical thinking, and comprehension abilities**, ensuring a strong performance in UGC NET Paper 1.

Tips to Score Well in Reading Comprehension

The Reading Comprehension section in **UGC NET Paper 1** requires a strategic approach to maximize accuracy and efficiency. Many candidates struggle with time management and selecting the most relevant answers. The following tips will help aspirants tackle passages with confidence and improve their overall performance.

1. Skim the Passage First

Read quickly to get the general idea before focusing on details.

Before diving into the questions, it is crucial to **skim the passage** to grasp its **overall theme and structure**. Skimming involves reading **at a faster pace** while focusing on **key ideas, headings, and the first and last sentences of paragraphs**.

How to Skim Effectively:

- Read the first and last **two sentences** of the passage carefully.
- Identify the **subject** of discussion (e.g., education, technology, history).
- Ignore examples and unnecessary details in the first reading.
- Look for **transition words** that indicate the structure (e.g., "therefore," "however," "on the other hand").

Why It Helps:

- Gives a **big-picture understanding** of the passage.
- Helps **locate information quickly** when answering questions.
- Saves **time** by preventing unnecessary re-reading.

2. Identify Keywords

Highlight important terms related to the question.

Once you read a question, focus on identifying **keywords** in both the passage and the question. These words help in quickly locating relevant information and avoiding confusion.

Types of Keywords to Look For:

- **Names, Dates, and Places:** Example – "According to the passage, when did the Industrial Revolution begin?"
- **Numbers and Statistics:** Example – "What percentage of students prefer online education?"
- **Technical Terms:** Example – "The passage discusses the impact of 'cognitive learning theories' in education."
- **Words Indicating Author's Opinion:** Look for words such as **critical, beneficial, problematic, innovative**.

Why It Helps:

- Saves time by directing attention to relevant parts of the passage.
- Prevents misunderstanding by focusing on **precisely stated facts**.

3. Eliminate Wrong Options

Rule out extreme, irrelevant, or contradictory choices.

Many options in Reading Comprehension questions are designed to **mislead candidates**. Learning how to **eliminate wrong answers** increases the chances of selecting the correct one.

How to Identify Wrong Options:

- **Extreme Statements:** Options that use **absolute words** like *always, never, completely, totally* are usually incorrect.
- **Outside Information:** If an option introduces new information **not mentioned in the passage**, it is incorrect.
- **Contradictory Statements:** If an option states the opposite of what the passage says, eliminate it.
- **Too Specific or Too Broad:** If an option focuses on a minor detail instead of the passage's overall theme, it is likely incorrect.

Example Question:
What is the impact of technology on education, according to the passage?
A) Technology has completely eliminated traditional education. X (Too extreme)
B) Technology has improved access to learning resources. ✅ (Logical and moderate)
C) Technology is harmful to education. X (Contradictory to the passage)
D) The passage does not mention technology. X (Incorrect, as the passage does mention it)

Why It Helps:

- Reduces confusion by narrowing down choices.
- Helps in **guessing strategically** when unsure.

4. Understand the Author's Tone

This helps in answering inference and tone-based questions.

The **tone** of the passage reflects the **author's attitude** toward the subject. Identifying the tone helps in understanding **the purpose of the passage** and choosing the right answer in **tone-based** and **inference-based** questions.

Common Tones and Their Meaning:

- **Neutral:** Presents facts without any bias.
- **Optimistic:** Shows hope or positivity.
- **Pessimistic:** Reflects negativity or doubt.
- **Critical:** Analyzes or points out flaws.
- **Persuasive:** Tries to convince the reader about something.
- **Sarcastic/Ironic:** Uses humor or irony to express the opposite of what is meant.

Example Question:
What is the tone of the passage?
A) Neutral ✅ (If the passage is factual)
B) Critical X (If the passage does not criticize anything)
C) Sarcastic X (If the passage is serious)
D) Optimistic X (If the passage does not express hope)

Why It Helps:

- Aids in answering **inference-based questions** accurately.
- Prevents **misinterpretation** of the passage's intent.

5. Don't Assume Beyond the Passage

Answer based only on what is provided.

One of the biggest mistakes candidates make is **using outside knowledge** to answer a question. Even if you are familiar with the topic, your answer must be based **only on the passage**, not on your personal knowledge or opinions.

How to Avoid This Mistake:

- Stick to the **facts mentioned in the passage**.
- Avoid **making assumptions** beyond the given text.
- If an answer choice seems logical but is **not explicitly mentioned in the passage, it is incorrect**.

Example Question:
According to the passage, what is the effect of climate change on agriculture?
A) It has led to changes in crop production. ✅ (Correct if mentioned in the

passage)
B) It will completely destroy farming in the future. X (Incorrect unless stated explicitly)
C) The passage does not discuss agriculture. X (Incorrect if agriculture is mentioned)
D) Climate change is a myth. X (Extreme and contradicts scientific facts)

Why It Helps:

- Ensures **objective** answering based only on given information.
- Prevents **misinterpretation** by avoiding personal bias.

6. Practice with Mock Tests

Regular practice improves speed and accuracy.

Since Reading Comprehension involves **time management and critical thinking**, **consistent practice** with mock tests is essential.

How to Practice Effectively:

- Take **timed practice tests** to simulate exam conditions.
- Analyze **mistakes** to understand weak areas.
- Focus on **improving reading speed** without losing comprehension.
- Solve passages from different topics (education, science, politics, philosophy) to adapt to **diverse content**.

Example of a Study Plan:

- **Daily:** Solve at least **one passage** with detailed analysis.
- **Weekly:** Take a **full-length mock test** to evaluate progress.
- **Before the Exam:** Revise common question types and strategies.

Why It Helps:

- Increases **familiarity with question patterns**.
- Improves **speed and efficiency** in answering.
- Builds **confidence** before the actual exam.

Mastering Reading Comprehension requires **a combination of speed, accuracy, and analytical skills**. By following these techniques, aspirants can **effectively manage time, eliminate incorrect answers, and improve comprehension skills**, ensuring a high score in UGC NET Paper 1. Regular **practice and strategic answering** will lead to **better accuracy and confidence** in tackling reading passages successfully.

Steps to Solve Reading Comprehension (RC) Questions

Solving Reading Comprehension questions efficiently requires a systematic approach to quickly identify the correct answer while avoiding confusion. The following **step-by-step method** ensures accuracy and saves time during the exam.

1. Read the Question First

Why?

- It helps in identifying **what information** you need to look for in the passage.
- Saves time by directing attention to the **specific part** of the passage instead of reading everything in detail.

How to Do It:

- Read the **entire question** carefully before looking at the passage.
- Identify the **type of question** (Main idea, inference, fact-based, tone-based, etc.).
- Pay attention to **keywords** in the question (e.g., names, dates, concepts).

Example:
Question: *According to the passage, what is the main challenge of online education?*

- Here, the keyword is **"main challenge of online education"**, so you need to look for **problems associated with online education** in the passage.

2. Search for Related Words in the Passage

Why?

- Helps in **locating the relevant section** quickly.
- Reduces unnecessary reading of the entire passage.

How to Do It:

- Scan the passage to find **keywords or similar words** from the question.
- Look for **synonyms or paraphrased versions** of the keywords.
- If the question asks about **dates or figures**, locate **numerical values** in the passage.

Example:
If the question asks, *"What are the benefits of artificial intelligence in education?"*

- Look for terms like **"AI in education," "advantages," "benefits," "positive impact."**

3. Search for Related Sentences

Why?

- The correct answer is often **hidden within a sentence or two** in the passage.
- Helps in understanding the **context** of the answer.

How to Do It:

- Once the keyword is found, read **before and after** the keyword to understand the complete idea.
- If the passage is long, read **the first and last sentences of each paragraph** to locate relevant sections.
- If the passage has **subheadings or bullet points**, use them to quickly navigate.

Example:
If the keyword is **"challenges of online education,"** look for sentences that discuss:

- Problems students face while studying online.
- Technical or social issues related to online learning.

4. Underline the Sentence Containing the Answer

Why?

- Helps in **visually marking** important parts of the passage.
- Prevents re-reading the passage multiple times.

How to Do It:

- Underline or highlight the sentence that **directly answers** the question.
- If highlighting is not allowed, mentally note or **rewrite the key sentence** on rough paper.
- Pay attention to **transition words** (e.g., "however," "therefore," "in contrast") as they often signal **important ideas**.

Example:
If the passage states:
"One of the major challenges of online education is the lack of interaction between students and teachers, which affects learning engagement."

- Underline **"lack of interaction between students and teachers"** as this is the key information for answering the question.

5. Eliminate the Wrong Options

Why?

- Many options are **designed to confuse candidates** by using similar words or partial truths.
- Eliminating incorrect answers increases the probability of choosing the right one.

How to Do It:

- **Eliminate extreme options** – If an option uses words like *"always," "never," "completely,"* it is likely incorrect.
- **Eliminate unrelated options** – If an answer choice **introduces new information** not in the passage, discard it.
- **Eliminate contradictory options** – If an answer **directly opposes** the information in the passage, it is incorrect.
- **Compare remaining options** – If two options seem correct, compare them with the **underlined sentence** and choose the most relevant one.

Example:
Question: *What is the main challenge of online education?*

◆ Passage says: *"One of the major challenges of online education is the lack of interaction between students and teachers."*

Wrong options:
A) Online education is expensive. (Not mentioned in the passage)
B) Online education has no benefits. (Too extreme and incorrect)

Correct option:
C) Lack of interaction between students and teachers. (Matches the passage)

6. Select the Correct Answer

Why?

- After eliminating wrong options, selecting the best choice ensures accuracy.

How to Do It:

- Re-read the **underlined sentence** and check if it fully supports the chosen option.
- If two answers seem correct, select the one that **covers the passage's intent** more accurately.
- Avoid **overthinking** or adding outside knowledge—base your choice **only on the passage**.

Example:

Final answer: ☑ **C) Lack of interaction between students and teachers.**

Final Tip:
If unsure, **re-read the passage section** related to the question and **double-check** your choice.

By following this structured **6-step approach**, candidates can significantly **improve their accuracy** in solving Reading Comprehension questions in **UGC NET Paper 1**. This method ensures that answers are based on **logical reasoning and textual evidence**, rather than guesswork.

Summary of Steps:

1. **Read the question first** – Know what to look for.
2. **Search for related words** – Locate key terms in the passage.
3. **Search for related sentences** – Identify supporting sentences.
4. **Underline key sentences** – Mark the exact sentence that answers the question.
5. **Eliminate wrong options** – Rule out extreme, unrelated, or contradictory answers.
6. **Select the correct answer** – Choose the best-supported option based on the passage.

Practicing these steps regularly will help **increase speed and accuracy**, making Reading Comprehension questions easier to tackle in the exam.

Practice 1 August 2024 UGC NET English Shift II

A careful study of the Rig-Veda shows that even in the early times, karma and jnana were recognized as two separate factors in the spiritual progress of man. Karma is connected with the world immediately above the one in which we live; and jaana is connected with the world further above that. Agni and Indra are connected with sacrifices, and the gods of the highest world are connected with prayer, and jdana. Since the Vedic Samhitds are intimately connected with sacrifices, it's but natural that the gods connected with sacrifices, the gods of the two lower regions, should be more prominent in the Rig-Veda. It is only through jana that the soul can get into a state of everlasting bliss. This jaana is esoteric knowledge. At the time of the Rig-Veda, the rsis had evolved a highly complicated system of philosophy and that the value of jana as a means to final release from the world of physical bondage had been well established. The Yajur- Veda and the Sama-Veda are of little importance to a student of ancient Indian culture. One notes the same optimistic tone in the Yajur-Veda, regarding man's life in this world and his future in the other world. Material plenty is also quite noticeable. Gold and ornaments are spoken of freely as covetable objects. Cows are mentioned in thousands. So far as culture is concerned, so far as religion and philosophy go, there is no difference between the Rig-Veda and the other two Vedas.

Question

In Rig-veda, Agni is connected with.

1. The world immediately above the one in which we live in
2. Sacrifices
3. Souls with everlasting bliss
4. The gods of Wisdom

Explanations
Answer: 2. Sacrifices

Applying the 6-Step Method to Solve the Question

Step 1: Read the Question First

- The question asks about *Agni's connection in the Rig-Veda.*
- This is a **fact-based question** because it seeks **explicit information** from the passage.
- **Keyword:** *Agni*

Step 2: Search for Related Words in the Passage

- Scan the passage to locate the word **"Agni."**
- The passage states:
  "Agni and Indra are connected with sacrifices."

Step 3: Search for Related Sentences

- The **sentence clearly states** that Agni is connected with sacrifices.

- The relevant part in the passage is:
  "Agni and Indra are connected with sacrifices."
- This directly answers the question.

Step 4: Underline the Sentence

- If this were a physical test, you would underline:
  "Agni and Indra are connected with sacrifices."

Step 5: Eliminate Wrong Options

1. **The world immediately above the one in which we live in** ❌
   - The passage mentions that **karma** is connected with this world, but **Agni is not specifically linked to it**.
2. **Sacrifices** ✅
   - The passage directly states **"Agni and Indra are connected with sacrifices."**
3. **Souls with everlasting bliss** ❌
   - The passage mentions that **jnana** (knowledge) leads to everlasting bliss, **not Agni**.
4. **The gods of Wisdom** ❌
   - The passage states that **"the gods of the highest world are connected with prayer and jnana,"** but **Agni is not mentioned in that category**.

Step 6: Select the Correct Answer

Correct Answer: 2. Sacrifices

Question

The optimistic tone regarding man's ife in this world and his/her future in the world exists in:

1. The Yajur-Veda
2. The Sima-Veda
3. The Atharva Veda
4. Rig-Veda

Explanations

Answer: 1. The Yajur-Veda

Step 1: Read the Question First

- The question asks **which Veda has an optimistic tone** regarding **man's life and future**.
- This is a **tone-based question**, requiring recognition of the **author's perspective** on a specific Veda.
- **Keyword:** *Optimistic tone*

Step 2: Search for Related Words in the Passage

- Scan the passage for words like **"optimistic," "man's life," "future," and "Yajur-Veda."**
- The passage states:
  "One notes the same optimistic tone in the Yajur-Veda, regarding man's life in this world and his future in the other world."

Step 3: Search for Related Sentences

- The relevant part in the passage is:
  "One notes the same optimistic tone in the Yajur-Veda, regarding man's life in this world and his future in the other world."
- This directly answers the question.

Step 4: Underline the Sentence

- If underlining were possible, you would highlight:
  "One notes the same optimistic tone in the Yajur-Veda, regarding man's life in this world and his future in the other world."

Step 5: Eliminate Wrong Options

1. **The Yajur-Veda** ✅
   - **Correct** because the passage directly mentions the Yajur-Veda in relation to an **optimistic tone**.
2. **The Sama-Veda** ❌
   - Not mentioned in relation to an optimistic tone.
3. **The Atharva-Veda** ❌

    - Not discussed in the passage.
4. **The Rig-Veda** ❌
    - The passage compares it to the Yajur-Veda but does not specifically mention it as having an optimistic tone.

Step 6: Select the Correct Answer

☑ **Correct Answer: 1. The Yajur-Veda**

Question

At the time of Rig Veda, the rsis valued jiana as means.

1. To find signs of a gloomier side in man's life
2. To sacrifice and dissociate
3. To find release from the world of physical bondage
4. To rule and regulate

Explanations
Answer: 3. To find release from the world of physical bondage

Step 1: Read the Question First

- The question asks about **the purpose of jnana (knowledge) according to the Rig-Veda.**
- This is a **fact-based question** because the answer is explicitly stated in the passage.
- **Keyword:** *Jnana (knowledge) as a means*

Step 2: Search for Related Words in the Passage

- Scan the passage for the word **"jnana"** or any related phrase.
- The passage states:
  "The value of jnana as a means to final release from the world of physical bondage had been well established."

Step 3: Search for Related Sentences

- ➢ The relevant sentence in the passage is:
  "The value of jnana as a means to final release from the world of physical bondage had been well established."
- ➢ This directly answers the question.

Step 4: Underline the Sentence

- ➢ If underlining were possible, highlight:
  "The value of jnana as a means to final release from the world of physical bondage had been well established."

Step 5: Eliminate Wrong Options

1. **To find signs of a gloomier side in man's life** ❌
   - Incorrect. The passage does **not** associate jnana with a negative or gloomy outlook.
2. **To sacrifice and dissociate** ❌
   - Incorrect. Sacrifices are linked to **karma** (rituals), not **jnana**.
3. **To find release from the world of physical bondage** ✅
   - Correct. The passage **explicitly states this as the purpose of jnana**.
4. **To rule and regulate** ❌
   - Incorrect. The passage does not mention **jnana** as a tool for ruling or governance.

Step 6: Select the Correct Answer

✅ **Correct Answer: 3. To find release from the world of physical bondage**

Question

What is the original source of cultural life of the Hindus?

1. Itihasas
2. Puranas
3. Manu
4. Sacred Vedas

Explanations
Answer: 4. Sacred Vedas

Step 1: Read the Question First

- The question asks about the **original source of cultural life of Hindus**.
- This is a **fact-based question** because it seeks information explicitly mentioned in the passage.
- **Keyword:** *Original source of cultural life*

Step 2: Search for Related Words in the Passage

- Scan the passage for words like **"culture," "Hindus," "source," or "Vedas."**
- The passage discusses the **Rig-Veda, Yajur-Veda, and Sama-Veda**, emphasizing their **cultural and philosophical significance**.

Step 3: Search for Related Sentences

- The passage emphasizes:
  "The Yajur-Veda and the Sama-Veda are of little importance to a student of ancient Indian culture... So far as culture is concerned, so far as religion and philosophy go, there is no difference between the Rig-Veda and the other two Vedas."
- This means that the **Vedas collectively serve as the foundation of Hindu culture**.

Step 4: Underline the Sentence

- If underlining were possible, highlight:
  "So far as culture is concerned, so far as religion and philosophy go, there is no difference between the Rig-Veda and the other two Vedas."

Step 5: Eliminate Wrong Options

1. **Itihasas** ❌

   - The Itihasas (Ramayana and Mahabharata) are important historical epics but are **not the original source** of Hindu culture.
2. **Puranas** ❌
   - The Puranas contain **mythology and history** but were written **after the Vedas**.
3. **Manu** ❌
   - The **Manusmriti** (Laws of Manu) is a later **legal text**, not the foundation of Hindu cultural life.
4. **Sacred Vedas** ✅
   - The passage **repeatedly discusses the significance of the Vedas in shaping cultural, religious, and philosophical life**, making this the correct answer.

Step 6: Select the Correct Answer

✅ **Correct Answer: 4. Sacred Vedas**

Question

According to Rig-Veda, Jiana refers to.

1. Primitive culture
2. Predominance of sacrifice
3. Everlasting bliss
4. The gods of the highest world that are connected with sacrifices

Explanations
Answer: 3. Everlasting bliss

Step 1: Read the Question First

- The question asks about the meaning of **jnana (knowledge) in the Rig-Veda**.
- This is a **fact-based question**, as the passage explicitly discusses jnana.
- **Keyword:** *Jnana (knowledge) refers to what?*

Step 2: Search for Related Words in the Passage

- Scan the passage for the word **"jnana"** or any related concept.
- The passage states:
  "It is only through jnana that the soul can get into a state of everlasting bliss. This jnana is esoteric knowledge."

Step 3: Search for Related Sentences

- The relevant sentence is:
  "It is only through jnana that the soul can get into a state of everlasting bliss."
- This directly answers the question by linking jnana to **everlasting bliss**.

Step 4: Underline the Sentence

- If underlining were possible, highlight:
  "It is only through jnana that the soul can get into a state of everlasting bliss."

Step 5: Eliminate Wrong Options

1. **Primitive culture** ❌
   - The passage does **not** mention jnana in connection with primitive culture.
2. **Predominance of sacrifice** ❌
   - The passage states that **sacrifices are associated with karma, not jnana**.
3. **Everlasting bliss** ✅
   - **Correct** because the passage explicitly states that **jnana leads to everlasting bliss**.
4. **The gods of the highest world that are connected with sacrifices** ❌
   - The passage states that **the gods of the highest world are connected with prayer and jnana, but not sacrifices**.

Step 6: Select the Correct Answer

✅ **Correct Answer: 3. Everlasting bliss**

Practice 2 August 2024 UGC NET English Shift I

A. K. Ramanujan was one of those thinkers, like Freud (whom he greatly, though not uncritically, admired), who so transform our way of looking at a subject that we are in danger of undervaluing their contribution, since we have come to take for granted precisely what they taught us, as we view the subject through their eyes. At a time when the American Indo-logical establishment regarded native Indian scholars merely as sources of information about language and texts, like the raw fiber that were taken from India to be processed in British mills, but seldom as scholars who might have their on ideas about how to process those texts, Raman taught them all how to weave a theory, a folktale, a poem, a book. Raman taught the all how to weave a theory, a folktale, a poem, a book. Long before it was politically respectable, let alone politically correct, to study the works of women or of 'illiterate' peasants, Raman valued their poetry, their stories and their counter-systems. At a time when Indian literature meant Sanskrit. and Sanskrit meant Greek and Latin, Raman arrived in Chicago to join Edward C. Dimock and the other 'founding fathers" in proclaiming to the world the relevance of Tamil and Bengali and the other mother tongues. Without so much as raising his gentle voice, he blazed a great path through the centre of Indological studies. He gave us so many new paradigms that no Indologist can now think about India without thinking through his thoughts.

Question

The languages that Ramanujan tried to bring to limelight in Indological studies is

1. Greek and Latin
2. Only Sanskrit
3. Tamil, Bengali and other mother tongues
4. French and German

Explanations
Answer: 3. Tamil, Bengali and other mother tongues

Step 1: Read the Question First

- The question asks **which languages A.K. Ramanujan emphasized** in Indological studies.

- This is a **fact-based question**, requiring a direct reference from the passage.
- **Keyword:** *Languages Ramanujan highlighted*

Step 2: Search for Related Words in the Passage

- Scan for terms like **"languages," "Indological studies," "Tamil," "Bengali," or "Sanskrit."**
- The passage states:
  "*At a time when Indian literature meant Sanskrit, and Sanskrit meant Greek and Latin, Raman arrived in Chicago to join Edward C. Dimock and the other 'founding fathers' in proclaiming to the world the relevance of Tamil and Bengali and the other mother tongues.*"

Step 3: Find Related Sentences

- The key sentence is:
  "Raman arrived in Chicago to join Edward C. Dimock and the other 'founding fathers' in proclaiming to the world the relevance of Tamil and Bengali and the other mother tongues."
- This confirms that **Tamil, Bengali, and other Indian languages were his focus**.

Step 4: Underline Key Information

- If underlining were possible, highlight:
  "*Tamil and Bengali and the other mother tongues.*"

Step 5: Eliminate Wrong Options

1. **Greek and Latin** ❌
   - The passage states **Greek and Latin were traditionally emphasized, but Ramanujan focused on Indian languages**.
2. **Only Sanskrit** ❌
   - Incorrect. The passage explicitly states that Ramanujan brought **Tamil, Bengali, and other mother tongues** into focus.
3. **Tamil, Bengali and other mother tongues** ✅

    - **Correct**. This is exactly what the passage states.
4. **French and German** ✕
    - These languages are **not mentioned** in the passage.

Step 6: Select the Correct Answer

☑ **Correct Answer: 3. Tamil, Bengali and other mother tongues**

Question

Ramanujan emphasised on

1. The criticism on the British mills
2. Creating controversies in American Indological Studies
3. A path through Indological Studies
4. The study of Western languages only

Explanations
Answer: 3. A path through Indological Studies

Step 1: Read the Question First

- The question asks about **Ramanujan's emphasis** in his work.
- **Keyword:** *Emphasized on what?*

Step 2: Search for Related Words in the Passage

- Look for words like **"emphasized," "focused on," "path," "Indology."**
- The passage states:
  "Without so much as raising his gentle voice, he blazed a great path through the centre of Indological studies."

Step 3: Find Related Sentences

- The phrase **"blazed a great path through Indological studies"** confirms his focus.

Step 4: Underline Key Information

- **"He blazed a great path through Indological studies."**

Step 5: Eliminate Wrong Options

1. **The criticism on the British mills** ❌ (Used as an analogy, not his emphasis)
2. **Creating controversies in American Indological Studies** ❌ (No mention of controversy)
3. **A path through Indological Studies** ✅ (Directly stated in the passage)
4. **The study of Western languages only** ❌ (He focused on Tamil, Bengali, etc.)

Step 6: Select the Correct Answer

✅ **Correct Answer: 3. A path through Indological Studies**

Question

Who were the 'Founding Fathers' that Ramanujan joined in Chicago?

1. British Mill Owners
2. American Indo-logical establishment leaders
3. Edward C. Dimock and others
4. Greek and Latin scholars

Explanations
Answer: 3. Edward C. Dimock and others

Step 1: Read the Question First

- The question asks who the **'Founding Fathers'** were in the passage.

Step 2: Search for Related Words in the Passage

- Look for **"Founding Fathers"** and **"Chicago."**

Step 3: Find Related Sentences

- The passage states **"Raman arrived in Chicago to join Edward C. Dimock and the other 'founding fathers'."**

Step 4: Underline Key Information

- **"Edward C. Dimock and the other 'founding fathers'."**

Step 5: Eliminate Wrong Options

- ❌ *British Mill Owners* (Not related to Indological studies).
- ❌ *American Indo-logical establishment leaders* (They viewed Indian scholars as sources, not collaborators).
- ✅ *Edward C. Dimock and others* (Explicitly mentioned in the passage).
- ❌ *Greek and Latin scholars* (Not mentioned in this context).

Step 6: Select the Correct Answer

✅ **Correct Answer: 3. Edward C. Dimock and others**

Question

What did Ramanujan teach in America?

1. Process raw fibers in British mills
2. Weave theories, folktales, poems and books
3. Only Sanskrit literature
4. Only English Literature

Explanations

Answer: 2. Weave theories, folktales, poems and books

1. Read the question first: It asks what **Ramanujan taught in America**.
2. Search for related words in the passage: Look for **"teach," "weave," "theory," "folktale," "poem," "book."**
3. Find related sentences: The passage states **"Raman taught them all how to weave a theory, a folktale, a poem, a book."**
4. Underline key information: **"Weave a theory, a folktale, a poem, a book."**

5. Eliminate wrong options:
6. Select the correct answer: **Weave theories, folktales, poems, and books.**

Question

Who is A.K Ramanujan compared to in the text?

1. Chomsky
2. Sigmund Freud
3. Brunvand
4. British Mill Owners

Explanations
Answer: 2. Sigmund Freud

- Read the question first: It asks **who A.K. Ramanujan is compared to** in the passage.
- Search for related words in the passage: Look for **"compared to," "like," "similar to."**
- Find related sentences: The passage states **"A.K. Ramanujan was one of those thinkers, like Freud (whom he greatly, though not uncritically, admired)."**
- Underline key information: **"Like Freud (whom he greatly, though not uncritically, admired)."**
- Eliminate wrong options:
    - ❌ *Chomsky* (Not mentioned in the passage).
    - ✅ *Sigmund Freud* (Explicitly mentioned as a comparison).
    - ❌ *Brunvand* (Not discussed in this context).
    - ❌ *British Mill Owners* (Used as an analogy, not a comparison to Ramanujan).
- Select the correct answer: ✅ **Sigmund Freud.**

Practice 3 June 2024 UGC NET English Shift II

According to a World Health Organization report, about 80 percent of the world population uses traditional medicine systems in some or the other way. India has a distinctive and unique traditional medicine base, with each system having its own ancient philosophy, medicinal knowledge, perception and practices that align with the regional cultures, traditions and beliefs. The traditional medicine systems in India include Ayurveda, Yoga, Naturopathy, Unani, Siddha, Sowa Rigpa and Homeopathy which is known as Ayush. All these systems were formulated, practised and perfected in a continuum much before the advent of modern health science.

In many countries of the world, medical pluralism is the norm and traditional medicine is one of the surest means to achieve total healthcare coverage for the world population using acceptable, safe and economically-feasible methods. No system of medicine can single-handedly address all health concerns, but an integrative approach incorporating the positives of each can surely benefit mankind. The holistic patient-centered and individualised approach is the trademark of tractional systems and enables the patient-physician partnership to design or customise treatment and lifestyle advice in order to achieve the highest potential for well-being. This awareness combined with the increase in use of traditional medicine has brought the systems to the fore. The diverse activities ranging from the provision of prophylactic care to the management of disease and the effective implementation and integration of AyliSh system to the public healthcare during the pandemic has garnered global attention to Ayush systems. This has enabled the signing of the Host Country Agreement for the establishment of Global Centre for Traditional Medicine (GCTM) at Jamnagar.

Question

The Global Centre for Traditional Medicine has been established in:

1. World Health Organization
2. Jamnagar
3. New Delhi
4. Haridwar

Explanations

Answer: 2. Jamnagar

1. Read the question first: It asks where the **Global Centre for Traditional Medicine (GCTM)** has been established.
2. Search for related words in the passage: Look for **"Global Centre for Traditional Medicine," "established," "location."**

3. Find related sentences: The passage states **"This has enabled the signing of the Host Country Agreement for the establishment of Global Centre for Traditional Medicine (GCTM) at Jamnagar."**
4. Underline key information: **"GCTM at Jamnagar."**
5. Eliminate wrong options:
    - ❌ *World Health Organization* (WHO supports it but didn't establish it there).
    - ✅ *Jamnagar* (Clearly stated in the passage).
    - ❌ *New Delhi* (Not mentioned).
    - ❌ *Haridwar* (Not mentioned).
6. Select the correct answer: ✅ **Jamnagar.**

Question

According to a World Health Organization report, the percentage of the world population that uses traditional medicine systems in some way or the other is:

1. About 20%
2. About 50%
3. About 100%
4. About 80%

Explanations
Answer: 4. About 80%

1. It asks for the **percentage of the world population using traditional medicine** according to WHO.
2. Look for **"World Health Organization," "percentage," "traditional medicine."**
3. The passage states **"According to a World Health Organization report, about 80 percent of the world population uses traditional medicine systems in some way or the other."**
4. **"About 80 percent of the world population uses traditional medicine."**
5. Eliminate wrong options:
    - ❌ *About 20%* (Incorrect; too low).
    - ❌ *About 50%* (Incorrect; not mentioned).
    - ❌ *About 100%* (Incorrect; too high).

- ☑ *About 80%* (Directly stated in the passage).

6. Select the correct answer: ☑ **About 80%.**

Question

Choose the appropriate title for the passage:

1. Allopathy
2. Holistic Healthcare
3. Ayurveda
4. Homeopathy

Explanations

Answer: 2. Holistic Healthcare

1. Read the question first: It asks for the **most appropriate title** for the passage.
2. Search for related words in the passage: Look for **"holistic," "healthcare," "integrative approach."**
3. Find related sentences: The passage states **"The holistic patient-centered and individualized approach is the trademark of traditional systems."**
4. Underline key information: **"Holistic patient-centered and individualized approach."**
5. Eliminate wrong options:
   - ✕ *Allopathy* (The passage focuses on traditional medicine, not modern allopathy).
   - ☑ *Holistic Healthcare* (Matches the passage's emphasis on integrative, patient-centered medicine).
   - ✕ *Ayurveda* (Ayurveda is mentioned, but the passage covers multiple traditional systems).
   - ✕ *Homeopathy* (It is only one part of Ayush, not the central focus).
6. Select the correct answer: ☑ **Holistic Healthcare.**

Question

Which of the following facts about the traditional Indian medicine systems are false?

A. Each system is Unique.
B. They include Ayurveda, Naturopathy, Yoga, Unani, Siddha, Sowa Rigpa and Homeopathy.
C. Modern Health Science preceded them.
D. Each system has an essentially similar philosophy.

Choose the most appropriate answer from the options given below:

1. A, B and D only
2. B and C only
3. C and D only
4. B, C and D only

Explanations
Answer: 3. C and D only

1. Read the question first: It asks which **facts about traditional Indian medicine systems are false**.
2. Search for related words in the passage: Look for "**traditional medicine systems," "modern health science," "philosophy," and "unique."**
3. Find related sentences: The passage states **"Each system has its own ancient philosophy"** and **"All these systems were formulated, practiced, and perfected much before the advent of modern health science."**
4. Underline key information: **"Each system has its own ancient philosophy"** and **"Much before modern health science."**
5. Eliminate wrong options
6. Select the correct answer: ✅ **C and D only.**

Question

In many countries of the world, medical pluralism is the norm because:

1. Traditional systems of medicine are useless.
2. Traditional systems of medicine befool the public.
3. No single system of medicine can single-handedly address all health concerns.
4. An integrative approach incorporating the positives of each system of medicine can in no way benefit mankind.

Explanations

Answer: 3. No single system of medicine can single-handedly address all health concerns.

1. Read the question first: It asks why **medical pluralism is the norm in many countries**.
2. Search for related words in the passage: Look for **"medical pluralism," "health concerns," "integrative approach."**
3. Find related sentences: The passage states **"No system of medicine can single-handedly address all health concerns, but an integrative approach incorporating the positives of each can surely benefit mankind."**
4. Underline key information: **"No system of medicine can single-handedly address all health concerns."**
5. Eliminate wrong options
6. Select the correct answer: **No single system of medicine can single-handedly address all health concerns.**

Practice 4 June 2024 UGC NET English Shift I

Micron's $800 million semiconductor plant followed by recent approval to Tata Group and CG Power for fabrication and Assembly, Testing and Packaging (ATP) plants with an investment of Rs 1.30.000 crore (and more in the pipeline) are the beginning of a transformational global supply chain shift centered around chip manufacturing in India. This will create a multiplier effect on talented and skilled workforce inside India. It's a matter of pride that almost one-third of the global semiconductor talent pool is Indian. However; the need for a domestic semiconductor workforce is estimated to be around 3,00,000 by 2026. In addition, there is also a huge manpower requirement of almost six million in the electronics manufacturing sector which will be the largest beneficiary of the chip boom. The current combined Science, Technology, Engineering and Mathematics (STEM) graduate output from India's higher education institutions is inadequate. The growth is certainly going to come from the non-IITians orbit and the policy path ways of the Ministries of Electronics and IT and Education converge to present bountiful opportunities for industry and academia to work together. This industry academia synergy was key to India's software success story. Now a similar trifecta of government industry-academia is needed to make this a winning semicon trio.

Question

As a result of the chip boom, the requirement of workforce in the electronics manufacturing sector will:

1. Remain Unchanged
2. Lead to Job Losses
3. Increase
4. Drastically go down

Explanations
Answer: 3. Increase

- The requirement of workforce in the electronics manufacturing sector will **increase** due to the chip boom.
- Look for **"manpower requirement," "electronics manufacturing sector," "chip boom."**
- The passage states **"There is also a huge manpower requirement of almost six million in the electronics manufacturing sector which will be the largest beneficiary of the chip boom."**
- **"Huge manpower requirement of almost six million."**

Question

The new talented skills workforce in India will come mainly from:

1. STEM Graduates
2. The Non-IlTians orbit
3. The IIT's
4. Unskilled Labour Force

Explanations
Answer: 2. The Non-IlTians orbit

- The new talented skills workforce in India will come mainly from **the Non-IITians orbit.**
- Look for **"talented workforce," "growth," "non-IITians orbit."**
- The passage states **"The growth is certainly going to come from the non-IITians orbit."**
- **"Growth is certainly going to come from the non-IITians orbit."**

Question

India's share in the semiconductor global talent pool is:

1. Two-thirds
2. One-third
3. Three-fourths
4. One-fifth

Explanations

Answer: 2. One-third

- India's share in the semiconductor global talent pool is **one-third.**
- Look for **"global semiconductor talent pool," "India's share."**
- The passage states **"Almost one-third of the global semiconductor talent pool is Indian."**
- **"One-third of the global semiconductor talent pool is Indian."**

Question

Micron set up a:

1. Fabrication plant
2. An ATP plant
3. A semiconductor plant
4. An engineering college

Explanations

Answer: 3. A semiconductor plant

- Micron set up **a semiconductor plant.**
- Look for **"Micron," "set up," "plant."**
- The passage states **"Micron's $800 million semiconductor plant."**
- **"Micron's $800 million semiconductor plant."**

Question

The need for additional talented and skilled workforce in the domestic semiconductor sector has been created by:

A. The approval given to Tata Group and CG Power for fabrication and ATP plants
B. Micron's $800 million semiconductor plant
C. Setting up of new Universities
D. The global supply chain shift centered around chip manufacturing in India
E. Choose the most appropriate answer from the options given below:

1. A and B only
2. A, C and D only
3. B, C and D only
4. A, B and D only

Explanations
Answer: 4. A, B and D only

The need for additional talented and skilled workforce in the domestic semiconductor sector has been created by **A, B, and D only.**

Look for **"need for workforce," "factors contributing to demand."**

The passage states **"Micron's $800 million semiconductor plant followed by recent approval to Tata Group and CG Power for fabrication and ATP plants... are the beginning of a transformational global supply chain shift centered around chip manufacturing in India."**

"Micron's plant, Tata Group and CG Power approval, and global supply chain shift."

✅ *A (Approval to Tata Group and CG Power)* (Mentioned).
✅ *B (Micron's semiconductor plant)* (Clearly stated).
❌ *C (Setting up of new universities)* (Not mentioned).
✅ *D (Global supply chain shift)* (Clearly stated).

Practice 5 DEC 2024 UGC NET English Shift II

Handicraft is about processing materials by hand with hand tools. The results can be helpful things or decorative things. The materials utilized in the product are natural, industrially processed or may be recycled. The models of the product are ancient, revised, traditional and fashionable. Handicraft is deeply frozen in society and contributes to the idea of preserving and perpetuating traditions. In their product. Crafters transfer an area of their cultural heritage in ideas, forms. materials and work ways. similarly as their own values, philosophy of life, fashion and self-image. Crafts people also known as artisans possess technical data of materials and work ways. They are skilled employees whose profession relies on manual skills. Handicrafts contain plenty of implicit data which grows every year, aboard with skills. The order and apprentice system has been widely used to transfer skills and implicit data.

Question

The world 'apprentice implies:

1. Carpenter
2. Plumber
3. Trainee
4. Artist

Explanations
Answer: 3. Trainee

It asks for the meaning of the word **"apprentice."**

Look for **"apprentice," "transfer skills," "order and apprentice system."**

The passage states **"The order and apprentice system has been widely used to transfer skills and implicit data."**

"Apprentice system... used to transfer skills."

❌ *Carpenter* (A specific profession, not the meaning of "apprentice").
❌ *Plumber* (A skilled worker, but not the meaning of "apprentice").
✅ *Trainee* (An apprentice is someone learning a skill).
❌ *Artist* (Not related to learning under someone).

✅ **Trainee.**

Question

Identify the central theme of the passage.

1. Inventions of India
2. Creations and designs of India
3. Architecture of India
4. Handicrafts of India

Explanations
Answer: 4. Handicrafts of India

It asks for the **central theme** of the passage.

Look for **main idea, repeated concepts, key focus of discussion.**

The passage discusses **handicrafts, traditional skills, and craftsmanship in India.**

"The passage highlights India's rich handicraft traditions and skill transfer systems."

❌ *Inventions of India* (Not focused on scientific or technological inventions).
❌ *Creations and designs of India* (Too broad, not specific to handicrafts).
❌ *Architecture of India* (Architecture is not the main focus).
✅ *Handicrafts of India* (Clearly the passage's main subject).

✅ **Handicrafts of India.**

Question

Pick the statements which is not true.

1. Craftsmen transfer their values and philosophy of life
2. There is a no implicit data in the craftsmanship
3. The materials utilized for the crafts are generally recycled
4. The models prepared by craftsmen are very fashionable

Explanations
Answer: 2. There is no implicit data in the craftsmanship & The models prepared by craftsmen are very fashionable.

It asks for the **statement that is NOT true.**

Look for **contradictions, incorrect information, or statements not supported by the passage.**

The passage states **"Craftsmen transfer their values and philosophy of life,"** confirming it as true. It also mentions **"implicit data in craftsmanship,"** making the second statement false. **Recycled materials are commonly used,** making the third statement true. However, **fashionable models** are not mentioned, making the fourth statement likely false.

"There is a no implicit data in the craftsmanship" is incorrect as implicit data exists in craftsmanship.

❌ *Craftsmen transfer their values and philosophy of life* (True, mentioned in the passage).
✅ *There is no implicit data in the craftsmanship* (False, passage states implicit data exists).
❌ *The materials utilized for the crafts are generally recycled* (True, commonly practiced in handicrafts).
✅ *The models prepared by craftsmen are very fashionable* (False, not mentioned).

✅ **There is no implicit data in the craftsmanship & The models prepared by craftsmen are very fashionable.**

Question

The importance behind the idea of crafts is

1. Gainful employment
2. To make new products
3. to preserve the tradition
4. to spend quality time

Explanations
Answer: 3. to preserve the tradition

It asks for the **importance behind the idea of crafts.**

Look for **key reasons mentioned in the passage related to craftsmanship.**

The passage emphasizes **preserving traditional skills and cultural heritage.**

"Crafts play a role in preserving tradition and passing down skills."

❌ *Gainful employment* (Not the primary focus of the passage).
❌ *To make new products* (Craftsmanship is more about tradition than innovation).
✅ *To preserve the tradition* (Directly aligns with the passage's emphasis).
❌ *To spend quality time* (Not the main reason for craftsmanship).

✅ **To preserve the tradition.**

Question

The materials used in the products are.

1. Natural only
2. Industrially processed and natural only
3. Recyclable and natural only
4. Natural, Recyclable and Industrially processed

Explanations
Answer: 4. Natural, Recyclable, and Industrially processed.

It asks about the **materials used in the products.**

Look for **mentions of materials like natural, recyclable, or industrially processed in the passage.**

The passage highlights **the use of natural, recyclable, and industrially processed materials.**

"Crafts often use a mix of natural, recyclable, and industrially processed materials."

❌ *Natural only* (Too limited, excludes other materials).
❌ *Industrially processed and natural only* (Excludes recyclable materials).

❌ *Recyclable and natural only* (Excludes industrially processed materials).
✅ *Natural, Recyclable, and Industrially processed* (Includes all materials mentioned).

✅ **Natural, Recyclable, and Industrially processed.**

Practice 6 DEC 2024 UGC NET Computer Shift I

A radical new surgery procedure, laughed at not long ago, is holding out fresh hope for patients of cardiac myopathy, or enlargement of the beart. The technique, now in India. allows patients to go home two weeks after the operation, to lead a near-normal sedentary lite. Cardiomyopathy is a condition that has a variety of causative factors. An attack from one of the 20 identified viruses, parasite infection, long-term alcohol abuse and blood pressure could bring it on, and in rare cases. It could follow childbirth and is even known to run in families. The condition is marked by an increase in the size of the heart's chambers
and a decrease in the efficieney of pumping.

Question

Cardiomyopathy is a medical condition related to

1. The heart
2. The eyes
3. The muscles of the legs
4. Body movement

Explanations
Answer: 1. The Heart

Cardiomyopathy is a medical condition related to the heart.

Look for **"cardiomyopathy," "medical condition," "affected organ."**

The passage states **"Cardiomyopathy, or enlargement of the heart."**

"Enlargement of the heart."

☑ *The heart* (Clearly stated in the passage).
✕ *The eyes* (Not mentioned).
✕ *The muscles of the legs* (Irrelevant).
✕ *Body movement* (Not related).

☑ **The heart.**

Question

Which of the following is incorrect about the causative factors of cardiomyopathy?

1. Attack by certain identified viruses
2. Long-term alcohol abuse
3. Overeating
4. Heredity

Explanations
Answer: 3. Overeating

The incorrect causative factor of cardiomyopathy is overeating.

Look for **"causative factors," "what brings it on."**

The passage states **"An attack from one of the 20 identified viruses, parasite infection, long-term alcohol abuse, and blood pressure could bring it on. In rare cases, it could follow childbirth and is even known to run in families."**

"Viruses, alcohol abuse, blood pressure, heredity."

☑ *Attack by certain identified viruses* (Mentioned).
☑ *Long-term alcohol abuse* (Clearly stated).
✕ *Overeating* (Not mentioned in the passage).
☑ *Heredity* (Mentioned as a factor).

☑ **Overeating.**

Question

Which of the following is true about cardiomyopathy surgery?

1. The radical new surgery procedure is now available in India.
2. It was unsuccessfully tried in India in the past.
3. Earlier patients had to stay in hospital for 4 weeks after surgery.
4. Earlier the surgery was available in only a few cities in India.

Explanations
Answer: 1. *The radical new surgery procedure is now available in India.*

The true statement about cardiomyopathy surgery is that the radical new surgery procedure is now available in India.

Look for **"surgery," "India," "new procedure."**

The passage states **"The technique, now in India, allows patients to go home two weeks after the operation."**

"The technique, now in India."

✅ *The radical new surgery procedure is now available in India.* (Clearly stated).
❌ *It was unsuccessfully tried in India in the past.* (No mention of failure).
❌ *Earlier patients had to stay in hospital for 4 weeks after surgery.* (No reference to 4 weeks).
❌ *Earlier the surgery was available in only a few cities in India.* (Not mentioned).

✅ **The radical new surgery procedure is now available in India.**

Question

Which of the following is NOT mentioned as a possible cause of cardiomyopathy?

1. Blood pressure issues
2. Parasite infection
3. Excessive sugar intake

4. Childbirth in rare cases

Explanations
Answer: 3. Excessive sugar intake

The passage states **"An attack from one of the 20 identified viruses, parasite infection, long-term alcohol abuse and blood pressure could bring it on, and in rare cases, it could follow childbirth."**

Excessive sugar intake is not mentioned.

Question

What is a key characteristic of cardiomyopathy?

1. The heart's chambers enlarge, reducing pumping efficiency.
2. The lungs become inflamed, causing breathing issues.
3. The muscles of the arms weaken over time.
4. The brain's neural activity slows down.

Explanations
Answer: 1. The heart's chambers enlarge, reducing pumping efficiency.

The passage states **"The condition is marked by an increase in the size of the heart's chambers and a decrease in the efficiency of pumping."**

✅ **The heart's chambers enlarge, reducing pumping efficiency.**

Practice 7 DEC 2023 UGC NET English Shift I

The most important part of a person's life is his childhood. The learning our young citizens receive at home, in school and in society between the ages of five and sixteen will shape them for the rest of their lives. During this phase, they need a good value based education to become enlightened humans. Parents and teachers need to have an integrated mission: education with a good value system at home and in school. Education is fundamental to building the nation of our dreams. All our aspirations as a society are tied to the capabilities of our youngsters, who form such a large part of our population. A child's individuality and creativity need to be given due importance in our education. The curriculum needs to be innovative and the examination system overhauled so that it recognizes and evaluates creativity and new thinking rather than the memorization of facts. Schools must move away from being centres of education alone, instead becoming centres of knowledge and skill development.

Question

What is essential for building the nation of our dreams?

1. More schools
2. Value based education
3. Democracy
4. Rapid Urbanization

Explanations
Answer: 2. Value based education

Value-based education is essential for building the nation of our dreams.

Look for **"education," "building the nation," "value system."**

The passage states "*They need a good value-based education to become enlightened humans. Education is fundamental to building the nation of our dreams.*"

"Education is fundamental to building the nation."

❌ *More schools* (Quantity is not the focus; quality matters).
✅ *Value-based education* (Clearly emphasized).
❌ *Democracy* (Not the main subject).
❌ *Rapid urbanization* (Not mentioned in this context).

✅ **Value-based education.**

Question

Given below are two statements:

Statement I: Schools should only be centres of education.
Statement II: Youngsters form a minimal part of our population.

In the light of the above statements, choose the most appropriate answer from the options given below:

1. Both Statement I and Statement II are correct.
2. Both Statement I and Statement II are incorrect.
3. Statement I is correct but Statement II is incorrect.
4. Statement I is incorrect but Statement II is correct.

Explanations
Answer: 2. Both Statement I and Statement II are incorrect.

Both Statement I and Statement II are incorrect.

Look for **"schools as centres of education" and "youngsters' population share."**

The passage states *"Schools must move away from being centres of education alone, instead becoming centres of knowledge and skill development." and "Youngsters form such a large part of our population."*

"Move away from being centres of education alone."
"Youngsters form such a large part of our population."

Question

A good examination system should:

A. Recognize a child's creativity
B. Recognize a child's individuality
C. Encourage rote learning
D. Encourage new thinking

Choose the correct answer from the options given below:

1. (A), (B) & (D) Only
2. (B) & (C) Only
3. (A), (B) & (C) Only
4. (C) & (D) Only

Explanations

Answer: 1. (A), (B) & (D) Only

A good examination system should recognize a child's creativity, individuality, and encourage new thinking.

Look for **"examination system," "creativity," "new thinking."**

The passage states "*The curriculum needs to be innovative and the examination system overhauled so that it recognizes and evaluates creativity and new thinking rather than memorization.*"

"Recognizes creativity and new thinking."

Question

A child becomes an enlightened human being as a result of the value based education received:

A. At home only
B. In school only
C. At home, in school and in society
D. In society only
E. Between the ages of five and sixteen

Choose the correct answer from the options given below:

1. (A) & (E) Only
2. (A), (D) & (E) Only
3. (C) & (E) Only
4. (A) & (B) Only

Explanations
Answer: 3. (C) & (E) Only

A child becomes an enlightened human being as a result of the value-based education received at home, in school, and in society between the ages of five and sixteen.

Look for **"value-based education," "home, school, society," "age range."**

The passage states *"The learning our young citizens receive at home, in school and in society between the ages of five and sixteen will shape them for the rest of their lives."*

"At home, in school, and in society between the ages of five and sixteen."

Question

Who needs to have an integrated mission: education with a good value system at home and in school?

1. Politicians
2. Philanthropists
3. Parents and Teachers
4. Businessmen

Explanations
Answer: 3. Parents and Teachers

Parents and teachers need to have an integrated mission: education with a good value system at home and in school.

Look for **"who is responsible for value-based education."**

The passage states **"Parents and teachers need to have an integrated mission: education with a good value system at home and in school."**

"Parents and teachers need to have an integrated mission."

❌ *Politicians* (Not mentioned).
❌ *Philanthropists* (Not stated).
✅ *Parents and Teachers* (Directly stated in the passage).
❌ *Businessmen* (Not relevant to the passage).

✅ **Parents and Teachers.**

Practice 8 June 2023 UGC NET English Shift I

Read the passage and answer the next five questions. Choose the most appropriate options from the options given:

As part of the great cultural renaissance generated during the post-independence period, there has occurred a most meaningful encounter with tradition in various fields of creative activity. The return to and discovery of tradition was inspired by a search for roots and a quest for identity. This was a part of the whole process of decolonization of our lifestyle, values, social institutions, creative forms and cultural modes. The modern Indian theatre, product of a colonial theatrical culture, felt the need to search for roots most intensely to match its violent dislocation from the traditional course. Directors like B.V. karanth, K.N. Panikar and Ratan Thiyam have had a most meaningful encounter with tradition and, with their work, have reversed the colonial course of contemporary theatre and put it back on the track of the great Natyashastra tradition. It sounds paradoxical, but their theatre is both avant-garde in the context of conventional realistic theatre, and still belongs to the Natyashastra theatrical tradition.

Question

The most significant contribution of Directors like BV Karanth, K. N. Panikkar and Ratan Thiyam was

1. Making Indian theatre totally traditional
2. Making Indian theatre backward
3. Dislocating Indian theatre from the traditional Indian theatre
4. Bringing about an amalgamation of the Indian theatrical tradition with Western realistic theatre

Explanations
Answer: 4. Bringing about an amalgamation of the Indian theatrical tradition with Western realistic theatre

The most significant contribution of directors like B.V. Karanth, K.N. Panikkar, and Ratan Thiyam was bringing about an amalgamation of the Indian theatrical tradition with Western realistic theatre.

Look for **"directors," "contribution," "theatrical tradition."**

The passage states "*Directors like B.V. Karanth, K.N. Panikkar, and Ratan Thiyam reversed the colonial course of contemporary theatre and put it back on the track of the great Natyashastra tradition.*"

"Reversed the colonial course and brought it back to the Natyashastra tradition."

Question

Decolonization is the process of

1. Becoming independent from
2. Becoming dependent on
3. Relying on
4. Learning from

Explanations
Answer: 1. Becoming independent from

Decolonization is the process of becoming independent from.

Look for **"decolonization," "process," "meaning."**

The passage states **"Decolonization of our lifestyle, values, social institutions, creative forms, and cultural modes."**

"Decolonization... freeing from colonial influences."

Question

The return to and discovery of traditional in post- independence era was inspired by

A. Search for values
B. Search for roots
C. Search for realism
D. Search for identity

Choose the correct answer from the options given below:

1. A & B only
2. D & C only
3. B, C & D only
4. B & D only

Explanations
Answer: 4. B & D only

The return to and discovery of tradition in the post-independence era was inspired by a search for roots and a search for identity.

Look for **"return to tradition," "post-independence," "search for."**

The passage states **"The return to and discovery of tradition was inspired by a search for roots and a quest for identity."**

"Search for roots and a quest for identity."

Question

The Natyasastra tradition refers to

1. The colonial tradition
2. Avant-garde theatre
3. Conventional realistic theatre
4. Indian theatrical tradition

Explanations
Answer: 4. Indian theatrical tradition

The Natyashastra tradition refers to Indian theatrical tradition.

Look for **"Natyashastra tradition," "theatrical tradition."**

The passage states "*Put it back on the track of the great Natyashastra tradition*."

"Natyashastra tradition refers to Indian theatre."

Question

Post- Independence cultural renaissance in Indian theatre focused on

1. Development of Western theatre
2. Return to traditional Western theatre
3. Search for traditional Indian theatre
4. Modern Western theatre

Explanations
Answer: 3. Search for traditional Indian theatre

Post-independence cultural renaissance in Indian theatre focused on a search for traditional Indian theatre.

Look for **"post-independence," "cultural renaissance," "theatre focus."**

The passage states "*The return to and discovery of tradition was inspired by a search for roots and a quest for identity.*"

"Search for roots and identity led to rediscovery of traditional Indian theatre."

Practice 9 June 2023 UGC NET English Shift II

Man is the only animal that laughs and weeps, for he is the only animal that is struck with the difference between what things are and what they ought to be. We weep at what exceeds our expectations in serious matters; we laugh at what disappoints our expectations in trifles. We shed tears from sympathy with real and necessary distress; as we burst into laughter from want of sympathy with that which is unreasonable and unnecessary. Tears are the natural and involuntary response of the mind overcome by some sudden and violent emotions. Laughter is the same sort of convulsive and involuntary movement, occasioned by mere surprise or contrast. The serious is the stress which the mind lays upon the expectations of a given order of events and the weight attached to them. When this stress is increased beyond its usual intensity and strains the feelings by the violent opposition of good and bad, it becomes tragic. The ludicrous is the unexpected relaxing of this stress below its usual intensity, by an abrupt transposition of ideas that takes the mind by surprise and startles it into a lively sense of pleasure.

Question

We shed tears when

A. Something is tragic
B. Something is ludicrous
C. Something is surprising

D. Seriousness exceeds our expectations.

Choose the correct answer from the options given below:

1. C & D only
2. A & B only
3. A & D only
4. A, B & D only

Explanations
Answer: 3. A & D only

We shed tears when **something is tragic and when seriousness exceeds our expectations.**

Look for **"tears," "weeping," "serious matters," "exceeds expectations."**

The passage states "*We weep at what exceeds our expectations in serious matters" and "Tears are the natural and involuntary response of the mind overcome by some sudden and violent emotions.*"

"Weep at serious matters exceeding expectations."

Question

The author implies that animals lack the ability to

1. Perceive emotional changes in humans
2. Laugh or weep
3. Evoke sorrow or laughter in humans
4. Respond strongly to external stimuli

Explanations
Answer: 2. Laugh or weep

The author implies that animals lack the ability to **laugh or weep.**

Look for **"animals," "lack of emotions," "differences."**

The passage states "*Man is the only animal that laughs and weeps.*"

"Man is the only animal that laughs and weeps."

Question

The author develops the passage primarly by

1. Disproving a theory
2. Citing authorities
3. Presenting counter example
4. Defining terms

Explanations
Answer: 4. Defining terms

The author develops the passage primarily by **defining terms.**

Look for **"structure of explanation," "how the passage is written."**

The passage explains **tears, laughter, seriousness, and the ludicrous** through definitions.

"Defines tears, laughter, serious, and ludicrous."

Question

It can be inferred from the passage that the ludicrous is most nearly opposite to the

1. Serious
2. Surprise
3. Pleasure
4. Unexpected

Explanations
Answer: 1. Serious

It can be inferred from the passage that the ludicrous is most nearly opposite to the **serious.**

Look for **"ludicrous," "opposite meaning," "contrast."**

The passage states "*The serious is the stress which the mind lays upon the expectations of a given order of events.*" *and "The ludicrous is the unexpected relaxing of this stress."*

"Serious = stress, Ludicrous = unexpected relaxation of stress."

Question

According to the passage, which of the following is not true is the case of tears and laughter?

1. They are both involuntary reaction
2. They are both the result of violent emotions
3. They are both natural emotions.
4. They are both reaction to experiences of the world

Explanations
Answer: 2. They are both the result of violent emotions

According to the passage, **tears and laughter are not both the result of violent emotions.**

Look for **"tears and laughter," "comparison," "differences."**

The passage states "*Tears are the natural and involuntary response of the mind overcome by some sudden and violent emotions.*" *but "Laughter is a convulsive and involuntary movement, occasioned by mere surprise or contrast.*"

"Tears result from violent emotions, laughter from surprise or contrast."

Practice 10 March 2023 UGC NET English Shift II

Read the following passage and answer the question given below:

Around the age of 2 children have a sense of intention, at least of their own intentions. They will announce, "I wanna peanut butter sandwich". As children develop a theory of mind, they also can understand that other people have intentions of their own. Older pre-schoolers who get along well with their peers can separate intentional from unintentional actions and react accordingly. For example, they will not get angry when another child accidentally knocks over their block tower. But aggressive children have more trouble assessing intention.

They are likely to attack anyone who topples their tower, even accidently. As children mature, they are more able to assess and consider the intentions of others.

With a developing theory of mind, children are increasingly able to understand that other people have different feelings and experiences and therefore may have a different viewpoint or perspective. This perspective taking ability develops over time until it is quite sophisticated in adults. Being able to understand how others might think and feel is important in fostering cooperation and moral development, reducing prejudice, resolving conflicts, and encouraging positive social behaviours in general. Some coaching in perspective taking from the teacher might help if children mistreat peers and the mistreatment is not part of a deeper emotional or behavioural disorder.

Question

Children of Which of the following ages would generally have the best perspective taking ability?

1. 3 years
2. 8 years
3. 13 years
4. 18 years

Explanations
Answer: 4. 18 years

Children of **18 years** would generally have the best perspective-taking ability.

Look for **"perspective-taking," "age development," "sophistication in adults."**

The passage states "*This perspective-taking ability develops over time until it is quite sophisticated in adults.*"

"Sophisticated in adults" implies full development at 18 years.

Question

Given below are two statements:

Statement I: Aggressive children can assess the intention of others with ease.
Statement II: Different persons may have different viewpoints.

In the light of the above statements, choose the most appropriate answer from the options given below.

1. Both Statement I and Statement II are correct.
2. Both Statement I and Statement II are incorrect.
3. Statement I is correct but Statement II is incorrect.
4. Statement I is incorrect but Statement II is correct.

Explanations
Answer: 4. Statement I is incorrect but Statement II is correct.

Statement I is incorrect, but Statement II is correct.

Look for **"aggressive children," "different viewpoints."**

The passage states "*Aggressive children have more trouble assessing intention" and "People may have a different viewpoint or perspective.*"

"*Aggressive children struggle with assessing intention*" **confirms Statement I is incorrect.**
"Different viewpoint or perspective" confirms Statement II is correct.

Question

Understanding how others feel is important in

A. Developing empathy
B. Reducing prejudice
C. Conflict resolution
D. Encouraging Selfishness
E. Enhancing cooperation

Choose the most appropriate answer from the options given below:

1. A, B, C and D Only
2. A, B, C and E Only
3. B, C, D and E Only

4. A, B, D and E Only

Explanations
Answer: 2. A, B, C and E Only

Understanding how others feel is important in developing empathy, reducing prejudice, conflict resolution, and enhancing cooperation.

Look for **"understanding others," "positive social behaviors."**

The passage states "*Being able to understand how others might think and feel is important in fostering cooperation, moral development, reducing prejudice, resolving conflicts.*"

"Encouraging selfishness" is not mentioned.

Question

Given below are two statements: One is labelled as Assertion A and the other is labelled as Reason R.

Assertion A: Older pre-schoolers have better chances of getting along well with their peers as compared to young pre-schoolers.
Reason R: Older pre-schoolers generally have a better understanding of the intentions of others.

In the light of the above statements, choose the most appropriate answer from the options given below.

1. Both A and R are correct and R is the correct explanation of A
2. Both A and R are correct but R is NOT the correct explanation of A
3. A is correct but R is not correct.
4. A is not correct but R is correct.

Explanations
Answer: 1. Both A and R are correct and R is the correct explanation of A

oth A and R are correct, and R is the correct explanation of A.

Look for **"older pre-schoolers," "understanding intentions," "peer relationships."**

The passage states "*Older pre-schoolers who get along well with their peers can separate intentional from unintentional actions and react accordingly.*"

"Better understanding of intentions helps them get along well" confirms R explains A.

Question

Given below are two statements:

Statement I: A 2 years old child is likely to have a better understanding of his own intentions than those of others.
Statement II: It is always helpful to coach a child in perspective-taking if the child has the habit of mistreating others because of some behavioural disorder.

In the light of the above statements, choose the most appropriate answer from the options given below.

1. Both Statement I and Statement II are correct.
2. Both Statement I and Statement II are incorrect.
3. Statement I is correct but Statement II is incorrect.
4. Statement I is incorrect but Statement II is correct.

Explanations
Answer: 4. Statement I is incorrect but Statement II is correct.

Statement I is incorrect, but Statement II is correct.

Look for **"2-year-old's understanding of intentions," "coaching in perspective-taking."**

The passage states "*Around the age of 2, children have a sense of intention, at least of their own intentions.*" but "**T***hey develop a theory of mind and understand others' intentions later.*"

It also states "*Some coaching in perspective-taking might help if children mistreat peers, unless it is part of a deeper disorder.*"

Statement I is incorrect because 2-year-olds do not understand others' intentions well.

Statement II is correct because coaching is not always effective if mistreatment is due to a disorder.

End

Usage Policy for NerdSchool Notes

Created by: Instructors from NerdSchool
Owned by: NERDSTABLE PVT LTD

The following notes are the intellectual property of **NERDSTABLE PVT LTD** and are made available exclusively to students who have paid for access. By using these notes, you agree to the terms and conditions outlined below:

Policy of Usage:

Personal Use Only: These notes are intended for your **personal study and exam preparation**. You are permitted to **read** and **print** them for your own reference.

No Unauthorized Distribution or Sale: You **may not sell**, **distribute**, or **replicate** these notes in any form, whether digitally or physically. This includes sharing copies with others, regardless of the medium (online platforms, printed materials, etc.).

No Plagiarism: You **may not claim** the contents of these notes as your own. Any form of direct publication or submission under your name, without proper citation, is strictly prohibited.

Non-Transferable Access: Access to these notes is restricted to the individual purchaser. **Sharing your login credentials** or any other means of access to these materials with others is a violation of this policy.

Additional Guidelines:

For Educational Use Only: These notes are designed to help students succeed in their academic exams and should be used responsibly. They are meant to supplement your learning, not to replace the guidance of instructors or textbooks.

No Commercial Use: The content in these notes cannot be used for **commercial purposes**. This includes using the material in any form of paid tutoring or educational courses that you offer without the explicit permission of NERDSTABLE PVT LTD.

www.ingramcontent.com/pod-product-compliance
Ingram Content Group UK Ltd.
Pitfield, Milton Keynes, MK11 3LW, UK
UKHW062310290726
14090UKWH00018B/977

9 798897 441532